CLOUD
COMPUTING
AND
ELECTRONIC
DISCOVERY

The Wiley CIO series provides information, tools, and insights to IT executives and managers. The products in this series cover a wide range of topics that supply strategic and implementation guidance on the latest technology trends, leadership, and emerging best practices.

Titles in the Wiley CIO series include:

Strategic IT: Best Practices for Managers and Executives by Arthur M. Langer and Lyle Yorks

Trust and Partnership: Strategic IT Management for Turbulent Times by Robert Benson, Piet Ribbers, and Ronald Billstein

Transforming IT Culture: How to Use Social Intelligence, Human Factors, and Collaboration to Create an IT Department That Outperforms by Frank Wander

Unleashing the Power of IT: Bringing People, Business, and Technology Together (Second Edition) by Dan Roberts

The U.S. Technology Skills Gap: What Every Technology Executive Must Know to Save America's Future by Gary J. Beach

Founded in 1807, John Wiley & Sons is the oldest independent publishing company in the United States. With offices in North America, Europe, Asia, and Australia, Wiley is globally committed to developing and marketing print and electronic products and services for our customers' professional and personal knowledge and understanding.

CLOUD COMPUTING AND ELECTRONIC DISCOVERY

James P. Martin

Harry Cendrowski

WILEY

Cover image: © istock/polygraphus
Cover design: Wiley

Published by John Wiley & Sons, Inc., Hoboken, New Jersey.
Published simultaneously in Canada.

For general information on our other products and services or for technical support, please
contact our Customer Care Department within the United States at (800) 762-2974, outside
the United States at (317) 572-3993 or fax (317) 572-4002.

Wiley publishes in a variety of print and electronic formats and by print-on-demand. Some
material included with standard print versions of this book may not be included in e-books or in
print-on-demand. If this book refers to media such as a CD or DVD that is not included in the
version you purchased, you may download this material at http://booksupport.wiley.com. For
more information about Wiley products, visit www.wiley.com.

Library of Congress Cataloging-in-Publication Data:
Martin, James P., author.
  Cloud computing and electronic discovery/James P. Martin, Harry Cendrowski.
    pages cm
  Includes bibliographical references and index.
  ISBN 978-1-118-76430-5 (cloth); ISBN 978-1-118-94745-6 (ebk); ISBN 978-1-118-94744-9
(ebk)   1. Cloud computing—Law and legislation—United States.   2. Electronic discovery
(Law)—United States.   3. Privacy, Right of—United States.   4. United States. Electronic
Communications Privacy Act of 1986.   I. Cendrowski, Harry, author.   II. Title.
  KF390.5.C6M365 2014
  347.73'72—dc23
                                                                    2014013668

Printed in the United States of America

10 9 8 7 6 5 4 3 2 1

CONTENTS

CHAPTER 12 Compelled Production of Cloud Computing Data: Fifth Amendment Concerns   171

Matthew P. Breuer and James P. Martin

PREFACE

In general, *cloud computing* describes technologies that allow applications and data to be hosted on a computer external to a business's own computing resources and firewall (i.e. a "remote computer"). From a personal perspective, it means that an individual can have access to convenient solutions for little or no cost, for example, to host family photos or videos. One of the promises of cloud computing is the end user doesn't really need to know how it works, or where the data resides; it just works, and will be available when you need it, wherever you need it. This promise has also resulted in profound misunderstandings of what cloud computing actually involves, and what it means from a litigation perspective.

Cloud computing services provide computing resources on an as-needed basis; this is why cloud computing was sometimes referred to as *utility computing*, a term that certainly did not have the marketing cachet of *cloud computing*. Cloud computing solutions generally require a reasonable periodic service fee and little additional hardware cost to access a computing solution. The reduction of costly IT assets, avoidance of software license costs, and removal of software maintenance tasks provide an attractive economic model; the end user is given a turnkey solution supported and maintained by the service provider, and hosted at a remote location. Cloud computing is enabled by rapid, reliable Internet and mobile data communications, which means that applications and data are available "everywhere," simultaneously, and transparently. The convenience and financial benefits of cloud solutions are changing business models fundamentally and have resulted in mass migration of data to the cloud. Much of this data, of course, would be of interest to parties during criminal proceedings or civil litigation.

A key issue from a legal perspective is that an investigator or litigant cannot access data held in the cloud through traditional discovery techniques. Discovery of data within a cloud computing solution likely falls under the restrictions of the Electronic Communications Privacy Act of 1986 (ECPA),[1] and specifically, Title II of the ECPA, which is called the Stored Communications Act (SCA).[2] Under the SCA, third parties that provide communication services or remote computing services to the public are generally prohibited from releasing the data; the SCA defines a series of procedures for the government to access

---

[1] 18 U.S.C. §§2510–2522.
[2] 18 U.S.C. §§2701–2712, although the term "Stored Communications Act" does not appear anywhere within the body of the legislation.

the data. This law, now almost 30 years old, is the primary law that regulates disclosure of such data. It was written at a time when telephones actually rang, when e-mail was considered a novel new technology for computer geeks, and when conversations on portable phones could be intercepted with a standard FM radio. Today, judges use this law to rule on cases involving data created and stored by devices that would have been considered magic (or certainly at least in the realm of science fiction) in 1986.

This book is our attempt to briefly explain the way that data held by a third-party provider (i.e., in a cloud computing solution) potentially affects legal proceedings and discovery of electronic information. This work is divided into three topical sections:

Section One explains the basics of cloud computing technologies, how data is stored, and (at a high level) the technical aspects of hosted solutions that can affect production of data. This is intended to be a technical guide for non-technicians, offering a brief glimpse behind the technological curtain.

Section Two describes the SCA as well as the prior laws that protected technological communications of the day. This will hopefully provide the reader with insights into legal concepts that still shape cases today, and the common themes of privacy issues. We also describe some of the limitations of the current laws in interpreting modern systems and devices.

Section Three surveys many of the precedent-setting cases involving interpretation of hosted data and access of such data by litigants or the government. Many of these cases are still active and may be modified on appeal. Rapid technological advancements mean that issues may arise that have not been previously considered by the courts in the current context, and interpretation in those situations can widely vary.

The issues presented here often walk hand-in-hand with privacy issues. However, we limit this discussion primarily to litigation settings. Recent revelations of widespread government surveillance programs are well beyond the scope of this work. We sincerely hope this book provides practical insight into the current world of hosted data and its potential impact on legal proceedings, and wish you the best as you encounter these issues in the future.

James P. Martin
Harry Cendrowski
May 2014

ACKNOWLEDGMENTS

We are sincerely grateful to many individuals for their unique contributions to this book as well as their steadfast support and encouragement. First and foremost, we would like to thank the Wiley team, including John DeRemigis, Sheck Cho, Stacey Rivera, and the staff at John Wiley & Sons for their assistance and support during the development and writing process.

We would also like to thank all the contributing authors and advisors to the process, without whom the production of this book would not have been possible:

Matthew P. Breuer
Deirdre Fox
Virginia Kim
Sarah Marmor
Christopher Thieda

Their professional insights and advice were instrumental in the production of this work, and their dedication and commitment are sincerely appreciated. Thank you also to the countless individuals who provided perspectives on the use of emerging technologies, expectations of privacy, and the proliferation of smart devices.

Cloud Computing: Basics of Technologies and Applications

CHAPTER 1

Cloud Computing Definitions and Technical Considerations

Christopher Thieda

The introduction of cloud computing has taken technology users by the hand and brought them into a new realm of possibilities. Whether the purpose is for personal, corporate use, or anything in between, today's everyday tech users have been exposed to a multitude of cloud practicalities. Cloud computing applications allow computer users to conveniently rent access to fully featured applications, to software development and deployment environments, and to computing infrastructure assets such as network-accessible data storage and processing. Those that have exposure to common applications such as Google Apps or Microsoft Office 365 likely already have experience with cloud computing, even though they may not have realized it.

The term *cloud computing* has a variety of definitions, mostly because it has become a powerful marketing term. The National Institute of Standards and Technology, the federal technology agency that works with industry to develop and apply technology, offers this definition:

> Cloud computing is a model for enabling convenient, on-demand network access to a shared pool of configurable computing resources (e.g., networks, servers, storage, applications, and services) that can be rapidly provisioned and released with minimal management effort or service provider interaction.[1]

Today, technical questions remain that occasional users might not dare to ask regarding how virtualized models actually operate, where data actually resides, or who actually controls access to the data and applications, but for some users that are financially dependent on or have sensitive data involved with their cloud solution, those questions should be addressed. Parties to litigation will also naturally be concerned with the answers to those questions as well. Of course, there are numerous advantages to cloud computing from the perspective of the customer. Scalability, cost efficiency, ease of implementation, and optimal resource allocation are some of the main benefits that stem from virtualization. Conversely, concerns have risen concerning cloud practices regarding security, storage location, and intrusion protection. For parties and their counsel involved in litigation, cloud computing has increased the complexity of electronic discovery. In this chapter, we will address the different cloud computing models, the issues of cloud computing applications, and the legal regulations involving virtual data capture. Cloud computing is a developing area, and the strengths, weaknesses, delivery models, and legal implications of its use are constantly in flux.

Virtualization is the key technology involved in cloud computing. In a virtual computing model, an organization can obtain the exact hardware and/ or software solutions required, at the exact time it is required, without the need for a large capital commitment. Virtualization allows hardware and software owners to partition their resources and provide the exact quantity of resources needed to satisfy their customers. This model has existed for a while, but has been advancing in recent years due to the common availability of low-cost, high-speed data communications infrastructure.

There are three main service models seen in today's cloud computing environments. We will focus on: cloud Infrastructure as a Service (IaaS), which allows organizations to outsource hardware, cloud Platform as a Service (PaaS), which allows organizations to outsource operating systems and web infrastructure, and cloud Software as a Service (SaaS), which allows companies to outsource applications. These layers create the core of cloud computing. Since they share the commonality as components of the cloud, each of the three layers accomplish specific tasks and have the capabilities to complement one another in an entirely virtual environment. IaaS is the substitution of virtual solutions for hardware that is commonly used within a company's network. PaaS is created for users to be able to build and implement their own virtual, web-based solutions. SaaS is centered around supporting users entirely through web-based resources, and it is the most commonly seen model in today's cloud market. Every cloud layer provides a differentiation factor versus standard enterprise networking while providing a broad range of possibilities for users looking to delve into the world of virtualization. Most consumers will typically contract with an SaaS vendor to provide a web solution, and may not be aware that the infrastructure and platform levels have also, in turn, been outsourced to other cloud vendors.

IaaS

Cloud computing has provided organizations with the advantage of configuring their network based on using resources in the most efficient manner. IaaS is the foundation of the three cloud layers. It is a virtualized availability of hardware that can substitute for pertinent networking items such as servers, firewalls, and load balancers. Instead of purchasing a physical server and firewall with a set amount of data capacity, virtual network solutions are available where storage and computing power is scalable depending on the organization's requirements. Virtual machines have also created a way for users to obtain similar functionality to preexisting hardware while eliminating data center space and recurring physical support costs including maintenance, power consumption, and expertise to operate the hardware. The elimination of overhead costs and flexibility are the main reasons why companies choose to source their infrastructure through the cloud.

Although there are many benefits of virtualizing an environment, network administrators must have a thorough knowledge of networking and how infrastructures should be constructed in order to properly configure their cloud requirements. Administrators must be well-versed in dealing with different virtualized operating systems and interfaces. An example of an important resource to be familiar with when dealing with a cloud-based infrastructure is a hypervisor. A hypervisor is software that enables users to monitor and control servers that are built on hosted environments. Hypervisors are an extremely useful technology piece to remotely allocate shared resources that can have a large impact concerning how efficiently data is transferred.

There are two types of hypervisors, depending on how they are implemented. The first is a type-1 hypervisor, which is built directly on the server platform and communicates with resources designated by the service provider. The second is a type-2 hypervisor, which is built on a preexisting host operating system and can interact with associated virtual systems thereafter. A type-1 hypervisor is more commonly used in business practices, as it minimizes any latency potential and maximizes networking efficiency from its direct source of interaction with the server. Type-2 hypervisors are still a useful way to virtually manage servers and can be effective when the operating system is communicating with input-output style computing processes, similar to how personal web surfing is conducted. VMware, a popular cloud service provider, offers both type-1 and type-2 hypervisors with their operating systems. VMware's ESXi is an example of a type-1 hypervisor, whereas their VMware Server software is a type-2.

It is important to understand hypervisors and how they work, as it could aid in reducing potential security threats. If an organization is looking to minimize risk against their virtualized infrastructure, they could implement an efficient hypervisor strategy to stop any malicious attacks from taking down their entire network. Hypervisors can be set up by separating virtual servers with the intention of preventing compromised network channels from negatively impacting other servers. Instead of an attack on a host causing a severe security breach for all virtual machines associated with it, hypervisors can be set up by segregating how information is transferred. Hypervisors also provide the advantage of transferring data using encrypted communication methods such as Internet Protocol Security, commonly referred to as IPsec.

The most significant element concerning cloud computing infrastructure is that there are differences regarding how cloud networks can be implemented. This breakdown is categorized into three cloud computing groups: public, private, or hybrid. Each is distinctively separated in terms of how the software, firmware, or infrastructure is hosted.

Public Cloud

Public cloud computing provides users with the availability of hosted online resources through service providers. This is the most common cloud application seen in today's market due to the integration ease for new users and its convenient bundles that can be purchased according to requirements and usage. Instead of having hardware on site and needing to constantly create data center space, public cloud computing is an alternative hosting solution.

Because it is externally hosted, the added benefit of network flexibility also comes along with vagueness regarding how data is stored and where it resides. As previously mentioned, public cloud is a service provided and sourced entirely through a service provider's infrastructure; the service provider is providing services to hundreds if not thousands of organizations. Thus, public cloud solutions are hosted through an infrastructure with a mixture of data from other entities. In a traditional computing model, organizations operate with enterprise hardware they actually own and control, and have the benefit of physically knowing where data is being stored at all times. Cloud users operate with the hindrance of not having direct physical control over the hosted network (i.e., the actual hardware) within which their data lies. During discovery, this limits the ability of investigators to directly access the data of interest. This transparency limitation can also cause the potential for unfavorable variances with data security.

Not only is there a lack of direct control over hardware resources with public cloud computing, but there is also the limitation of knowledge regarding how data is being secured. Most cloud service providers have security precautions in place, but for the wellness of your network and your data there should be an audit of the service provider's security measures prior to any solutions being implemented. Users should address vendors with questions asking about the set of security standards by which they abide. An example of an information privacy standard is the ISO/IEC 27000, which is a series of security regulations recommending best practices regarding maintaining information security management procedures. Guidelines like these provide insight into minimizing vulnerabilities and constantly being aware of new security threats. It is important to implement information security business practices that help protect against threats compromising information relating to their company, their employees, or their customers.

With this data being stored through a public cloud service, organizations must have a way to obtain data when needed. Accessing externally hosted data is made possible through cloud application program interfaces, or APIs. APIs allow users to communicate with a multitude of software components to be able to properly transfer data from one source to the next. These APIs are created to conform to interfaces such as Representational State Transfer (REST) and Simple Object Access Protocol (SOAP). REST and SOAP are web-based protocols created to oversee the sending and receiving of HTTP data between operating systems.

Continuing further, APIs are entitled to communicate with cloud storages to specify what data users are looking to obtain. An API that conforms to REST can use HTML requests to obtain data quickly and easily. Things become more complicated when archived data stores must be accessed from a cloud service provider. These actions can take much longer periods of time to retrieve, as cloud archival data stores are created to be accessed only on an occasional basis, and typically only for a file or two at a time. A wholesale restore from archival data can require a surprising amount of time.

Hosted archives can provide an additional discovery point during litigation, and the existence, location (i.e., host name), and chronology of those archives should be cataloged as part of the discovery process.

Private Cloud

The private cloud is a way of implementing a cloud infrastructure for the use and management of a single organization. The purpose of private cloud computing is to have the benefits of virtualization, such as the elimination of multiple servers, while having an infrastructure dedicated to one entity. It can either be hosted internally or externally, meaning that their infrastructure could be served through their internal resources or through a private cloud service provider. Private cloud solutions are typically utilized by larger organizations who wish to control potential risks that come from operating with a public cloud.

From a discovery standpoint, private clouds are more akin to traditional computing models. Hardware is typically directly controlled by the organization, and, because the private cloud does not involve a service provider offering service to the public, the disclosure restrictions of the Stored Communication Act do not apply. Technical issues may still be present as servers and archives are virtualized, however, the legal restrictions placed upon a third party responsible for the data should not be present.

Self-hosted private cloud solutions serve as a tool for organizations to obtain a singularly dedicated environment that is internally managed. It creates a highly secure network structure while giving administrators more control over the configurations of the network in comparison to public cloud computing. If hosted internally, it would require on-premise hardware for the cloud architecture to function, thus creating initial and recurring operating costs for the organization.

With external hosting, there is still only one entity being managed through the cloud. The main difference between self-hosting and external private cloud hosting is the lack of control and insight with regard to data management and storage. Despite this, utilizing these computing resources can be a potential option for organizations that prefer to operate with the flexibility that comes with the public cloud while addressing the security risks that come along with sharing service provider resources.

Hybrid Cloud

Those who see cloud computing as a pertinent piece to introduce into their network but wouldn't particularly benefit from a completely externally or internally hosted infrastructure can pursue hybrid cloud computing. Hybrid cloud computing is a flexible way of combining on- and offsite applications without running the risk of exposing potential vulnerabilities or accruing unnecessary physical maintenance costs. Therefore, this style of configuration can help organizations choose what network resources they feel should be privately managed and those that should be publicly hosted for less security-sensitive applications.

For example, a company is looking to deploy an architecture that would efficiently and securely correspond to their sector and customer needs. They could utilize hybrid cloud computing through using multiple deployment models, obtaining the most ideal resources from each model. The company could use a more traditional private cloud environment for their internal portals and network servers. Additionally, their website could be externally hosted, considering the information is already made for public viewing and is less of a security concern if those information stores were to be breached. Minimizing exposure to security risks is one of the fundamental elements that differentiates hybrid computing from a standalone public or private cloud architecture. For discovery purposes, it will be important to understand the relationship between the organization and the service provider. If the service provider is providing services to the public, restrictions of the Stored Communication Act may be in play with regard to the data.

PaaS

PaaS is one of the most powerful ways that cloud computing has changed how applications and resources are created and maintained. This cloud layer provides developers with the architecture to which they can construct their own applications; PaaS vendors provide a ready-to-go hosting area for applications. This ability is generated through virtually hosted services supplied by a cloud service provider. PaaS has made it easy for web developers, software developers, and others to create their own solutions without owning any hardware or installing any tools on their computer. Regardless of the complexity of the applications that are being developed, users can then deploy these applications without the need for enterprise networking or technical skills. Many popular cloud applications are hosted on PaaS platforms owned by another provider.

PaaS providers offer a multitude of offerings to help aid in the development. There are platforms available where users are guided through a simple, step-by-step process that eliminates the need for a technical understanding of the framework. Users can also choose to build their platform based on a preexisting architecture, which can remove any initial layout confusion. Through its flexible development procedure, if users need to make alterations to their platform after it has already been deployed, they can easily retain or exclude necessary features without accruing high-level costs. PaaS services are frequently utilized through subscriptions where users are only expected to pay for what they need. PaaS is an efficient way to allocate resources by using what is necessary to develop and manage the application.

PaaS is highly suitable for developers interested in creating a web-based application. It can be a very useful tool involving scenarios where the automation of testing and deployment proves to be a primary advantage. Additionally, PaaS can become a fundamental resource when collaboration is an important factor in the applications building process. However, the service can be counterproductive if large data must be incorporated within the application.

SaaS

The term *Software as a Service* originated in the 1990s and therefore predates the current term *cloud computing*. While many variations of SaaS are possible, a simple explanation is that it is software deployed as a hosted service and accessed via the Internet.

The rapid rise in consumer needs and expectations has caused the ongoing development of efficient ways to deliver data through on-demand and rapidly responsive applications. Thus, information service providers and organizations have introduced services through the SaaS cloud model. SaaS applications are frequently developed as a broad solution for users of all demands and technical backgrounds. Added with the scalability of these services, consumers can easily upgrade their level of service, such as storage and data capacity, while still using the same functionality and maintaining fluency within the tool. Thus, clients only pay for what they need, creating an elastic financial solution. This "pay-as-you-need" model is a staple for SaaS and has been a major reason why it is so commonplace in the consumer technology sector.

Despite its applicability, SaaS is very interchangeable from one solution to the next. It is difficult for information service providers to present a unique benefit that would help draw consumers toward their solution versus comparable services. For most successful SaaS platforms, intuitiveness and ease for users within the tool has seemed to be fundamental for its success. Customer resource management providers such as Salesforce and e-mail providers such as Google were some of the early implementers of SaaS. Thus, they have garnered the benefits as first-movers by being two of the top resources in their respective categories.

Despite its advantages, the SaaS cloud layer is still not yet a universally reliable tool. Thus, disagreement has arisen regarding when SaaS should be applied in business practice. SaaS is commonly utilized when remote data storage and virtualization outweigh the costs associated with having onsite hardware. The advantage of having service providers supply the application software through the cloud eliminates necessary maintenance. However, SaaS might not be appropriate when speed is of the essence. Due to the hosting of the layer, data is only transferred as fast as Internet speeds allow. This latency could be substantial for organizations of larger sizes or those that deal with urgent applications.

Considerations for Discovery

Data in a cloud computing solution may be contained within assets owned by up to three different companies: an IaaS vendor who owns and operates the actual physical server hosting the data, a PaaS vendor who controls the operating system and distribution of the data, and the SaaS vendor who controls the application. In a public cloud model, the end customer will typically only have a relationship with the SaaS vendor, however, in some circumstances, and certainly in a private cloud model, the end customer would have relationships with the other layers as well. Parties to litigation should consider the relationships with cloud vendors across the platforms when crafting their discovery strategy.

To the extent that the cloud vendor is providing service to the public, discovery may be restricted by the provisions of the Electronic Communications Privacy Act, as discussed later in this chapter.

Service level agreements will likely be in place between the end customer, and directly or indirectly between vendors in the different layers of the cloud computing platforms. Parties to litigation should understand the terms of the service agreements as they define the relationship and responsibilities between the parties, including the duties of the cloud customer and those of the cloud provider. They will also potentially describe the procedures to access data in the event of litigation. The following are excerpts from the Gmail (Google-hosted e-mail) cloud e-mail application:

Information we share

We do not share personal information with companies, organizations, and individuals outside of Google unless one of the following circumstances applies:

■ With your consent

We will share personal information with companies, organizations or individuals outside of Google when we have your consent to do so. We require opt-in consent for the sharing of any sensitive personal information.

■ For legal reasons

We will share personal information with companies, organizations, or individuals outside of Google if we have a good-faith belief that access, use, preservation, or disclosure of the information is reasonably necessary to:

■ Meet any applicable law, regulation, legal process, or enforceable governmental request.
■ Enforce applicable Terms of Service, including investigation of potential violations.

- Detect, prevent, or otherwise address fraud, security, or technical issues.
- Protect against harm to the rights, property, or safety of Google, our users, or the public as required or permitted by law.[2]

The terms of service agreement should also define the vendor's data preservation requirements. Many agreements specify that if a subscriber's access to cloud services is terminated "for cause," (i.e., because the subscriber has violated the cloud's acceptable use policies or for nonpayment) the provider may state that they have no obligation to preserve any consumer data remaining in cloud storage. The terms of service agreement should also indicate the disposition of data in the event the subscriber stops using the service, for example, if they did not log into their hosted e-mail account for a period of time; providers generally state that they will suspend the service after an interval, but will not intentionally erase the consumer's data for a period of 30 days beyond that interval. Some providers indicate they will preserve only a snapshot of consumer data, or recommend that consumers: (1) back up their data outside that provider's cloud inside another provider's cloud, or (2) back it up locally.

Most cloud services require acceptance of the terms of service during the subscription process. This can help identify the subscribing party who might be deemed in control of the contents for purposes of compelled disclosure.

Providers generally reserve the right to change the terms of the service agreement at any time, and to change pricing with limited advanced notice; notice would typically be given to the subscriber of the service. For standard service agreement changes, notice is generally given by a provider by posting the change to a website, and it is the consumer's responsibility to periodically check the website for changes. Changes may take effect immediately or after a delay of several weeks. Litigation involving customer account information should consider that changes could be made to the terms of service over time, and that it might be essential to determine the terms of service applicable during the time frame of the litigation period.

Data Transfer Regulations

The movement of data around the world through cloud computing solutions is technically quite easy. However, it can be heavily limited through global restrictions. There are policies in place to prevent the misuse and unnecessary disclosure of data pertaining to individuals, but these regulations are created on a sectorial basis or, in other words, promulgated by particular countries. However, just because they are created by one country doesn't mean that they aren't applicable internationally. Cloud computing is highly correlated in this sense, as it relates to the global ease of data transfer and storage. With cloud computing solutions, data could reside within multiple different entities or countries equating to the potential need of complying with multiple different data regulation policies.

The Electronic Communications Privacy Act (ECPA) is the primary law regulating disclosure of information in the United States. Courts have determined that law applies to user information of foreign nationals, even if they themselves have never been to the United States. In *Beluga Shipping v. Suzlon Energy Ltd*,[3] Suzlon claimed that three former employees had formed an independent company and profited from shipping Suzlon's cargo. The former employees used Gmail accounts to communicate with each other and with potential customers. Suzlon petitioned for leave to conduct discovery in aid of foreign judicial proceedings pursuant to 28 U.S.C. §1782; Google moved to intervene and opposed the petition. The U.S. District Court, Northern District of California, San Jose Division held:

> Suzlon seeks, inter alia, the contents of the individual cross-defendants' email accounts. Pursuant to Electronic Communications Privacy Act (18 U.S.C §§2701-2712), non-party Google states that consent from the individual cross-defendants is required, and that until, and unless, their consents are obtained, it is unable to comply with the subpoenas. *See* 18 U.S.C. §2702 (the ECPA's description of the voluntary disclosure of customer communications or records); *see also Theofel v. Farey-Jones*, 359 F.3d 1066, 1073 (9th Cir. 2004) (the ECPA protects users whose electronic communications are in electronic storage with an ISP or other electronic communications facility); *O'Grady v. Superior Court*, 139 Cal. App. 4th 1423, 1447 (2006) (the discovery must be directed to the owner of the data, not the bailee to whom it was entrusted). A subpoena can be permissible if it seeks the identity of specific emails or of accounts. *See O'Grady*, 139 Cal. App. 4th at 1447. The ECPA, however, prohibits a subpoena if it seeks the content of any email account absent a consent. *See* 28 U.S.C. §1782 (2010). Because Google knows that it cannot comply with the subpoenas, it seeks to intervene at this stage of the proceedings and to oppose the petition, even though the subpoenas or deposition requests have not yet been issued.
>
> Suzlon contends that the ECPA does not apply to foreign citizens, and, therefore, Google may comply with the subpoenas. Specifically, Suzlon relies on Zheng v. Yahoo! Inc., which held that the ECPA does not apply to electronic communications of foreign citizens. *See Zheng v. Yahoo, Inc*, 2009 U.S. Dist. LEXIS 111886 (N.D. Cal. Dec. 2, 2009)

(M. Chesney). However, the court in Zheng found that because the email interceptions and disclosures occurred outside of the United States by a company whose servers were located outside the United States, the ECPA would not apply or extend to the foreign nationals. In the present case, however, Google and its servers are located within the United States and, therefore, the ECPA applies. As such, the ECPA prohibits Google from disclosing the contents of those email accounts until it receives consents from the email account holders. Therefore, it is futile for the subpoenas to issue until notice has been served and consent has been obtained from the cross-defendants. Accordingly, it is appropriate for non-party Google to intervene at this juncture to oppose the petition and to deny the petition insofar as it seeks the content of the specific email accounts set forth above.[4]

Another example of this type of data regulation is the European Union's Data Protective Directive 95/46/EC. This policy heavily restricts the data transfer of global organizations due to its rigid guidelines. The directive was created to limit and protect the personal data of European Union residents. This legislation not only applies to entities that lie within the European Union but also to non-European organizations. Additionally, those that use equipment located within those said EU boundaries must comply with this policy. Thus, cloud service providers must abide by these regulations when providing solutions to organizations located in the European Union, or while using hardware resources and data centers located within the European Union.

There are a number of requirements within the EU Directive that are highly applicable to cloud computing processes and services. If data is shared, organizations must obtain consent from the subjects whose data is being shared. Organizations must also have procedures in place to keep data safe and secure from potential threats, including security breaches and unauthorized intrusions. Involved subjects also must be made aware that their information is being collected and stored by the parties involved in the storage of said data. These are just a few of the necessary protocols that must be institutionally implemented to conform to the EU Directive.

The distributed nature of cloud computing makes understanding the applicable regulations and abiding by those regulations challenging. A primary example is the sourcing of public cloud computing resources. Since public cloud computing solutions can be globally sourced, there are numerous difficulties involved with security of information, along with users not knowing where their data lies. For example, an application developer may contract space with a PaaS vendor, and in turn the PaaS vendor may host their platform with an IaaS vendor who owns and operates data centers in a foreign country. The application developer may not even know that the data centers are hosted there, but could be responsible for conformity with legal standards in that country. If a cloud service provider has international data centers, there could be a possibility that it may be hosted through a country that has its own set of compliance rules and regulations.

The European Union is currently looking to fully adopt a new data protection policy by 2016, called the General Data Protection Regulation, which is a revision of the original Data Protective Directive 95/46/EC. With the increase in cloud computing practices, non-European organizations are troubled that this new legislation will make data transfer within member countries of the European Union even more difficult and come with even greater penalties for nonconformance. These revisions call for the potential erasing of data if it is misused, the prevention of personal data being sent outside of the borders of the European Union and larger fines for noncompliant businesses. Fines could cap out at 5 percent of an organization's total revenue if they do not abide by these new regulations, replacing the previous policy's max fine of 2 percent. These data protection policies could cause a massive hit to internationally operating tech companies that supply cloud services. Increasing global regulation is just one of the many ways that the use of cloud computing is changing not only how technology environments are created but also how compliant business must be with regard to data handling.

Notes

1. NIST Cloud Computing Definition, NIST SP 800-145.
2. Gmail, Privacy Policy, retrieved January 29, 2014, www.google.com/intl/en/policies/privacy.
3. *Beluga Shipping GMBH & Co. KS "Beluga Fantastic" v. Suzlon Energy Ltd*, Federal Court Proceedings, NSD 1670 OF 2008 Before the Federal Court, New South Wales, Australia.
4. *Beluga v. Suzlon* 09-23-10, Order.

CHAPTER 2

The Proliferation of Data Available for Discovery

*James P. Martin and
Harry Cendrowski*

The same technologies that make cloud computing possible (i.e., the pervasive availability of high-speed wide-area network connections for devices of all kinds) have also enabled the capture of data related to virtually every aspect of our lives. Smart devices are in communication with central data repositories exchanging information about our personal habits and preferences, where we go, and what we do. E-mail and other communication are available at our fingertips, no matter where we are, and a host of social media applications keep us in constant communication with friends and business contacts; this data is also correlated in databases designed to help marketers serve us with advertising intended to be specific to our needs.

The industry and technologies that capture and collate this expansive set of personal information is often referred to as *Big Data*. Big Data vendors promise enhanced customer interactions, more specifically, the ability to more accurately target potential buyers at the moment they are considering a purchase; this is their stated reason for collecting all that data. Device and operating system manufacturers design their systems to capture and share data with Big Data, and, in turn, utilize big data to refine their offerings. Advertising revenue driven by Big Data is the engine that makes many of the services available in the cloud "free" of cost.

From a litigation and investigation perspective, there is more data available about a subject than at any previous time in history. Much of the data captured would be of direct interest to investigators or parties to litigation depending on the particular legal issue at hand. Cases emerge every day in which attorneys and investigators apply an innovative investigative analysis to data to create a picture of the subject or to support theories about events leading up to the case. Today, investigators and attorneys need to understand the types of data available about subjects, and how to access such data.

Data can reside on a local device, for example, a personal computer, tablet, or smartphone, or it can reside in the hands of a third-party service provider, like Google, or other third party. Technically, accessing data on a local device is relatively easy, and accepted forensic procedures are defined to allow such data to be used in a legal forum. From a legal perspective, accessing data on a local device can become complicated depending on specific circumstances of the case and the device; many of the nuances of such discovery are covered in detail in this book.

For civil litigation, discovery often hinges on ownership or control of a device. Some devices have clear ownership: for example, a company-owned computer installed at an employee's workstation. Many companies have computer use policies that clarify the ownership of the device and all data included on the device. Under current laws and regulations in the United States, a company should have little trouble examining the device for relevant data and using that discovery for litigation purposes.

On the other hand, some companies allow employees to bring a personal tablet or smartphone to the workplace, and allow them to be used for business purposes. This has become known as *Bring Your Own Device* (or BYOD), and it tends to muddy the discovery process. Courts are still deciding whether the company has a right to access the device without the owner's permission, and to what extent such data can be used. Divorce cases frequently involve the family computer, one that is used by both parties to the litigation, and may contain financial information about the family unit, or each party individually. Under many circumstances, either party would be able to access the device and obtain the underlying data; however, in certain circumstances, access may become complicated.

On the criminal side, examination of a device may fall under criminal search and seizure procedures that may not yet be universally applied. If a suspect is arrested, do the police have a right to examine the contents of a smartphone found in his possession? What about computer drives or flash drives? Some law enforcement agencies have claimed a digital device is a "container" that is subject to search the same as a suitcase or purse. Courts have differed on the interpretation, with some jurisdictions requiring an additional search warrant and some that allow the search.

Accessing hosted applications, including e-mail systems, social media sites, and cloud computing solutions, is often driven by identification of the "subscriber" who would have control over the account. The subscriber is often the person who can authorize disclosure of the contents of the systems, and courts differ on the procedures for compelled disclosure. Discovery of data hosted by third-party service providers is generally covered by the restrictions of the Stored Communications Act (SCA) of 1986, which prohibits a service provider from releasing information to a third party. Accessing data held by a third-party provider is frequently the subject of litigation, and courts frequently differ about the type of data protected by the SCA and procedures to access that data.

An Example of Third-Party Data: Google Search Engine

Google is not exclusive in their data-gathering activities; these are highlighted here as an illustration of the extensive types of information captured.

The Google search engine records and collates every search a user has ever performed when logged into Google services, irrespective of the device with which the search was initiated or the Google service that was used. Google services include web search, image search, news search, Gmail (both personal and corporate), YouTube, and Maps, among others. Once a user signs into Google services on a device, Google starts tracking search activity. Let's say a user signs into their personal Gmail account at work, and performs some web searches using Google. Then they go to lunch and use Google maps to find the restaurant. Both searches will be recorded in the search history for that Google account. Google also accesses and stores information directly from the mobile device, including call information and location data.

Google describes collecting such information in terms of providing a better experience, like providing advertising specific to your interests or finding the people who matter most to you online. The extent of data collected by Google is expansive, and is described in their privacy policy:

- **Information we get from your use of our services**. We may collect information about the services that you use and how you use them, like when you visit a website that uses our advertising services or you view and interact with our ads and content. This information includes:

- **Device information**

   We may collect device-specific information (such as your hardware model, operating system version, unique device identifiers, and mobile network information including phone number). Google may associate your device identifiers or phone number with your Google Account.

■ **Log information**

When you use our services or view content provided by Google, we may automatically collect and store certain information in server logs. This may include:

- Details of how you used our service, such as your search queries.
- Telephone log information like your phone number, calling-party number, forwarding numbers, time and date of calls, duration of calls, SMS routing information, and types of calls.
- Internet protocol address.
- Device event information such as crashes, system activity, hardware settings, browser type, browser language, the date and time of your request, and referral URL.
- Cookies that may uniquely identify your browser or your Google Account.

■ **Location information**

When you use a location-enabled Google service, we may collect and process information about your actual location, like GPS signals sent by a mobile device. We may also use various technologies to determine location, such as sensor data from your device that may, for example, provide information on nearby Wi-Fi access points and cell towers.

■ **Local storage**

We may collect and store information (including personal information) locally on your device using mechanisms such as browser web storage (including HTML 5) and application data caches.

■ **Cookies and anonymous identifiers**

We use various technologies to collect and store information when you visit a Google service, and this may include sending one or more cookies or anonymous identifiers to your device. We also use cookies and anonymous identifiers when you interact with services we offer to our partners, such as advertising services or Google features that may appear on other sites.[1]

A user's Google search history is available at www.google.com/history; the user must sign in with their Google credentials to view their account. Once in the account, specific items may be flagged and removed by the user.

Consideration of Data Points in Discovery

In a data-driven world, discovery procedures must be updated to consider data points from new sources. They should also be flexible, based on the particular circumstances. The age-old concept of "modus operandi" now should include a subject's interface with the digital world; in many cases, the subject may not even realize he is creating data points. Considering available data points is a different process than attempting to access the data, which will present technical and legal hurdles; the first step is to consider what data may be available regarding the subject. Like many other areas of litigation, this is an arduous task, as the possibilities may seem limitless. However, to facilitate the process, it is often helpful to break the possibilities down into more manageable subcategories. Below are common examples of data created in the category described; it would be impossible to innumerate all possible data sources within a single book. Also, please consider that systems and applications change extremely rapidly, and newly introduced technologies create new categories of data.

User-Created Data

This category includes data that is overtly created by the subject, and includes things like e-mail accounts and social media accounts. Depending on the nature of the case, accessing data of this type could be helpful to prove intent, prior knowledge of an event, involvement, or planning with others. Social media is commonly thought of as Facebook, Twitter, and LinkedIn. However, many other sites should be given consideration in certain circumstances:

- *Photo hosting sites.* A common cloud application is the photograph server. These sites allow a user to host pictures and videos for free or for an annual fee. In certain cases, such photographs or videos may provide valuable evidence regarding the case.
- *Dating sites.* An offshoot of social media is the dating site; many sites exist that cater to a particular market segment, for example, christianmingle.com, ourtime.com, or farmersonly.com. One site, ashleymadison.com, is specifically intended for married persons to meet other married persons. Particularly in divorce actions, identification of a dating profile could be key to the case.
- *People-meeting sites.* As more of an informal dating site, apps like Tinder or Skout allow a user to "broadcast" their picture and brief biographical information to the surrounding area. Users may "like" a profile, and users that like each other are placed together in a chat.

While many online users are careful with their online posts, others are not so cautious. Many cases are solved through social media content. For example, Anthony James Lescowitch, Jr. was wanted by Freeland, Pennsylvania, police for several months. Lescowitch was apprehended within two hours of sharing the police department's wanted poster of himself on Facebook. An officer posed as a woman wanting to meet Lescowitch, and when he arrived at the meeting was promptly arrested.[2]

E-mail accounts are most frequently identified by cross-e-mailing from known e-mail accounts (e.g., a person uses their work e-mail account to forward a document to a personal e-mail account). Additionally, it is common for an e-mail site to use another e-mail site as a password recovery option. For example, in the event of a forgotten password, a Yahoo! account may forward a password recovery link to the user's Gmail account; the Gmail account may have content identifying the Yahoo! account. In such a case, the recovery email account would have been sent a confirming email that may still exist on the account. Web searches including the subject's name and interests may also identify previously undiscovered e-mail accounts. Many hosted e-mail platforms also come with document storage capabilities, for example Google Drive or Microsoft Hosted SharePoint. Identification of an e-mail account should include determining what other services are provided with the account that may be of interest to the case.

Another cloud application with particular importance to litigation is hosted accounting and financial systems. These may range from detailed ledger systems to financial tracking applications to online investment accounts. These are frequently discovered by analysis of e-mail records that provide updates and sales information to the user.

Given the wide variety of sites and applications available through the cloud, it is impossible to create an exhaustive list of all potential sites of interest. Clues to the use of a cloud application may be found in e-mail accounts, as well as through the devices themselves. For example, examination of browser favorites may reveal saved links to dating sites or financial sites. Desktop icons may link to web pages of interest. Internet browser history may additionally reveal prior visits to sites of interest. Also, credit card statements should be examined for payments to online services, including dating sites, financial sites, and online archives.

It has become increasingly common to provide an interrogatory asking the person to identify any and all cloud-based solutions utilized by the subject, including social media and e-mail accounts, and including account information (such as handle or user ID) and dates the accounts were defined. The resulting list can be compared to the results of investigative actions for accuracy and completeness.

Data Created about the User

This category includes data created through different real-world transactions and events that may be important to a case. We create data as we move throughout the world and conduct routine business transactions; often we don't even stop to think about the data we create and what it says about us. Depending on the nature of the case, this data can be extremely interesting.

Different courts have interpreted data of this type in different ways. Some courts have held that this is data protected by the Stored Communications Act, while others have held that these are the business records of the company, and that authorization to capture the data is provided as a part of using the service. Care should be exercised when attempting to access data of this type:

- *Electronic security systems.* Electronic security systems have become pervasive, and have replaced keys in many environments. These systems provide a near-field token or RFID chip in a card or key fob that is placed in proximity to a reader (card reader or proximity sensor) to activate the locking mechanism. The security system can be defined to limit access based on the day of the week or time of day. The system also maintains a log of the card or fob presented to the reader and the time stamp it was presented. This allows a report to be created of (1) all the cards that were presented at a reader and the time they were presented, and (2) the presentation history of a single card; in essence, a history of a person accessing doors within the organization.

  The use of such systems has grown beyond the corporate setting. Many colleges and universities have implemented an electronic security system that requires residents living in the residence calls to have a card to access their hall or floor.

- *Transportation systems.* Many manual toll collection facilities have been replaced by an electronic toll collection facility. On the tollway, transponders are available that capture the date and time the transponder moves through the sensor gate. Often this is at real time driving speeds; a common system is called E-ZPass. Subways, buses, and other mass-transit systems have implemented an electronic card linked to a bank account that can be used to pay the toll. These systems log the card swipes, including date, time, and location.

  A recent article in *Forbes* revealed that E-ZPass transponders are read throughout lower Manhattan, even where no toll is collected.

According to the TransCore spokesperson quoted by the article, the E-ZPass tag ID is scrambled to make the identity of the tag anonymous. The tag data is gathered and accumulated with data from other readers to measure traffic flow and conditions over an interval; the tag readers are placed at strategic locations to help measure the average travel times through the area. The spokesperson offered assurance that data pertaining to an individual are not retained:

- Tag sightings (reads) age off the system after several minutes or after they are paired and are not stored because they are of no value. Hence the system cannot identify the tag user and does not keep any record of the tag sightings.[3]

    Irrespective of the purpose of the New York system to read E-ZPass transponders, the article demonstrates the availability to read the devices at any time.

- *Frequent shopper cards.* Many stores require a person to register as a frequent shopper to obtain sale prices on merchandise; the frequent shopper has an electronic card or barcode tag that is presented at checkout to receive the discounts. These systems maintain a purchase history of items purchased, including date and time of purchase and location. At pharmacy chains, this includes prescription drug purchases.
- *Credit card metadata.* Beyond the amounts spent on a credit card, credit card statements include interesting information about the location, time, and type of purchase made. This can include travel information (e.g., airfare, auto rental, hotels), dining habits (type of restaurant preferred), and manner of dress.

Data in this category tends to indicate broad behavioral actions. Often, observation of data of this type over time can reveal changes in behavior that could be related to a case. For example, in a divorce action, changes in dining habits or travel could indicate marital stress prior to the divorce action. Drastic changes may also indicate intervention of another party. For example, when investigating an elder abuse case, behavioral information indicated the elder person was frugal, did not eat at restaurants very frequently or purchase expensive clothing. Credit card balances were minimal and paid off routinely. After care was transferred to a new person, transactional information changed, including meals at expensive restaurants and purchases at trendy clothing stores. Data of this type should be viewed with a long-term perspective.

Data Created by Devices with Which We Interact

Hardware devices include personal computers, tablets, and smartphones, and they create activity logs showing access times and other information that could be relevant to a case. Additionally, since local files on a device are not protected by the SCA, it may be important to identify, catalog, and request copies of all devices with which a subject may interact.

- *Smartphones and tablets.* Smartphones and tablets can be a treasure-trove of information from a litigation perspective. These devices interface with frequently used applications, including call logs, social media, e-mail, text messaging, calendaring, and photo and videos, and additionally can log where a user has been. Most smartphones have privacy notification procedures that tell a user when an app enables GPS tracking; however, researchers have found log files indicating that iOS (Apple's operating system) continuously tracks and records the device's location.[4]

  Industry standard procedures are utilized by digital forensics specialists to "image" a smartphone, allowing analysis of all contents and application data. Digital search tools can also be employed by the specialist to automate the review of the phone contents.

- *Automobiles.* Higher-end automobiles frequently include an "infotainment" system that syncs with smart devices in the vehicle via cord or Bluetooth connection. An emerging area of eDiscovery includes analysis of these infotainment systems. Specialty vendors are currently introducing analytical tools and procedures to image and analyze vehicle systems. Vendors claim they can acquire forensic artifacts including: tracking points, tracking logs, recent destinations, favorite locations, paired device history, contacts, call logs, analysis of speed, altitude, direction of travel, and time-line analysis.

  Device information is often critical to a case; smartphones are emerging as a first-person witness in many criminal and civil cases. Device acquisition, however, can become expensive, and care must be exercised based on the nature and magnitude of the case to ensure that digital forensic expenditures are in line with the case objectives.

Creating an eDiscovery Plan in a Cloud-Based World

Cloud computing means that important systems and data may be hosted outside the four walls of the organization. Traditionally, investigators could image key computers and servers within the organization and have a copy of all the organization's data. Today, cloud applications mean that key applications and archives may not be easily identifiable. However, a methodical approach should still identify all key systems. One key difference is that investigators will be looking for clues to the existence of relationships with cloud systems, not necessarily the systems themselves. Additionally, discovery may become a multistep process, with identification of systems separate from attempts to access the data. As more data is produced, additional hosted systems may be discovered.

The following is a generic outline for considerations developing a discovery process considering the possibility of cloud-based systems. Based on the wide variety of litigation and criminal investigations, this should not be considered definitive for a particular matter and does not constitute legal advice:

1. Provide interrogatories and production requests regarding use of hosted systems and cloud-based applications; interrogatories should require identification of the system, vendor, purpose, subscriber to the service, and internal administrator of the service.
   a. As a key system, specific interrogatories should ask about e-mail systems employed by the organization. If the matter is related to an individual, interrogatories should ask them to identify each and every e-mail account utilized by the individual.
   b. The interrogatories should be as broad as possible, and differentiate between systems subscribed by (under the control of) the company versus systems subscribed by the individual.
   c. Interrogatory answers may not identify all the cloud systems in place, but will be important to attempt to extend discovery if additional systems are noticed late in discovery.
2. Interrogatories should specifically identify document retention and archival procedures and vendors used in the retention process for both paper-based and electronic documents. Cloud solutions frequently include data archive systems, and archive information may contain useful information. Identify the vendors used, retention requirements, and litigation hold procedures.
3. Categorize systems between internal systems and cloud-based systems.
   a. Internal systems and data may generally be accessed through production requests and traditional discovery procedures.
   b. Data hosted with third-party service providers (i.e., cloud-based systems) may fall under the restrictions of the SCA, and may require authorization of the opposing party to allow the third party to produce the data.
4. Catalog all devices used by a subject. The device list should include assigned computers and workstations, company-issued tablets, and smartphones.
   a. Additionally, identify any personal device used to conduct business transactions, including home computers or BYOD devices.

    b. Prioritize devices for examination; work with a digital forensics specialist to obtain images of key devices.

    c. Images of the devices should be examined for evidence of undisclosed cloud systems, including shortcuts, saved favorites, and browsing history.

5. Obtain and examine e-mail records for evidence of other systems. This may include discussion e-mails, updates from the vendor, changes in service notifications, etc. Be sure to follow up on any previously unknown systems.

6. Examine payables records and credit card statements for payments to cloud vendors.

7. Deposition questions should be based on an understanding of the business, and include questions about how key transactions are processed.

    a. Note and follow up on any differences from previous discovery procedures.

    b. Consider deposing a lower level person in the organization for questions regarding procedures to record transactions and process functions; often they will be the users of systems and will describe the systems used.

Production of Cloud Data

Beyond the restrictions of the SCA, production of data from a cloud system is different than traditional eDiscovery procedures. Traditionally, an investigator could image the entire computer and obtain a copy of the entire drive; procedures could then be applied to the data to find content related to the case. In a cloud computing model, organizational data is stored in a virtual server containing the data of possibly thousands of other clients; obtaining an image of the entire server is neither technically nor legally feasible. Investigators typically do not directly search the cloud computers for the information requested. Instead, the warrant, subpoena, or authorization by the subscriber directs the service provider to produce all the content of the account or accounts desired, and the information produced is then reviewed by investigators for items that fall within the scope of items to be produced.

As the cloud computing market is still under development, forensic procedures to be applied to a cloud-hosted system are still being built as well. As more data is moved from internally hosted devices to the cloud, the challenges of litigation will continue to grow. Vendors of analytical toolsets will continue to improve and expand their product offerings as demand will grow, and it is a good practice to remain abreast of developments in the cloud computing market as well as in the digital forensics solutions market.

Notes

1. www.google.com/policies/privacy, accessed March 1, 2014.
2. *USA Today*, January 21, 2014.
3. Kashmir Hill, "E-ZPasses Get Read All Over New York (Not Just At Toll Booths)," *Forbes Online*, September 12, 2013, www.forbes.com/sites/kashmirhill/2013/09/12/e-zpasses-get-read-all-over-new-york-not-just-at-toll-booths/.
4. Jacqui Cheng, "How Apple Tracks Your Location without Consent, and Why It Matters," *Ars Technica*, April 20, 2011, http://arstechnica.com/apple/2011/04/how-apple-tracks-your-location-without-your-consent-and-why-it-matters/.

CHAPTER 3

Cloud Migration and Planning for Retention

James P. Martin and Harry Cendrowski

Data Retention and the Cloud

Businesses maintain books and records so an accounting of business activities may be performed. Whether for an audited financial report, a compilation, a review, a tax return, or a specific management report, businesses must gather, summarize, and analyze facts and figures to support reports, tax returns, and conclusions. After the report is issued and/or the tax return is filed, supporting documentation must be maintained for a prescribed period of time depending on the particular circumstances of the organization. Organizations moving to a cloud computing solution must carefully plan the service level offerings to ensure that they still meet all data retention requirements applicable to their organization; hosting data in a cloud-based product does not change these requirements. Additionally, organizations need to ensure their cloud solution includes capability to process a litigation hold should they become embroiled in litigation.

Likely the most far-reaching requirement for retention is Treasury Regulation 1.6001, which requires taxpayers to retain information to support their tax return information:

> Except as provided in paragraph (b) of this section, any person subject to tax under subtitle A of the Code (including a qualified State individual income tax which is treated pursuant to section 6361(a) as if it were imposed by chapter 1 of subtitle A), or any person required to file a return of information with respect to income, shall keep such permanent books of account or records, including inventories, as are sufficient to establish the amount of gross income, deductions,

credits, or other matters required to be shown by such person in any return of such tax or information.[1]

Not very many years ago, record retention requirements were satisfied by retaining boxes of paper documents, folders, and file cabinets, and moving older items to an offsite storage archive. Onsite storage of paper documents was cumbersome and time consuming to manage. The costs of office floor space were significant. Offsite storage costs, including third-party management of offsite storage, were quite expensive as well. Today, many pertinent business records are retained in source computer files, and paper records are scanned for electronic storage. Cloud vendors abound that can host document archives remotely, provide search and retrieval capabilities, all for costs typically below the costs incurred to store paper documents. This has created an entirely new concern for organizations: Technology has advanced to the point that it is now possible to store "everything" on a long-term basis. The decreased cost of computer storage means that it is often perceived to be cheaper to acquire additional digital storage archive space than it would be to manually determine what should be archived and what should be deleted.

An IBM whitepaper highlighted a concern with sprawling data archives in 2006:[2]

> E-mail has proved to be one of the first sources of this corporate pain. Once seen as nothing more than a quick and flexible communications tool, e-mail is now estimated to be the platform for as much as 75% of company intellectual property. E-mail documents figure in some 75% of all cases of corporate litigation. Sheer weight of usage means that the medium has in many organizations become the primary record repository, a fact recognized by legislation requiring the long-term retention of messages.
>
> Companies are now learning the hard way about the need to take e-mail storage seriously. Five US banks were recently fined US$1.25 million each when they failed to retrieve e-mails that were demanded of them. One Fortune 500 company had to spend US$750,000 to dig e-mails out of an archive in response to a legal subpoena. A pharmaceuticals company was forced to devote time and people to searching through 30 million messages for a court case.
>
> Regulatory insistence on data retention looks set to continue unabated in the future. Along with factors like the introduction of megabitrated mobile communications services for consumers, citywide wireless Internet access, and ultra-broadband wireless networking inside homes and offices, this regulatory insistence will add still more momentum to today's roaring inflation in the demand for data.

Companies and other organizations face an increasingly urgent choice about how to respond to this enterprise-threatening challenge. They can carry on dumping, creating ever bigger and more incoherent "data pits" and paying a soaring price when they need to retrieve items of value. Or they can face up to the problem and find out what it takes to actively manage information from cradle to grave, weeding out the mass of ephemera early on and keeping only what is likely to be of long-term value.[3]

Cloud computing archival solutions could add to the problem of growing data volumes if not properly managed. Cloud-based archives are based on storage volumes, and the provider will send a summary of the total amount of storage used, year over year. Some solutions may not offer robust file management tools that would allow a manual review and purge of data that no longer needs to be retained. Without such tools an organization can lose visibility into how much data they actually have under their control.

System backup procedures are responsible to ensure that lost or damaged data can be restored when needed, preventing the business costs of corrupt or destroyed data. Although these are not the same as document retention policies, the two go hand in hand. The retention policies must consider the existence of the catalog of backup data, and the time it must be retained. Backup procedures, likewise, create an archive that can support the objectives of the retention policies, but may not address all the data that needs to be archived within the organization. Careful coordination of the system backup procedures and document retention policies is required.

Electronic documents are easier and cheaper to copy, distribute, and store than paper documents. Exact duplicates of electronic documents can be created at the touch of a button, without regard to the length of the document or the cost of creating the printed copy. These copies may be stored in a different location than the original, on a different device or different platform. Attempting to catalog and control these cascading volumes of information can be difficult.

Organizations should develop and maintain a robust document retention policy, and this policy should be extended to the cloud-based storage solution when the organization migrates to the cloud. This policy should clearly define the retention period for classes of documents, both paper-based and electronic, as well as procedures to ensure documents are destroyed when their retention periods have expired. These policies should address all types of information, including documents, e-mail content, and other data as well as all storage locations within the organization, including paper archives, server storage space, cloud-based storage space, personal computer drives, removable media (such as flash drives and optical disks), and smart devices.

The document retention policy should be driven by the regulatory requirements that drive the need to retain documents for a specified period. Additionally, the policy should consider the special retention needs for documents related to litigation events.

The retention policy should be supported by a record retention solution to help the organization implement and manage compliance with the retention policy. A single point of retention is ideal, but may not be practical for all organizations. The solution will likely involve a combination of technical infrastructure as well as operational procedures for how to archive and how to purge records who have reached the end of their retention periods. Additionally, procedures must define procedures to retain all records subject to litigation requirements (i.e., litigation hold procedures). These procedures must ensure that normal retention procedures are suspended for records irrespective of the platform or media upon which they are stored.

Management must also implement procedures to monitor compliance with the document retention policies, including consideration of new data sources and storage platforms. Monitoring procedures should help the organization ensure that data continues to be retained according to requirements as the organization's technology and business process continue to grow and change. Simply having a retention policy is not good enough; an organization must be able to demonstrate that it is implemented and followed by all members of the organization.

Document retention is not an IT responsibility; it is management's responsibility to ensure an adequate retention policy is developed and executed, and an organization-wide responsibility to ensure the approved procedures are followed consistently. IT is frequently charged with providing the archival solutions to support the procedures, but they cannot be successful without organizational support.

The low cost of cloud solutions can also create entirely new storage areas; these should be included in the document policies to ensure that documents records in that storage is appropriately managed. For example, if a company moves to corporate Gmail as their e-mail solution, users will be provided with storage space in Google Drive, which is an online data storage area within the user account. Microsoft 365, Microsoft's hosted e-mail application, similarly provides online space in the form of a hosted SharePoint database. Policies should clearly define the appropriate use of this storage and include any data stored in these archives under the overall retention policy. The policies must be resilient enough to consider the appropriate handling of information stored in new data repositories, or outright specify allowable storage locations and forbid the use of ad hoc storage.

Courts have responded harshly to companies that fail to preserve data relevant to litigation matters. In the case of *Laura Zubulake v. UBS*

Warburg LLC & UBS AG, United States District Court Judge Shira A. Scheindlin ruled:[4]

> Defendants also argue that none of the correspondence between counsel on discovery matters is relevant to plaintiff's claims or the adverse inference instruction and seek to preclude plaintiff from introducing this evidence. In *Zubulake v. UBS Warburg LLC*, No. 02 Civ. 1243, 2004 WL 1620866, at *5 (S.D.N.Y. July 20, 2004) ("Zubulake V"), I found that "UBS personnel unquestionably deleted relevant e-mails from their computers after August 2001, even though they had received at least two directions from counsel not to." I also found that "UBS acted willfully in destroying potentially relevant information, which resulted either in the absence of such information or its tardy production. . . ." Id. at *12. I therefore concluded that the appropriate remedy was an adverse inference instruction with respect to e-mails deleted after August 2001. See id. at *13. The text of the adverse inference instruction I intend to give the jury in this case is set forth at the end of Zubulake V. It states, in pertinent part, as follows: "You may also consider whether you are satisfied that UBS's failure to produce this information was reasonable."
>
> In light of the above, plaintiff may introduce correspondence between counsel on discovery matters if defendants open the door by introducing evidence as to whether their failure to produce was reasonable. If defendants decide not to offer proof that their failure to produce certain e-mails (or late production of other e-mails) was justified, plaintiff will not be permitted to introduce any of the correspondence between counsel in her case in chief.

> 2. Back-Up Tapes

> Defendants seek to preclude any evidence concerning the failure by UBS to preserve several monthly back-up tapes. In *Zubulake v. UBS Warburg LLC*, 220 F.R.D. 212, (S.D.N.Y.2003) ("Zubulake IV"), I stated the following:

> Whether a company's duty to preserve extends to backup tapes has been a grey area. As a result, it is not terribly surprising that a company would think that it did not have a duty to preserve all of its backup tapes, even when it reasonably anticipated the onset of litigation. Thus, UBS's failure to preserve all potentially relevant backup tapes was merely negligent, as opposed to grossly negligent or reckless. Id. at 220.[5]

Developing procedures to manage document retention practices can be time-consuming and detailed; however, given the high cost of production during litigation and the potential costs of non-conformance, they are an essential management tool.

Considerations for Litigation

Rule 34. Producing Documents, Electronically Stored Information, and Tangible Things, or Entering onto Land, for Inspection and Other Purposes

(a) In General. A party may serve on any other party a request within the scope of Rule 26(b):

   (1) to produce and permit the requesting party or its representative to inspect, copy, test, or sample the following items in the responding party's possession, custody, or control:

   (A) any designated documents or electronically stored information—including writings, drawings, graphs, charts, photographs, sound recordings, images, and other data or data compilations—stored in any medium from which information can be obtained either directly or, if necessary, after translation by the responding party into a reasonably usable form; or

   (B) any designated tangible things; or

   (2) to permit entry onto designated land or other property possessed or controlled by the responding party, so that the requesting party may inspect, measure, survey, photograph, test, or sample the property or any designated object or operation on it.[6]

In litigation, sweeping requests for production of documents can cause an organization to identify, locate, and catalog large categories of records. In today's electronic world, records may be considered in a variety of sources, platforms, and media types forming a matrix of items that might be responsive to the request. The list below is merely a sample of the types of data that might be available within an organization.

Source

- Electronic office documents, such as Microsoft Word and Microsoft Excel
- Business applications, including enterprise resource planning (ERP) and financial systems
- E-mail records
- Paper documents, and paper documents scanned into digital archives

- Relational databases, such as customer relationship management (CRM) applications, timekeeping records, security access records
- Automotive infotainment systems

Storage Platform

- Internal server repositories
- Cloud-based repositories
- Local computer drives (e.g., laptop or desktop computers)
- Mobile devices (iOS, Android, Blackberry, Windows)

Media Type

- Removable media, including hard drives and flash drives
- Optical storage disks
- Magnetic tapes

Without proper planning, efforts to gather records responsive to the request and simultaneously limit the production to only those records responsive to the request can become a fairly large project. In practicality, many organizations formulate well-intentioned document retention procedures. However, the vast number of sources of data and storage locations for data often can outgrow the capabilities of the organization to handle all data according to those procedures. The document retention procedures of an organization, and the extent to which they are thoroughly executed, are key to identifying data that might be available to parties in a litigation setting; discovery needs and requests will naturally vary with the nature of litigation and the parties involved.

Discovery should include understanding the document retention procedures in place within the organization. This is most easily accomplished by requesting the organization's document retention policies. All organizations are faced with retention requirements, if only those imposed by the taxing authorities. As organizations grow and become more complex, other retention requirements may come into play. The Securities and Exchange Commission (SEC) has a number of retention requirements placed on the issuers of financial statements; these were enhanced and clarified by the Sarbanes–Oxley Act. Other regulatory agencies, including the Occupational Safety and Health Administration (OSHA) and the Food and Drug Administration (FDA), also mandate retention standards for other organizations. Understanding the specific requirements that are mandated for an organization can provide adverse parties to litigation insight into data types that should be available for discovery and the periods for which such data should be available. Procedures should also define the method of retention, including the technical systems used to perform archival of data. Where cloud computing solutions are utilized for document retention, it will be important to understand the party that controls the relationship with the vendor, as that party would be considered in control of the data. Discovery requests should include the working storage location for the data, for example, a shared network drive, as well as the archival solution used for document retention.

Discovery should also include understanding, to the extent practicable, the systems that generate and store data that might be relevant to a case. If e-mail correspondence is relevant to a case, for example, requests should be made to identify the type of mail server employed by the organization (e.g., Microsoft Exchange), whether it is internally hosted or cloud based; if cloud based, the identity of the host; and whether a client program is used to locally access e-mail content (e.g., Microsoft Outlook). Understanding the technical implementation of systems can help clarify production requests, and provide a benchmark for data that would be expected to be available in response to those production requests.

Production requests should be written to include as many storage platforms and media types as are believed to be used by the organization. It is often possible that data has been removed from one storage platform, either intentionally or accidentally, but may still be available on a different platform or medium. For example, a critical document might have been stored on the network server, but is not available for production at the time a request is issued. A key employee, however, loaded the document on a flash drive to work on the document while on vacation, and returned from vacation and placed the drive in his or her desk. Likewise, relevant data may be available in system backup files and archive volumes. By considering all available data sources, the litigation team increases the chances that key information is produced.

A thorough understanding of the organization's system backup procedures and document retention policies can enhance the discovery process for litigants and help ensure that all data relevant to the litigation is produced. Often, the use of specialists can help interpret the technological aspects of the document storage, as well as to help manage the volumes of data that may be produced. Robust document requests can be a double-edged sword: they can cause the opposing party to produce a large volume of data, however, that data will eventually need to be read or analyzed to provide value to the litigation team.

Notes

1. 26 CFR 1.6001-1—Records.
2. IBM Global Technology Services, "The Toxic Terabyte: How Data-Dumping Threatens Business Efficiency," white paper, July 2006. Reprint Courtesy of International Business Machines Corporation, © 2006 International Business Machines Corporation.
3. *Ibid.*
4. *Zubulake v. UBS Warburg LLC*, 382 F. Supp. 2d 536—Dist. Court, SD New York 2005.
5. *Ibid.*
6. Federal Rules of Civil Procedure, Rule 34.

SECTION TWO

Current Laws Affecting Discovery

CHAPTER 4

Brief History of Privacy and Selected Electronic Surveillance Laws

James P. Martin

The framers of the Constitution established into law the basic right of privacy through the Fourth Amendment:

The right of the people to be secure in their persons, houses, papers, and effects, against unreasonable searches and seizures, shall not be violated, and no warrants shall issue, but upon probable cause, supported by oath or affirmation, and particularly describing the place to be searched, and the persons or things to be seized.

While the framers likely did not consider the technological advancements that would be forthcoming over the coming years and centuries, the interpretation of the Constitution continued to evolve. New technologies often create issues that exceed the definitions within existing law, and courts must attempt to rationalize the new technology allegorically to an understood and defined issue until new laws are passed. The framers understood written correspondence, and the importance of privacy in the mail. The telegraph represented a leap forward in communication in the mid-1800s, as did telephone communication in the late 1800s.

As technology advanced, so did the law enforcement capabilities of the U.S. government. The U.S. Marshal Service began on September 24, 1789, when President George Washington appointed the first 13 U.S. Marshals following the passage of the first Judiciary Act. The Secret Service Division was created on July 5, 1865, in Washington, D.C., to suppress counterfeit currency. In 1908, President Theodore Roosevelt transferred Secret Service agents to the Department of Justice; they formed the nucleus of what is now the Federal Bureau of Investigation (FBI). The scope of enforcement of the federal law enforcement agencies grew in the 20th century to include pursuit of organized crime, drug trafficking, political insurgencies, and terrorism, among others.

New communication technologies provide benefit to the users of such technology, and also create new potential sources of evidence in the investigation of criminal activities. Law enforcement investigation and surveillance techniques have been adept at exploiting emerging technologies, often because legal limits regarding access to the contents carried by the new technology have not yet been defined.

Legislation in the 20th century and beyond became a struggle to balance the protection of an individual's right of privacy from government intrusion and the legitimate needs of law enforcement in the conduct of their duties. At a federal level, numerous laws were passed dealing with privacy and access issues. Several of the notable acts in this area are discussed below.

Communications Act of 1934

In the early part of the 20th century, radio and telephone were bourgeoning industries in the United States, and law enforcement had already begun to mine these communications for evidence. Roy Olmstead, an alleged bootlegger from the Pacific Northwest, was convicted on evidence including wiretapped telephone conversations obtained by federal agents without judicial approval.[1] The Supreme Court of the United States determined that obtaining such evidence did not violate the Fourth or Fifth Amendment rights of the defendant. (For additional discussion of this case, see Chapter 10.)

By 1930, telephones were installed in more than 40 percent of homes. Radios were in more than 35 percent of homes, and adoption rates approached 10 percent per year.[2] The government felt it was time to bring increased organization and oversight to these technologies and passed the Communications Act of 1934.

Notably, this act created the Federal Communications Commission (FCC), including procedural and administrative provisions to enforce the orders of the commission, and codified the government's oversight of the broadcast spectrum. The act also transferred oversight of the telephone industry from the interstate commerce commission to the FCC. The act was signed by President Franklin Roosevelt on June 19, 1934.

The Act provided protection for communication via wire or radio, however, communication could be revealed "in response to a subpena[*sic*] issued by a court of competent jurisdiction, or on demand of other lawful authority":

> SEC. 605. No person receiving or assisting in receiving, or transmitting, or assisting in transmitting, any interstate or foreign communication by wire or radio shall divulge or publish the existence, contents, substance, purport, effect, or meaning thereof, except through authorized channels of transmission or reception, to any person other than the addressee, his agent, or attorney, or to a person employed or authorized to forward such communication to its destination, or to proper accounting or distributing officers of the various communicating centers over which the communication may be passed, or to the master of a ship under whom he is serving, or in response to a subpena[*sic*] issued by a court of competent jurisdiction, or on demand of other lawful authority; and no person not being authorized by the sender shall intercept any communication and divulge or publish the existence, contents, substance, purport, effect, or meaning of such intercepted communication to any person; and no person not being entitled thereto shall receive or assist in receiving any interstate or foreign communication by wire or radio and use the same or any information therein contained for his own benefit or for the benefit of another not entitled thereto; and no person having received such intercepted communication or having become acquainted with the contents, substance, purport, effect, or meaning of the same or any part thereof, knowing that such information was so obtained, shall divulge or publish the existence, contents, substance, purport, effect, or meaning of the same or any part thereof, or use the same or any information therein contained for his own benefit or for the benefit of another not entitled thereto: Provided, That this section shall not apply to the receiving, divulging, publishing, or utilizing the contents of any radio communication broadcast, or transmitted by amateurs or others for the use of the general public, or relating to ships in distress.[3]

The Communications Act of 1934 was replaced by the Telecommunications Act of 1996, which redefined the regulatory oversight of communications in the United States, but privacy issues were reconsidered much earlier than that.

Title III—Omnibus Crime Control and Safe Streets Act, 1968

The 1960s were a time of change in the United States, and the law enforcement process was no exception. New laws and court decisions focused on the procedures employed by law enforcement agencies in the conduct of their duties, including renewed interest in the rights of the accused.

The problem of crime in the United States became a campaign issue in the 1964 election. Lyndon B. Johnson was reelected by a landslide, and soon after, he acknowledged the need for a federal response to crime and public safety. On July 23, 1965, Johnson established the President's Commission on Law Enforcement and Administration of Justice through executive order 11236.[4] In February 1967, eighteen months after receiving Johnson's mandate, the Commission issued its report, "The Challenge of Crime in a Free Society."

The Commission examined every facet of crime and enforcement in the United States.[5] Relative to wiretapping and electronic eavesdropping the commission noted the struggle to balance the protection of an individual's right of privacy from government intrusion and the legitimate needs of law enforcement in the conduct of their duties. The report observed "the state of the law in this field is so thoroughly confused that no policeman, except in States that forbid both practices totally, can be sure about what he is allowed to do."[6]

The great majority of law enforcement officials believe that the evidence necessary to bring criminal sanctions to bear consistently on the higher echelons of organized crime will not be obtained without the aid of electronic surveillance techniques. They maintain these techniques are indispensable to develop adequate strategic intelligence concerning organized crime, to set up specific investigations, to develop witnesses, to corroborate their testimony, and to serve as substitutes for them— each a necessary step in the evidence-gathering processes in organized crime investigations and prosecutions.[7]

Enactment of Section 605 of the Federal Communications Act in 1934 precluded interception and disclosure of wire communications. The Department of Justice has interpreted this section to permit interception so long as no disclosure of the content outside the Department is made. Thus, wiretapping may presently be conducted by a Federal agent, but the results may not be used in court. When police officers wiretap and disclose the information obtained, in accordance with State procedure, they are in violation of Federal law.[8]

In a democratic society privacy of communication is essential if citizens are to think and act creatively and constructively. Fear or suspicion that one's speech is being monitored by a stranger, even without the reality of such activity, can have a seriously inhibiting effect upon the willingness to voice critical and constructive ideas. When dissent from the popular view is discouraged, intellectual controversy is smothered, the process for testing new concepts and ideas is hindered and desirable change is slowed. External restraints, of which electronic surveillance is but one possibility, are thus repugnant to citizens of such a society.[9]

The report concluded that "The present status of the law with respect to wiretapping and bugging is intolerable. It serves the interests neither of privacy nor of law enforcement. One way or the other, the present controversy with respect to electronic surveillance must be resolved. The Commission recommends: Congress should enact legislation dealing specifically with wiretapping and bugging."[10]

Congress passed legislation to implement many of the recommendations of the Commission on Law Enforcement and Administration of Justice in the Omnibus Crime Control and Safe Streets Act of 1968. This act was a broad legislative work, including the establishment of federal resources and funding for local law enforcement efforts, additional controls over firearm sales, and provisions that a court may authorize limited interception of electronic communications if certain procedural requirements are met.[11]

The procedures under the Act stated, "The Attorney General, or any Assistant Attorney General specially designated by the Attorney General, may authorize an application to a Federal judge of competent jurisdiction for, and such judge may grant in conformity with section 2518 of this chapter an order authorizing or approving the interception of wire or oral communications by the Federal Bureau of Investigation, or a Federal agency having responsibility for the investigation of the offense as to which the application is made," when such interception may provide evidence of certain crimes, including violations of the Atomic Energy Act, espionage, sabotage, treason, and activities of organized crime.[12] Additionally, the Act defined that a state Attorney General could authorize an application to a State Judge for interception of communication if such interception may provide evidence of felony offenses.[13]

The Act specified several restrictions to ensure that surveillance procedures were focused and limited. To be approved, the application needed to state details of the offense that had been or was about to be committed; a description of the facilities from which the interception was to take place; description of the type of communication to be intercepted; the identity of the, person, if known, whose communications were to be intercepted; and the length of time the interception would continue. There also needed to be a showing that other investigative procedures had been tried and failed, or would probably fail or be too dangerous, and if other interceptions involving the same individuals or facilities had taken place.[14]

The Act also made clear that the results of legally obtained intercepted communications could be shared with other law enforcement personnel engaged in the conduct of their duties, or to a state or criminal proceeding or Grand Jury.[15]

Despite the number of considerations that would need to be documented within the application to authorize the interception of communications, President Johnson did not believe the restrictions were adequate to protect the rights of citizens. Comments made by President Lyndon B. Johnson upon signing the Omnibus Crime Control and Safe Streets Act on June 9, 1968, noted his concern with several of the Act's provisions:

> Title III of this legislation deals with wiretapping and eavesdropping.
>
> My views on this subject are clear. In a special message to Congress in 1967 and again this year, I called—in the Right of Privacy Act—for an end to the bugging and snooping that invade the privacy of citizens.
>
> I urge that the Congress outlaw "all wiretapping and electronic eavesdropping, public and private, wherever and whenever it occurs." The only exceptions would be those instances where "the security of the Nation itself was at stake—and then only under the strictest safeguards."
>
> In the bill I sign today, Congress has moved part of the way by
>
> > –banning all wiretapping and eavesdropping by private parties;
> >
> > –prohibiting the sale and distribution of "listening-in" devices in interstate commerce.
>
> But the Congress, in my judgment, has taken an unwise and potentially dangerous step by sanctioning eavesdropping and wiretapping by Federal, State, and local law officials in an almost unlimited variety of situations.
>
> If we are not very careful and cautious in our planning, these legislative provisions could result in producing a nation of snoopers bending through the keyholes of the homes and offices in America, spying on our neighbors. No conversation in the sanctity of the bedroom or relayed over a copper telephone wire would be free of eavesdropping by those who say they want to ferret out crime.
>
> Thus, I believe this action goes far beyond the effective and legitimate needs of law enforcement. The right of privacy is a valued right. But in a technologically advanced society, it is a vulnerable right. That is why we must strive to protect it all the more against erosion.

I call upon the Congress immediately to reconsider the unwise provisions of Title III and take steps to repeal them. I am directing the Attorney General to confer as soon as possible with the appropriate committee chairmen and warn them of the pitfalls that lie ahead, in the hope that the Congress will move to repeal the dangerous provisions of this title.

Until that can be accomplished we shall pursue–within the Federal Government–carefully designed safeguards to limit wiretapping and eavesdropping. The policy of this administration has been to confine wiretapping and eavesdropping to national security cases only–and then only with the approval of the Attorney General.

This policy, now in its third year, will continue in force. I have today directed the Attorney General to assure that this policy of privacy prevails and is followed by all Federal law enforcement officers.

Many States have protected the citizen against the invasion of privacy by making wiretapping illegal. I call upon the State and local authorities in the other States to apply the utmost restraint and caution if they exercise the broad powers of Title III. We need not surrender our privacy to win the war on crime.[16]

Title III remained the law governing the interception of communications for the next 19 years.

Advancements in Telephone System Technologies

The telecommunications industry continued to evolve and grow through the 1970s and 1980s. In 1971, Erna Schneider Hoover, a researcher at Bell Labs, received a patent for a computerized switching system for telephone call traffic. This ushered in the age of digital switched voice communications, where voice traffic was transmitted in digital format rather than in analog format. Telephone companies soon began offering ISDN (Integrated Services Digital Network) services that included both voice traffic and data traffic, and computer networking continued to grow.

The Electronic Mail Association, a Washington-based trade association of the fledgling industry, was created in 1983, and by 1985 included over 60 members. The association predicted that "during the next decade, electronic mail will become a regular part of the communications mix that a substantial number of Americans use in the workplace, and increasingly at home as well."[17]

Surveillance techniques continued to grow as well. A pen register is a device that surreptitiously records the numbers of all outgoing calls dialed on a telephone line. In 1979, the Supreme Court of the United States held that such a device was not a search within the meaning of the Fourth Amendment, and, thus, no warrant was required to use such a device.[18] Trap and trace devices were similarly used to capture the numbers of inbound calls.

The emergence of data communications (i.e., computers and devices transmitting data between themselves, the digitization and transmission of voice traffic, and communication through microwave broadcast) substations exceeded the definitions within Title III of the Omnibus Crime Control and Safe Streets Act. In 1977 the Supreme Court held that the Act only covered communication that could be heard.[19] The court opined "Title III is concerned only with orders 'authorizing or approving the interception of a wire or oral communication. . . .'" Congress defined "intercept" to mean "the aural acquisition of the contents of any wire or oral communication through the use of any electronic, mechanical, or other device." Thus, the gathering of number dialed, such as through the use of a pen register, or accessing digital communications was not covered by the Act. There were also unresolved issues related to communication interception by non-law enforcement personnel.

The Foreign Intelligence Surveillance Act (FISA) of 1978 defines procedures for requesting judicial authorization for electronic surveillance by law enforcement of persons believed to be engaged in espionage or international terrorism against the United States on behalf of a foreign power; this was a question unanswered by Article 3 of the Omnibus Crime Control Act. The FISA required probable cause to believe that "the target of the electronic surveillance is a foreign power or an agent of a foreign power; provided, that no United States person may be considered a foreign power or an agent of a foreign power solely upon the basis of activities protected by the first amendment to the Constitution of the United States."[20] Article 3 of the Omnibus Crime Control Act also was not clear on penalties for electronic eavesdropping by non-law-enforcement personnel; this remained unanswered by the FISA:

> The criminal provisions in FISA only apply to law enforcement officers inasmuch as they state that a person is guilty of an offense only if he engages in electronic surveillance "under color of law" except as authorized by statute. Thus, a private person who without authority makes a nonaural acquisition of information from a telephone line between two computers, or from a radio transmission between two computers for the purpose of personal financial gain does not violate either the criminal provisions in FISA or in Title III, while an FBI agent who does the same thing in the course of a complicated criminal investigation, is himself in violation of the law.[21]

The Congressional Office of Technology Assessment (OTA) conducted a review of the technology and policy history of electronic surveillance, and the mid-1980s technological environment. Their observations included:

- The contents of phone conversations that are transmitted in digital form or calls made on cellular or cordless phones are not clearly protected by existing statutes.
- Data communications between computers and digital transmission of video and graphic images are not protected by existing statutes.
- There are several stages at which the contents of electronic mail messages could be intercepted: (1) at the terminal or in the electronic files of the sender, (2) while being communicated, (3) in the electronic mailbox of the receiver, (4) when printed into hard copy, and (5) when retained in the files of the electronic mail company or provider for administrative purposes. Existing law offers little or no protection at most of these stages.
- Legislated policy on electronic physical surveillance (e.g., pagers and beepers) and electronic visual surveillance (e.g., closed circuit TV and concealed cameras) is ambiguous or nonexistent.
- Legislated policy on database surveillance (e.g., monitoring of transactions on computerized record systems and data communication linkages) is unclear.
- There is no immediate technological answer to protection against most electronic surveillance, although there are emerging techniques to protect communication systems from misuse or eavesdropping (e.g., low-cost data encryption).[22]

The increasing complexity of telecommunications and the growth of computer networking and data services caused many in the legislature to wonder if eavesdropping and surveillance issues had outgrown Title III of the Omnibus Crime Control and Safe Streets Act. The year 1984 brought increased focus on and awareness of the issue of electronic surveillance, due to the famous book by George Orwell of the same name.

Electronic Communications Privacy Act of 1986

On January 26, 1984, Senator Patrick J. Leahey (D–Vermont) sent a letter to Attorney General William French Smith requesting clarification on the Justice Department's need for a court order to intercept electronic communications in light of the requirements of Title III of the Omnibus Crime Control and Safe Streets Act and FISA.

Assistant Attorney General Stephen S. Trott provided the response on behalf of the Attorney General on March 9, 1984, which included:

> Thus, the question whether a warrant or court order is legally required to conduct a nonaural interception of the radio portion of a hybrid wire-radio communication is, in our view, dependent upon whether there exists a reasonable expectation of privacy on the part of the individual whose communications are to be intercepted. If there exists such an expectation, a search warrant or court order is clearly necessary. If, however, the individual can claim no such justifiable privacy expectation in the communication, neither FISA nor the Fourth Amendment prohibits the warrantless interception of that communication. See Katz v. United States, 389 U.S. 347 (1967); Smith v. Maryland, 442 U.S. 735, 740-741 (1979).
>
> In this rapidly developing area of communications, which range from cellular non-wire telephone connections to microwave-fed computer terminals, distinctions such as that set out above are not always clear or obvious. Consequently, while we do not believe that there is currently a statutory requirement that a court order or search warrant be obtained in all instances involving nonaural interception, it is the policy of the Department of Justice to obtain such an order or warrant when nonaural electronic surveillance techniques are employed and our analysis indicates there is a reasonable expectation of privacy.[23]

On June 14, 1984, Mr. Trott sent a letter to clarify that:

> We [the Justice Department] wish to make clear that we believe that the microwave radio portion of a telephone call is normally accompanied by a justifiable expectation of privacy. Consequently, a judicial warrant would be required for the nonconsensual interception of such calls.[24]

On September 12, 1984, Senator Leahy chaired hearings by the Committee on the Judiciary, Subcommittee on Patents Copyrights, and Trademarks. Titled "Oversight on Communications Privacy," the hearings included testimony from representatives of American Telephone and Telegraph Co. (AT&T), Assistant Attorney General John C. Keeney, and representatives of the cellular communications industry.

Dr. Roy P. Weber, formerly of Bell Laboratories and currently division manager of service concepts at AT&T Communications, described the advancements taking place within the telecommunications industry, and why the definition of "aural communication" was becoming blurred:

> The key point that I will make, and I think is relevant to this subcommittee, is that the distinction between voice, data, image, and video is rapidly diminishing. What was once a telephone system that carried only voice is rapidly becoming an Integrated Services Digital Network, which carries the four forms of communication: voice, data, video, and image.[25]
>
> What you are doing today when you make an average call in this country, part of the voice is transmitted in an analog form, as represented on the top of that chart, and in many places in the network today in our switching machines, and over the wires that the voice is carried on, a process goes on where your voice is digitized and is represented as a string of bits and may go back and forth between analog and digital several times in an average conversation today.
>
> It is my belief that the way technology is going, it will soon be all bits; not in our lifetimes will it be all bits, but it will happen and that is the direction, but today it is a mixture.[26]

The Electronic Surveillance Act of 1984 was introduced in the U.S. House of Representatives on October 14, 1984, by Robert Kastenmeier (D–Wisconsin). In introducing the bill, Mr. Kastenmeier highlighted many of the issues with the current surveillance laws:

> Mr. Speaker, today I rise to introduce the Electronic Surveillance Act of 1984, a bill that I hope will serve as a study document in the remaining days of the 98th Congress and get the serious attention it deserves when the 99th Congress convenes in January.
>
> Mr. Speaker, for the past year the subcommittee I chair, the Subcommittee on Courts, Civil Liberties, and the Administration of Justice, has held a series of hearings entitled "1984: Civil Liberties and the National Security State." These hearings began on the eve of the Orwellian year, 1984, with the purpose of taking stock of the state of civil liberties in the very year Orwell used to warn us of the dangers of letting our precious freedoms slip away.
>
> Testimony at these hearings has made it clear that technology has outstripped existing law on electronic surveillance, leaving loopholes for wiretappers, public and private. My bill closes those loopholes, restoring the result intended by Congress when it passed

the law criminalizing wiretapping, the Omnibus Crime Control and Safe Streets Act of 1968.

The major loophole of that law is that it pertains only to aural communications, those capable of being heard by the human ear. Increasingly, however, telephone lines carry human conversation in digitized form, a series of computer signals that falls outside the law. Moreover, other forms of communications now carried over telephone lines, such as data transmissions and visual display, are also legally unprotected. My bill cures that, bringing all these forms of communication under legal protection.

My bill also sets legal standards for the use of video surveillance, which is currently unregulated, and for pen registers and electronic tracers. Subcommittee hearings early last session examined the operation of the Foreign Intelligence Surveillance Act. My bill, drawing on those hearings, makes a number of improvements, including the extension of the requirement of reporting to Congress, which otherwise would expire this year.

I urge my colleagues to consider the Electronic Surveillance Act of 1984 as a thoughtful response to changing technology; I welcome your suggestions and your support.[27]

The following year, after much discussion and debate, the Electronic Communications Privacy Act of 1985 was introduced simultaneously in the Senate and House of Representatives. On September 19, 1985, Senators Patrick J. Leahey (D–Vermont) and Charles McCurdy Mathias (R–MD) introduced the Act as Senate Bill 1667. As explained by Mr. Leahey:

"Let me describe a problem that grows as we sit here.

At this moment phones are ringing, and when they are answered, the message that comes out is a stream of sounds denoting one's and zero's. Nothing more. I am talking about the stream of information transmitted in digitized form, and my description covers everything from interbank orders to private electronic mail hookups.

By now this technology is nothing remarkable. What is remarkable is the fact that none of these transmissions are protected from illegal wiretaps, because our primary law, passed back in 1968, failed to cover data communications, of which computer-to-computer transmissions are a good example."

Mr. Mathias: "More than half a century ago, Justice Louis Brandeis sounded an eloquent warning about the challenge to privacy posed by technological advances. In his famous dissent in the

wiretapping case of Olmstead versus United States, Brandeis empha-
sized that if the right to privacy is to be meaningful, it must be strong
enough to meet this challenge. As he put it:

*The progress of science in furnishing the government with means of
espionage is not likely to stop with wiretapping. Ways may someday be developed by which the government, without removing papers from secret draw-
ers, can reproduce them in court, and by which it will be enabled to expose to
a jury the most intimate occurrences of the home.*

That prospect must have appeared fanciful to most of Brandeis'
contemporaries. But we know better. Brandeis' 'someday' has arrived,
and the law must respond.

Technological wizardry offers a variety of new communications
media: electronic mail, the cellular telephone, local area networks,
computer-to-computer data transmissions, and many more. Individuals and businesses are taking advantage of these new ways to share
information of every kind and description.

Some of the messages that these new media carry are highly
sensitive. A translation of the digital bits that race across our country by
wire, microwave, fiber optics, and other paths could reveal proprietary
corporate data, or personal medical or financial information. The users
of these networks—and that means more and more of us—expect
and deserve legal protection against unwarranted interceptions of
this data stream, whether by overzealous law enforcement officers or
private snoops.

The laws on the books today may not provide that protection.
The major statutory bulwark against one form of data interception—
wiretapping—forbids only the unauthorized 'aural acquisition' of wire
communications. This definition does not fully encompass the complex web of transmission media that have become the nervous system
of our economy and our society. Nor does it explicitly protect the
growing volume of messages that cannot be acquired 'aurally' because,
even though they may be intended as confidential, they never take the
form of the spoken word. Clearly, Brandeis' warning must be heeded;
the law must be brought up to date with the progress of science."[28]

On September 19, 1985, Congressman Kastenmeier introduced House
Resolution 3378, identical to the bill introduced in the Senate. Introducing
the bill, the Congressman stated:

Mr. Speaker, when Congress passed the wiretap law [Title III of the
Omnibus Crime Control and Safe Streets Act] in 1968, there was a

clear consensus that telephone calls should be private. Earlier Congresses had reached that same consensus regarding mail and telegrams.

But in the almost 20 years since Congress last addressed the issue of privacy of communications in a comprehensive fashion, the technologies of communication and interception have changed dramatically.

Today we have large-scale electronic mail operations, cellular and cordless telephones, paging devices, miniaturized transmitters for radio surveillance, light weight compact television cameras for video surveillance, and a dazzling array of digitized information networks, which were little more than concepts two decades ago.

These new modes of communication have outstripped the legal protection provided under statutory definitions bound by old technologies. The unfortunate result is that the same technologies that hold such promise for the future also enhance the risk that our communications will be intercepted by either private parties or the Government. Virtually every day the press reports on the unauthorized interception of electronic communications ranging from electronic mail and cellular telephones to data transmissions between computers. The communications industry is sufficiently concerned about this issue to have begun the process of seeking protective legislation. This bill is, in large part, a response to these legitimate business concerns." [29]

The bill was referred to the Subcommittee on Courts, Civil Liberties, and the Administration of Justice where hearings were held. The Justice Department opposed the broadening of the scope of the existing laws, indicating they appropriately balanced the need for privacy with the needs of law enforcement activities:

With respect to the legislation's attempt to bring within the proscriptions of Title III the newer types of non-aural transmissions such as computer transmissions and electronic mail, it is our current belief that with respect to authorization for the government to seize the contents of these transmissions, they are covered by an ordinary search warrant process based on probable cause pursuant to Rule 41 of the Federal Rules of Criminal Procedure. For example, if the government presently wishes to intercept a letter posted with the Postal Service, a search warrant under Rule 41 is procured. The Department believes that electronic mail is entitled to no greater protection than regular mail. Including these transmissions in Title III would, in effect, be adding an entire new scope to the existing statute. Had Congress intended that in 1968, it would have added non-aural communications such as ordinary mail in the statute at that time. The Department feels that changing the entire thrust of Title III is not warranted at this time and that intercepting this type of non-aural communication by private individuals could better be handled by separate legislation. The safeguards regulating government interception at this time are adequately covered by Rule 41 of the Federal Rules of Criminal Procedure. A similar analysis appears appropriate for computer transmissions.[30]

The results of the hearings and amendments were clean bill H.R. 4952, the Electronic Communications Privacy Act of 1986, which was introduced by Congressman Kastenmeier on June 24, 1986. An identical bill, S 2575, was simultaneously introduced in the Senate.

The following day, Assistant Attorney General John R. Bolton sent a letter to the Senate Committee on the Judiciary Chair Senator Strom Thurmond that the Justice Department strongly supported the enactment of S 2575.[31]

The bill passed the House on June 23, 1986, by voice vote, and passed the Senate on October 1, 1986, also by voice vote. On October 21, 1986, the law was signed by President Ronald Reagan.

More than 27 years later, the Electronic Communications Privacy Act remains the central legislation governing the interception and monitoring of electronic communications in the United States. Given the continuing evolution of telecommunications and computing over this time, many legislators and privacy advocates are again advocating an update to the Act to provide guidance and oversight that reflects modern technology.

Notes

1. *Olmstead v. United States*, 277 U.S. 438 (1928).
2. *Broadcasting and Cable Yearbook*, 1996; Federal Communications Commission.
3. Public Law Number 416, Act of June 19, 1934, Section 605.
4. President's Commission on Law Enforcement and Administration of Justice, "The Challenge of Crime in a Free Society" (report), U.S. Government Printing Office, February 1967, Foreword.
5. *Ibid.*
6. *Ibid.*, 94.
7. *Ibid.*, 201.
8. *Ibid.*, 202.
9. *Ibid.*, 202.
10. *Ibid.*, 203.
11. Omnibus Crime Control and Safe Streets Act of 1968, Pub. L. No. 90-351, 82 Stat. 197 (June 19, 1968).
12. Pub. L. No. 90-351, §2516(1).

13. Pub. L. No. 90-351, §2516(2).
14. Pub. L. No. 90-351, §2518(1).
15. Pub. L. No. 90-351, §2517(3).
16. Lyndon B. Johnson, "Statement by the President Upon Signing the Omnibus Crime Control and Safe Streets Act of 1968," June 19, 1928, www.presidency.ucsb.edu/ws/index.php?pid=28939.
17. "Electronic Communication and Privacy, Hearing before the Subcommittee on Patents, Copyrights, and Trademarks, November 13, 1985."
18. *Smith v. Maryland*, 442 U.S. 735 (1979).
19. *United States v. New York Telephone Co.*, 434 U.S. 159 (1977).
20. Foreign Intelligence Surveillance Act, Sec. 105(3).
21. Deputy Assistant Attorney General John C. Keeney, Prepared Statement before Subcommittee on Patents, Copyrights, and Trademarks, September 12, 1984, S. Hearing 98-1266.
22. *Federal Government Information Technology: Electronic Surveillance and Civil Liberties* (Washington, DC: U.S. Congress, Office of Technology Assessment, OTACIT-293, October 1985).
23. Letter to Hon. Patrick Leahy, March 9, 1984; presented before Subcommittee on Patents, Copyrights, and Trademarks, September 12, 1984, S. Hearing 98-1266.
24. Letter to Hon. Patrick Leahy, June 14, 1984; presented before Subcommittee on Patents, Copyrights, and Trademarks, September 12, 1984, S. Hearing 98-1266.
25. Transcript of S. Hearing 98-1266, p. 8.
26. Transcript of S. Hearing 98-1266, p. 9.
27. Congressional Record E4107.
28. Congressional Record–Senate, p.24365-p24371.
29. Congressional Record, p.24396
30. Deputy Assistant Attorney General James Knapp, Hearing before the Subcommittee on Patents, Copyrights, and Trademarks, November 13, 1985.
31. Electronic Communication and Privacy, Hearing before the Subcommittee on Patents, Copyrights, and Trademarks, November 13, 1985: Appendix, Documents Reflecting Developments on the Electronic Communications Privacy Act Subsequent to the Hearing on S. 1667.

CHAPTER 5

Electronic Communications Privacy Act

James P. Martin and
Harry Cendrowski

The Electronic Communications Privacy Act of 1986 (ECPA) amended the Omnibus Crime Control and Safe Streets Act to provide broader protection for electronic communications and increased penalties for violation. The ECPA closed many loopholes perceived in the Safe Streets Act and increased the protection of privacy of electronic communications. The ECPA is structured with a series of classifications meant to distinguish the type of information being communicated and stored, and to provide varying legal protection based on the perceived importance of the privacy interest of such information.

Title I of the ECPA defines federal penalties for the interception of communications for persons who intentionally intercept, endeavor to intercept, or procure any other person to intercept or endeavor to intercept, any wire, oral, or electronic communication. Penalties also apply to persons who disclose or use information that they knew or had reason to know was intercepted illegally, and also to persons who disclose communication gathered legally as part of a criminal investigation for purposes of impeding the investigation.[1] Title I prohibits interception of communication by *any* person not authorized, thus closing a loophole in the Safe Streets Act; the Safe Streets Act did not address nongovernmental interception.

The ECPA continues the distinction between contents and message data included in prior laws. Conceptually, contents of an electronic communication are analogous to the contents of a mailed letter sealed within the envelope; such contents have historically been protected under the Fourth Amendment. Under the ECPA, *contents* is defined as follows: "when used with respect to any wire, oral, or electronic communication, includes any information concerning the substance, purport, or meaning of that communication."[2] *Interception* under the ECPA is defined as "the aural or other acquisition of the contents of any wire, electronic, or oral communication through the use of any electronic, mechanical, or other device."[3] *Person* under the ECPA is defined as "any employee, or agent of the United States or any State or political subdivision thereof, and any individual, partnership, association, joint stock company, trust, or corporation"[4] The contents of a communication are perceived to have a greater privacy interest than the message data and thus are protected by greater legal safeguards.

The ECPA prohibits unlawful access to stored communications by prohibiting and penalizing whoever "intentionally accesses without authorization a facility through which an electronic communication service is provided;" or "intentionally exceeds an authorization to access that facility; and thereby obtains, alters, or prevents authorized access to a wire or electronic communication while it is in electronic storage in such system."[5]

Congress considered the definition of *storage* as it related to communications, and intended to provide protection of privacy irrespective of the medium on which the communication is stored:

> Subsection (a)(5) also provides a definition for electronic storage." That term means "any temporary intermediate storage of a communication incidental to the electronic transmission thereof and any storage of such communication by an electronic communication service for purposes of backup protection of such communication." Section 2510(17) defines "electronic storage" to mean any temporary, intermediate storage of a communication incidental to the electronic transmission thereof, and any storage of such communication by an electronic communication service for purposes of backup protection of such communication. Under Section 2710, computer storage is defined as an element of "remote computing service." These definitions are not intended to limit the terms "electronic storage" or "computer storage" to any particular medium of storage. While storage often takes place within the random access memory of a computer, the term applies equally to storage in any other form, including that on magnetic tape, disks, or other media. Thus, for example, the prohibitions against unauthorized access to a wire or electronic communication while it is in electronic storage, as set forth in Section 2701, would prohibit unauthorized access to such a communication while it is stored on magnetic tape or disk. The prohibitions would apply similarly to information held on magnetic tape or disk pursuant to an agreement to provide remote computing service.[6]

Title II—The Stored Communications Act

Title II of the ECPA created Chapter 121 of USC 18, "Stored Wire and Elec-tronic Communications and Transactional Records Access"; this is frequently referred to as the Stored Communications Act (SCA), although that term does not exist in the body of the ECPA. Many of the aspects defined within Title II were related to fledgling industries in 1986, however, the industries to which these terms apply have grown significantly ever since. Title II of the ECPA has tremendous relevance and applicability to cloud computing solu-tions as it governs data transmitted or held by a third-party service provider, which is essentially the definition of cloud computing.

Notably, Title II defines and makes the distinction between an *electronic communication service* (ECS) and a *remote computing service* (RCS). An ECS is defined as "any service that provides to users thereof the ability to send or receive wire or electronic communications"[7] while an RCS refers to providing storage or computing resources to a subscriber or customer. It is this section of the law that is most applicable to cloud computing solutions; cloud applica-tions by their very nature will either provide communications facilities, such as in an e-mail system or text message system, or provide storage and comput-ing, such as in photo hosting sites and social media sites. Many of the product offerings billed as "cloud computing" solutions could fall under the SCA as either an ECS, an RCS, or both.

The distinction between an ECS and an RCS was made in Congressional reports accompanying the Electronic Communications Privacy bill:

> Electronic mail differs from regular mail in three ways. First, e-mail is provided by private parties and thus not subject to governmental control or regulation under the postal laws. Second, it is interactive in nature and can involve virtually instantaneous "conversations" more like a telephone call than mail. Finally, e-mail is different from regular mail because the electronic communication provider as part of the service may technically have access to the contents of the mes-sage and may retain copies of transmissions.
>
> Any discussion of the application of current law governing interception of e-mail or the use of e-mail surveillance begins with the Fourth Amendment, which protects our reasonable expectation of privacy. There are no reported cases governing the acquisition of e-mail by the government, so an application of the Fourth Amendment to the interception of e-mail is speculative. It appears likely, however, that the courts would find that the parties to an e-mail transmission have a "reasonable expectation of privacy" and that a warrant of some kind is required.

As for statutory protection, while there may be some limits on government access to e-mail messages from an e-mail provider, there do not appear to be any federal statutes that directly address this issue. Title III would not apply, since it is limited to the "aural acquisition" of the contents of a communication, and e-mail usually does not involve the transmission of audible sound. The Communications Act might have some limited application, excepting, law enforcement officials. The Foreign Intelligence Surveillance Act, however, could be read to require federal law enforcement officials to obtain a court order before engaging in "electronic surveillance" that acquires the contents of e-mail communications. These criminal prohibitions do not apply to private persons.[8]

Congressional records also address RCS:

The use of remote computing services has also dramatically increased. Many persons use the facilities of these services to process and store their own data.

A subscriber or customer to a remote computing service transmits records to a third party, a service provider, for the purpose of computer processing. This processing can be done with the customer or subscriber using the facilities of the remote computing service in essentially a time-sharing arrangement, or it can be accomplished by the service provider on the basis of information supplied by the subscriber or customer.

As with electronic mail, remote computing services are still relatively new, and there is no case law directly on point. Proceeding by analogy, under current law a subscriber or customer probably has very limited rights to assert in connection with the disclosure of records held or maintained by remote computing services. It is likely, however, that contents of customer data enjoy a higher degree of Fourth Amendment protection.[9]

The ECPA provides:

(1) A person or entity providing an electronic communication service to the public shall not knowingly divulge to any person or entity the contents of a communication while in electronic storage by that service; and

(2) A person or entity providing remote computing service to the public shall not knowingly divulge to any person or

entity the contents of any communication which is carried or maintained on that service—

(A) On behalf of, and received by means of electronic transmission from (or created by means of computer processing of communications received by means of electronic transmission from), a subscriber or customer of such service; and

(B) Solely for the purpose of providing storage or computer processing services to such subscriber or customer, if the provider is not authorized to access the contents of any such communications for purposes of providing any services other than storage or computer processing.[10]

Notably, the law denotes that restrictions apply to services that are provided "to the public," that is, as a service that is available to any person after paying the requisite fees. The prohibition requirements of the ECPA are thus restricted to service providers and do not apply to private facilities such as internally hosted e-mail systems.[11] If the provider does not provide the applicable service "to the public," then the SCA does not place any restrictions on disclosure.

The petroleum company UOP hired the consulting firm Andersen Consulting and gave Andersen employees accounts on UOP's computer network. After the relationship between UOP and Andersen soured, UOP disclosed to the *Wall Street Journal* e-mails that Andersen employees had left on the UOP network. Andersen sued, claiming that the disclosure of its contents by the provider UOP had violated the SCA. The district court rejected the suit on the ground that UOP did not provide an electronic communication service to the public:

[G]iving Andersen access to [UOP's] e-mail system is not equivalent to providing e-mail to the public. Andersen was hired by UOP to do a project and as such, was given access to UOP's e-mail system similar to UOP employees. Andersen was not any member of the community at large, but a hired contractor.

Because UOP did not provide services to the public, the SCA did not prohibit disclosure of contents belonging to UOP's "subscribers."

For this reason, discovery of information held by a cloud service provider is vastly different than information held directly by a person or entity.

Providers of ECS, such as phone companies, e-mail services, and text message services, offer users the ability to send or receive wire or electronic communications. For example, a hosted e-mail system such as Gmail would be considered an ECS. *Contents* in "electronic storage" is defined as temporary, intermediate storage incidental to the communication (such as an inbox), and storage of such communication for system backup purposes.[12]

An RCS provides computer storage or processing services by means of an electronic communications system; this allows a user to obtain computer services in essentially a time-sharing arrangement. An RCS would include servers that allow users to store data for later retrieval, or a hosted application providing document editing and processing capabilities.

A service may be both an ECS and an RCS; the key is determining what role the provider has played, and is playing, with regard to the communication in question. For example, consider a hosted e-mail account through the Gmail service. When a communication is received for a user, and stored in the inbox, Gmail is an ECS with respect to the message. Once the message has been opened, and assuming the user does not delete the message, Gmail becomes an RCS with respect to the message. It is also important to note that if the message is downloaded or copied to the user's client computer, the restrictions of the SCA would no longer apply to the downloaded content, as it is no longer in the custody of the third-party provider.

The ECPA provides exceptions for the disclosure of communications:

(1) To an addressee or intended recipient of such communication or an agent of such addressee or intended recipient;

(2) As otherwise authorized in section 2517, 2511 (2)(a), or 2703 of this title; (these sections define the legal access to communications through court action, and are discussed below);

(3) With the lawful consent of the originator or an addressee or intended recipient of such communication, or the subscriber in the case of remote computing service;

(4) To a person employed or authorized or whose facilities are used to forward such communication to its destination;

(5) As may be necessarily incident to the rendition of the service or to the protection of the rights or property of the provider of that service;

(6) To the National Center for Missing and Exploited Children, in connection with a report submitted thereto under section 2258A;

(7) To a law enforcement agency if the contents
a. Were inadvertently obtained by the service provider; and
b. Appear to pertain to the commission of a crime; or

(8) To a governmental entity, if the provider, in good faith, believes that an emergency involving danger of death or serious physical injury to any person requires disclosure without delay of communications relating to the emergency.[13]

Exception (3) becomes significant for legal action, both civil and criminal, as the subscriber of the service can authorize disclosure of communications. RCS content may be provided with the consent of the subscriber. ECS content may be provided with the consent of the originator, addressee, or recipient. In civil litigation, some courts have concluded that contents of communications cannot be disclosed by the service provider to litigants when the service provider is presented with a civil subpoena.[14] In a recent decision however, the court noted that a subscriber could grant permission for the provider to release contents, or could not grant such permission, and the contents would not be provided. Therefore, the court reasoned that the information held by the provider was under the control of the subscriber, and therefore the party had an attendant duty to exercise this control and retrieve the content, or provide permission for the service provider to release the information.[15] For civil litigation, consent may be strongly encouraged by the court; in criminal matters, forcing consent could be considered a violation of the suspect's Fourth Amendment rights.[16]

Defining the subscriber is critically important, and may not always be clear. For individuals, it is likely fairly easy. An individual could be the sender or recipient, and the person who opened the e-mail would likely be deemed to be in control of the contents, and therefore could provide permission for disclosure. In a corporate setting, this becomes more complicated. A corporation may host a corporate e-mail system with a cloud computing vendor, but what about the e-mail accounts assigned through that same system to employees of a subsidiary entity? The definition of *control* is not yet fully established by the courts, and can vary from venue to venue, but is generally based on determining if the party has the right, authority, or practical ability to obtain the documents from a nonparty to the action.[17] The concept of control is a functional test rather than a categorical definition and is based on whether a party has actual access to relevant documents in the possession of the organization or stored in a cloud solution.

§2703—Required Disclosure of Customer Communication or Records

Section 2703 defines the procedures to compel disclosure of customer communication or records to government agencies, and defines greater privacy protection for materials in which there are greater privacy interests. Of note, §2730 distinguishes between e-mail content in storage less than 180 days, which may be disclosed only with a search warrant, and e-mail content in storage more than 180 days, which may be disclosed with a search warrant, a subpoena with notice, or court order with notice.[18] At the time, Congressional records describe the reason for treating content less than 180 days old with a higher privacy interest than older content:

> The Committee required the government to obtain a search warrant [for content in storage less than 180 days] because it concluded that the contents of a message in storage were protected by the Fourth Amendment. The Committee recognized that electronically stored communications can be of two types. The first type of stored communications are those associated with transmission and incident thereto. The second type of storage is of a back-up variety. Backup protection preserves the integrity of the electronic communications system and to some extent preserves the property of the users of such a system. Most—if not all—electronic communications systems (such as electronic mail systems), however, only keep copies of messages for a few months. To the extent that the record is kept beyond that point it is closer to a regular business record maintained by a third party and, therefore, deserving of a different standard of protection.[19]

The average cost of a gigabyte of computer storage in 1985 was approximately $105,000, which is why most communications were not maintained for long periods of time. Today the cost has decreased to around $0.05. Many privacy advocates note that the differentiation of protection of e-mail content based on days in storage is no longer appropriate given the pervasiveness of e-mail systems, and the tremendously decreased cost of computer storage, which means that content tends to be stored indefinitely, and all e-mail content should require a search warrant for disclosure.

§2703 defines the following three categories of information with increasing privacy interests; each category has different requirements to obtain the information:

1. Basic subscriber and session information
   a. Subscriber name
   b. Subscriber address
   c. Phone connection records or session duration information
   d. Length of service and service types
   e. Means and source of payments
2. Noncontent records and other information pertaining to customer;
   a. Transactional records
   b. Transaction and system logs
   c. Listing of e-mail accounts with whom subscriber communicated

3. Contents
   a. Actual files stored in the account
   b. E-mail text, headers
   c. Voicemail records
   d. Subject lines of e-mail
   e. Contents in electronic storage held by ECS
      i. Differs in the Ninth Circuit—see page 66
   f. Contents held by RCS

Section 2703 offers five mechanisms that a government entity, including law enforcement, can use to compel a provider to disclose certain kinds of information. They are described below in increasing order of power.

Subpoena

A subpoena will allow the government to compel disclosure of basic subscriber and session information, including: (a) name; (b) address; (c) local and long-distance telephone connection records, or records of session times and durations; (d) length of service (including start date) and types of service used; (e) telephone or instrument number or other subscriber number or identity, including any temporarily assigned network address; and (f) means and source of payment for such service (including any credit card or bank account number).[20]

A subpoena can also compel production of data not covered by the restrictions of the ECPA. The ECPA restricts production of data by third-party providers of service to the public. Production of internally stored data, including e-mail content, and local copies of data may be accomplished with a subpoena.

Subpoena with Prior Notice to the Subscriber or Customer

A subpoena with notice can compel production of all the materials allowed by a subpoena, and additionally the production of "the contents of a wire or electronic communication that has been in electronic storage in an electronic communications system for more than 180 days."[21]

The notice provisions can be met by providing the customer or subscriber prior notice of the disclosure. However, the court may grant an application to delay the notice for up to 90 days "upon the execution of a written certification of a supervisory official that there is reason to believe that notification of the existence of the subpoena may have an adverse result."[22]

The term *supervisory official* means "the investigative agent in charge or assistant investigative agent in charge or an equivalent of an investigating agency's headquarters or regional office, or the chief prosecuting attorney or the first assistant prosecuting attorney or an equivalent of a prosecuting attorney's headquarters or regional office."[23]

Adverse result is also a term defined in the ECPA. Potential adverse results include (a) endangering the life or physical safety of an individual; (b) flight from prosecution; (c) destruction of or tampering with evidence; (d) intimidation of potential witnesses; or (e) otherwise seriously jeopardizing an investigation or unduly delaying a trial.[24]

Many civil libertarians claim that the courts are much too free with the issuance of delayed notice orders, and the delay defeats the purpose intended by Congress in defining the notice requirement.

§2703(d) Court Order

A §2703(d) court order can compel production of all the materials covered by a subpoena with notice, and additionally the records and other information pertaining to a subscriber other than the contents of communications.[25]

A §2703(d) court order may be "issued by any court that is a court of competent jurisdiction and shall issue only if the governmental entity offers specific and articulable facts showing that there are reasonable grounds to believe that the contents of a wire or electronic communication, or the records or other information sought, are relevant and material to an ongoing criminal investigation. In the case of a State governmental authority, such a court order shall not issue if prohibited by the law of such State."[26] Under this standard, the government must explicitly identify the reasonable grounds and relevancy of the materials sought; it is not enough to merely certify that such grounds exist. The rationale behind the purpose of the §2703(d) court order was described in the House Report accompanying a 1994 amendment to the ECPA:

> This section imposes an intermediate standard to protect on-line transactional records. It is a standard higher than a subpoena, but not a probable cause warrant. The intent of raising the standard for access to transactional data is to guard against "fishing expeditions" by law enforcement. Under the intermediate standard, the court must find, based on law enforcement's showing of facts, that there are specific and articulable grounds to believe that the records are relevant and material to an ongoing criminal investigation.[27]

§2703(d) Court Order with Prior Notice to the Subscriber or Customer

A §2703(d) court order can compel production of all records within an account, except for unopened e-mail in the account for less than 180 days.[28]

This will allow production of all electronic communications in the account for more than 180 days, which would be considered communications held by an RCS.[29] Unopened e-mails remain covered by the restrictions defined for an ECS, as they have not yet been delivered to the recipient. Production of such e-mail content requires a search warrant.

In the Ninth Circuit, however, because of the interpretation of the court in the Theofel case, a §2703(d) court order with prior notice to the subscriber or customer would only compel production of communications in the system for 180 days or more, as the court held that opened e-mail in the account for less than 180 days would be a backup for the recipient, and thus the disclosure of the contents would require a search warrant. The Theofel decision is discussed below.

The notice requirements for a §2703(d) court order are the same as for a subpoena, as discussed above.

Search Warrant

Government investigators can compel disclosure of all information associated with an account through a search warrant; there is no notice requirement when a search warrant is obtained.

For discovery purposes the greater process generally includes access to information that cannot be obtained with a lesser process, and the additional work required to satisfy a higher threshold will often be justified because it can authorize a broader disclosure. For example, law enforcement will frequently obtain a search warrant as it can compel production of all records and contents, when the lessor processes cannot.

The following list summarizes the different production processes that can be employed, and the level of detail that can be produced with each:

Information Produced	Production Process
Basic subscriber, session, and billing information	Subpoena; 2703(d) order; or search warrant
Other transactional and account records	2703(d) order or search warrant
Retrieved communications and the content of other stored files	Subpoena with notice; 2703(d) order with notice; or search warrant
Unretrieved communications, including e-mail and voice mail (in electronic storage more than 180 days)	Subpoena with notice; 2703(d) order with notice; or search warrant
Unretrieved communications, including e-mail and voice mail (in electronic storage 180 days or less)	Search warrant

Backup Provisions

The ECPA allows for preservation of the sought records through a system backup pending resolution of the production issues or resolution of the matter:

> A governmental entity acting under section 2703(b)(2) may include in its subpoena or court order a requirement that the service provider to whom the request is directed create a backup copy of the contents of the electronic communications sought in order to preserve those communications. Without notifying the subscriber or customer of such subpoena or court order, such service provider shall create such backup copy as soon as practicable consistent with its regular business practices and shall confirm to the governmental entity that such backup copy has been made. Such backup copy shall be created within two business days after receipt by the service provider of the subpoena or court order.[30]

The data to be produced requires a 14-day notice period to the subscriber, during which time the subscriber can make a motion to quash the subpoena or vacate the court order with notice to the governmental agency and the service provider.[31] Such motion or application shall contain an affidavit or sworn statement:

(A) Stating that the applicant is a customer or subscriber to the service from which the contents of electronic communications maintained for him have been sought; and

(B) Stating the applicant's reasons for believing that the records sought are not relevant to a legitimate law enforcement inquiry or that there has not been substantial compliance with the provisions of this chapter in some other respect.[32]

Once the customer has complied with the challenge procedures, the court orders the government agency to file a sworn response, and the court conducts proceedings to determine if the request was appropriate or if the orders should be quashed.

Electronic Storage and the Ninth Circuit

The ECPA further divides contents into two categories: contents in electronic storage held by a provider of electronic communication service, and contents stored by a remote computing service. Importantly, *electronic storage* is a statutorily defined term. It does not simply mean storage of information by electronic means. Instead, *electronic storage* is defined as:

(A) Any temporary, intermediate storage of a wire or electronic communication incidental to the electronic transmission thereof; and

(B) Any storage of such communication by an electronic communication service for purposes of backup protection of such communication.[33]

As a result of the Ninth Circuit's decision in *Theofel v. Farey-Jones*, 359 F.3d 1066 (9th Cir. 2004), there are now two interpretations of *electronic storage*—a traditional narrow interpretation and an expansive interpretation supplied by the Ninth Circuit.

As traditionally understood, *electronic storage* refers to temporary storage made in the course of transmission by a service provider and to backups of such intermediate communications made by the service provider to ensure system integrity. These backups traditionally include transient copies of transmissions to verify the completeness and accuracy of transmission, and are often deleted as soon as the transmission is verified. It does not include posttransmission storage of communications. For example, e-mail that has been received by a recipient's service provider but has not yet been accessed by the recipient is in "electronic storage."[34] Before delivery, the communication is stored as a temporary and intermediate measure pending the recipient's retrieval of the communication from the service provider. Once the recipient retrieves the e-mail, however, the communication reaches its final destination. If the recipient chooses to retain a copy of the accessed communication, the copy will not be in "temporary, intermediate storage" and is not stored incident to transmission.

By the same reasoning, if the sender of an e-mail maintains a copy of the sent e-mail, the copy will not be in electronic storage. Messages posted to an electronic bulletin board or similar service are also not in electronic storage because the website on which they are posted is the final destination for the information.[35]

Traditionally, the *backup* component of the definition of *electronic storage* refers to copies made by an ISP to ensure system integrity. As one district court explained, the backup component "protects the communication in the event the system crashes before transmission is complete. The phrase 'for purposes of backup protection of such communication' in the statutory definition makes clear that messages that are in post transmission storage, after transmission is complete, are not covered by part (B) of the definition of 'electronic storage.'"[36] Additionally, Congressional records indicate the intent of the drafters of the ECPA that opened e-mail left on a provider's system be covered by provisions of the ECPA relating to remote computing services, rather than provisions relating to communications in electronic storage:

> Section 2702(a) protects communications "received by means of electronic transmission from * * * a subscriber or customer of such service" and kept "solely for the purpose of providing storage or computer processing services to such subscriber or customer * * *." In the case of either electronic mail or voice mail, the sender—a user of the service—has necessarily authorized the addressee's access to the message. The addressee's acquisition of the message is therefore clearly within the contemplation of section 2701(c). Sometimes the addressee, having requested and received a message, chooses to leave it in storage on the service for re-access at a later time. The Committee intends that, in leaving the message in storage, the addressee should be considered the subscriber or user from whom the system received the communication for storage, and that such communication should continue to be covered by section 2702(a)(2) [Remote Computing Service].[37]

The traditional interpretation of electronic storage was rejected by the Ninth Circuit in *Theofel v. Farey-Jones*,[38] in which the court held that e-mail messages were in electronic storage regardless of whether they had been previously accessed, because it concluded that retrieved e-mail fell within the backup portion of the definition of electronic storage. Although the Ninth Circuit did not dispute that previously accessed e-mail was not in temporary, intermediate storage within the meaning of §2510(17)(A), it determined that a previously accessed e-mail message fell within the scope of the backup portion of the definition of electronic storage, because such a message "functions as a 'backup' for the user."[39]

The impact of this decision is that, for litigation and proceedings within the Ninth Circuit, a search warrant would be required for all e-mail content, irrespective of whether it had been accessed by the recipient or had been in storage for more than 180 days. This ruling should not impact warrants and §2703(d) orders from jurisdictions outside the Ninth Circuit and served on service providers within the Ninth Circuit; however, it is possible some providers within the Ninth Circuit would resist production of such materials.

Pen Registers and Trap and Trace Devices

Title III of the Electronic Communications Privacy Act (ECPA) addresses pen register and trap and trace devices. A pen register is a device that captures the called numbers and information related to the calls made by the subject.

A trap and trace device captures the number and related information for incoming calls to the subject; today this would commonly be considered caller ID information. These devices do not intercept the contents of the call, only the information about the call itself. Today, both of these functions can easily be performed by a single device and are commonly called pen/trap devices.

Congress considered the need for protection of such data, as well as the expectation of privacy related to this data:

> The privacy of telephone customers can also be affected by the use of pen registers or other devices which record the numbers dialed from a telephone. Pen registers can be used by telephone companies for internal business purposes as well as by the government for law enforcement purposes. It is this governmental use which has posed the most difficult questions for Congress and the courts. The United States Supreme Court has on two occasions decided cases involving questions about the legality of installation and use of pen registers. *United States v. N.Y. Tel. Co.* presented the question whether an ordinary search warrant was sufficient to authorize government use of a pen register. The Court held that the existing federal wiretap law was not implicated by the use of a pen register, and that federal district judges have authority to issue warrants directing telephone company cooperation with the installation of pen registers.
>
> In *Smith v. Maryland* the Supreme Court found that law enforcement officials need not obtain a search warrant before securing telephone company cooperation in the installation of a pen register. The Court reasoned that because the person who used the telephone voluntarily disclosed the numbers dialed there was "no reasonable expectation of privacy," eliminating Fourth Amendment protection.
>
> The current practice of federal law enforcement agencies is to obtain a court order, under Rule 57 of the Federal Rules of Criminal Procedures, before using a pen register. This practice conforms with the Foreign Intelligence Surveillance Act, which created a requirement for a court order even in a domestic criminal case. Outside the limited context of foreign intelligence, Congress has specified no standard for obtaining a pen register court order. Thus, current case law and statutes leave federal law enforcement officials with virtually unchecked discretion to obtain information through the use of pen registers. All the government needs to do is make an application to a federal court; no independent judicial review of the facts is required.[40]

Title III of the ECPA prohibits the installation of a pen register or trap and trace device without obtaining a court order.[41] Additionally, Title III restricts the capabilities of such a device. "A government agency authorized to install and use a pen register or trap and trace device under this chapter or under State law shall use technology reasonably available to it that restricts the recording or decoding of electronic or other impulses to the dialing, routing, addressing, and signaling information utilized in the processing and transmitting of wire or electronic communications so as not to include the contents of any wire or electronic communications."

A federal pen/trap authorization order is effective across the country, and may be applied to anyone involved with the communications in question:

> The order, upon service of that order, shall apply to any person or entity providing wire or electronic communication service in the United States whose assistance may facilitate the execution of the order. Whenever such an order is served on any person or entity not specifically named in the order, upon request of such person or entity, the attorney for the Government or law enforcement or investigative officer that is serving the order shall provide written or electronic certification that the order applies to the person or entity being served.[42]

State-court orders authorizing a pen/trap device are limited to the jurisdiction of the court.[43]

The legal threshold to obtain such an order is fairly low. An attorney for the government may make an application to a court of competent jurisdiction, and must identify the law enforcement official and agency requesting the installation. The applicant must certify that the information likely to be obtained is relevant to an ongoing criminal investigation being conducted by that agency.[44] Additionally, the ECPA defines that a state law enforcement officer may also apply to a court of competent jurisdiction in that state to obtain an order approving the installation of a pen register or trap and trace device.[45] The applicant does not need to specifically identify the types of information they expect to capture.

The statute specifies that a service provider must provide assistance with the implementation of the order and must provide the results of the device in a reasonable period:

> A provider of a wire or electronic communication service, landlord, custodian, or other person shall install such device forthwith on the appropriate line or other facility and shall furnish such investigative or law enforcement officer all additional information, facilities, and technical assistance including installation and operation of the device

unobtrusively and with a minimum of interference with the services that the person so ordered by the court accords the party with respect to whom the installation and use is to take place, if such installation and assistance is directed by a court order. . . .[46]

The order does not need to identify the specific provider, which is significant for Internet communications. The very nature of the Internet means that traffic flows through a variety of providers, and each could provide an access point for a pen/trap device.

The pen register and trap and trace statute hold tremendous importance for modern communications. The statute permits law enforcement to obtain the addressing information of Internet communications much as it would addressing information for traditional phone calls. Internet communications are based on packets that are sent to a unique Internet Protocol (IP) address; this includes the way that e-mail contents are sent. Every e-mail message sent over the Internet (as opposed to e-mail sent within a company or local network) contains headers that specify address and routing information generated by the mail server, followed by the actual contents of the message. The header information includes the e-mail address of the sender and recipient, as well as the date and time the e-mail was sent and the IP address of the computer from which the e-mail was sent. Court decisions have held that the e-mail header information constitutes addressing information.[47]

Production Demands and the ECPA

Certain procedural aspects are different when implementing production demands under the ECPA.

First, §2711(3) defines "court of competent jurisdiction" as any district court of the United States (including a magistrate judge of such a court) or any U.S. court of appeals that has jurisdiction over the offense being investigated; or a court of general criminal jurisdiction of a State authorized by the law of that State to issue search warrants. This means that the ECPA permits federal judges to issue 2703(d) orders compelling providers to disclose information even if the judge does not sit in the district in which the information is stored or the service provider is headquartered. This is important given the nature of cloud computing; data may be stored in servers across the country or around the world, transparently to the end user or the courts. ECPA is silent, however, on whether state courts may issue orders to providers outside their districts.

Second, the presence of an officer is not required for service or execution of a §2703 warrant.[48] Investigators typically do not directly search the computers for the information requested. Instead, the warrant directs the provider to produce all the content of the account or accounts desired, and the information produced is then reviewed by law enforcement for items that fall within the scope of items to be seized.

While the ECPA generally prohibits voluntary disclosure of information by a third-party provider of services, there are several notable exceptions. If the provider does not provide services to the public, the ECPA does not apply. For example, consider a consultant who is provided an e-mail account by a company where they are assigned for work. Court decisions have determined that the company providing such an e-mail account is not covered by the ECPA, as they do not provide services to the public. In civil litigation, some courts have concluded that contents of communications cannot be disclosed to litigants even when the service provider is presented with a civil subpoena.[49] In a recent decision, the court noted that a subscriber could grant permission for the provider to release contents, or could not grant such permission, and the contents would not be provided. Therefore, the court reasoned that the information held by the provider was under the control of the subscriber, and therefore the party had an attendant duty to exercise this control and retrieve the content.[50]

The ECPA was primarily written to protect the end user of computing services from government surveillance, in essence reinforcing the Fourth Amendment right to be protected from searches when there is a reasonable expectation of privacy. The reasonable expectation of privacy is constantly being tested in a world of interconnected computers, social media applications, and mobile computing devices.

Courts have held that an individual will not retain a reasonable expectation of privacy in information that the person has made openly available. See *Katz v. United States*, 389 U.S. 347, 351 (1967) ("What a person knowingly exposes to the public, even in his own home or office, is not a subject of Fourth Amendment protection."); *Wilson v. Moreau*, 440 F. Supp. 2d 81, 104 (D.R.I. 2006) (finding no expectation of privacy in documents a user stored on computers available for public use in a public library); *United States v. Gines-Perez*, 214 F. Supp. 2d 205, 224-26 (D.P.R. 2002) (finding no reasonable expectation of privacy in information placed on the Internet); *United States v. Butler*, 151 F. Supp. 2d 82, 83-84 (D. Me. 2001) (finding no reasonable expectation of privacy in hard drives of shared university computers). This concept greatly complicates the privacy expectations over social media content, cell-tower data, and certain other computer activities; these issues are discussed in depth in other chapters of this book.

Investigators attempting to access information held by a third party will need to evaluate an appropriate course of action depending on the type of information received, as well as the relative cooperation of the subscribing party. The role of the ECPA will continue to grow in importance as more and more companies adopt cloud computing solutions, and solutions become more robust. The ECPA is more than 25 years old, and many believe that technology has again outstripped the capacity of the law to address current technological issues. Courts continue to evaluate aspects of the law, and case law continues to build around these issues. Several notable cases setting precedent in this area are discussed in later chapters of this book.

Notes

1. 18 USC §2511.
2. 18 USC §2510.
3. 18 USC §2510.
4. 18 USC §2510.
5. 18 USC §2701(a).
6. H.R. Rep. No. 99-647 (1986) at 38.
7. 18 USC §2510.
8. H.R. Rep. No. 99-647 (1986) at 22–23.
9. H.R. Rep. No. 99-647 (1986) at 23.
10. 18 USC §2702(a).
11. *Andersen Consulting LLP v. UOP*, 991 F. Supp. 1041 (N.D. Ill. 1998).
12. §2510(17)(A).
13. 18 USC §2702(b).
14. See *O'Grady v. Superior Court*, 139 Cal.App.4th 1423, 1448.
15. *Flagg v. City of Detroit*, 252 F.R.D. 346, 362 (E.D. Mich. 2008).
16. See *Juror No. 1 v. California*, 2011 U.S. Dist. LEXIS 16834.
17. *Victor Stanley, Inc. v. Creative Pipe, Inc.*, 269 F.R.D. 497, 523-24 (D. Md. 2010).
18. 18 USC §2703(a).
19. H.R. Rep. No. 99-647, at 68 (1986).
20. 18 U.S.C. §2703(c)(2).
21. 18 USC §2703(a).
22. 18 U.S.C. §2705(a)(1)(B).
23. 18 U.S.C. §2705(a)(6).
24. 18 U.S.C. §2705(a)(2).
25. 18 USC §2703(c).
26. 18 USC §2703(d).
27. H.R. Rep. No. 102-827 (1994).
28. 18 U.S.C. §2703(a).
29. 18 U.S.C. §2703(b).
30. 18 USC §2704.
31. 18 USC §2704(b).
32. 18 USC §2704 (b).
33. 18 USC §2510(17).
34. *Steve Jackson Games, Inc. v. United States Secret Service*, 36 F.3d 457, 461 (5th Cir. 1994).
35. *Snow v. DirecTV, Inc.*, 2005 WL 1226158.
36. *Fraser v. Nationwide Mut. Ins. Co.*, 135 F. Supp. 2d 623, 636 (E.D. Pa. 2001).
37. H.R. Rep. No. 99-647, at 65 (1986).
38. *Theofel v. Farey-Jones*, 359 F.3d 1066 (9th Cir. 2004).
39. *Ibid.*

40. H.R. Rep. No. 99-647 (1986).
41. 18 USC §3121(a).
42. 18 USC §3123(a)(1).
43. 18 USC §3123(a)(2).
44. 18 USC §3122.
45. 18 USC §3122(a)(2).
46. 18 USC §3124(b).
47. *United States v. Forrester,* 512 F.3d 500, 510 (9th Cir. 2008).
48. 18 U.S.C. §2703(g).
49. See *O'Grady v. Superior Court,* 139 Cal.App.4th 1423, 1448.
50. *Flagg v. City of Detroit,* 252 F.R.D. 346, 362 (E.D. Mich. 2008).

CHAPTER 6

Proposed Legislative Changes and Future Laws

James P. Martin

The year was 1986. The New York Mets won the World Series against the Boston Red Sox, a series that included a still infamous error by the Boston first baseman. In football, Jim McMahon led the Chicago Bears to a Superbowl win, and the still-forgettable song and video "The Superbowl Shuffle." A startup technology company called Quantum Computer Services Inc. was a year old and featured an online service called Q-Link that worked with the Commodore 64. Five years later, in 1991, the company would change their name to America Online Inc., also known as AOL. *Back to the Future* played in theaters; the second installment of that franchise featured Marty McFly traveling to the faraway future year 2015 to save his kids from peril. And in 1986, the Electronic Communications Privacy Act (ECPA) was passed by Congress and signed into law by President Reagan. Technology has advanced tremendously since 1986, however, the primary law that regulates disclosure of contents of computer communications and stored data is still the law of the land.

Few would have predicted in 1986 that e-mail would primarily replace paper-based mail as the primary means of communication, and that people would send business transactional and financial documents over e-mail. Fewer still might have predicted that cellular telephone technology would advance to the point that everyone would carry one at all times and they would be far more powerful than microcomputers of the day, or that a phone could be used as a tracker to determine its exact location. It should be no surprise, then, that many people believe the current safeguards against disclosure offered by the 1986 laws fall short in the current environment.

Calls for updates to the existing law are advanced by privacy experts, technology companies, and even the Department of Justice. Elana Tyrangiel,

Acting Assistant Attorney General for the Office of Legal Policy, provided testimony to the House Judiciary Committee's Subcommittee on Crime, Terrorism, Homeland Security, and Investigations, stating:

> Acknowledging that the so-called "180-day rule" and other distinctions in the SCA [a provision within ECPA] no longer make sense is an important first step, the harder question is how to update those outdated rules and the statute in light of new and changing technologies while maintaining protections for privacy and adequately providing for public safety and other law enforcement imperatives.[1]

Points for Improvement

Several deficiencies in the current law are frequently discussed as imperatives for change. Discussions of shortfalls and priorities for modernization of the 1986 Act frequently include:

- *Treat all content consistently.* Remove the distinction between content under 180 days old (which requires a search warrant) and content opened and over 180 days old (which requires a subpoena to be released). In an age where computer storage rates have dropped to the point of immateriality, and virtually unlimited storage space is available through cloud computing solutions, the difference between the ageing of content should be removed.
- *Develop a suppression remedy.* The suppression of evidence remedy under the Wiretap Act (Title III of the Omnibus Crime Control and Safe Streets Act of 1968) is provided pursuant to 18 U.S.C. §2515:

> "Whenever *any wire or oral communication* has been intercepted, no part of the contents of such communication and no evidence derived therefrom may be received in evidence in any trial, hearing, or other proceeding in or before any court, grand jury, department, officer, agency, regulatory body, legislative committee, or other authority of the United States, a State, or a political subdivision thereof if the disclosure of that information would be in violation of this chapter."[2] [italics for emphasis added by authors]

> Federal circuits have found that suppression of evidence is an unavailable remedy for violations of ECPA and interceptions of "electronic

communications"[3] and that the ECPA only provides a civil remedy for a violation of §2703.[4]

Many people believe the same rules should apply for electronic and nonelectronic information: If evidence is illegally obtained, it should not be used against an individual in court.

- *Determine required protection of location data.* Smartphones can currently be used as personal tracking devices through (1) internal GPS data; (2) their connections to cell towers; and (3) portable tracking devices such as the StingRay (see Chapter 8). The treatment of such data was not considered in 1986 and is not covered by the Act. Courts have developed varying implementations of the safeguards over such data, but differ as to the degree of protection afforded such data. Refinements to the law should specifically address the procedures and authorizations required to access location data and connection information.
- *Develop reporting mechanisms for discovery requests.* Current laws define reporting requirements for wiretap orders, but do not specify reporting requirements for other types of surveillance requests.
- *Define civil procedures for data access.* The current law speaks to data release to a government agency, and offers no guidance for civil litigants to access cloud-stored data of opposing parties. Additionally, the current law specifies that the orders of any federal judge may authorize disclosure, but is silent on the powers of state-level judges outside of their jurisdiction.

Congressional Action

Congress has advanced several bills in recent years to amend the law. However, they have not advanced beyond the committee stage as of this writing.

On August 2, 2012, HR 6339 was introduced to the U.S. House of Representatives. The Electronic Communications Privacy Act Modernization Act of 2012 was referred to committee and was not advanced. The bill included proposals to require a search warrant for the production of any data:

Section 2703(a) of title 18, United States Code, is amended to read as follows:

(a) Contents of Wire or Electronic Communications:

(1) A governmental entity may require the disclosure by a provider of electronic communication service or remote

computing service of the contents of a wire or electronic communication that is stored, held, or maintained by that service only pursuant to:

(A) a warrant complying with the Federal Rules of Criminal Procedure and issued by a court with jurisdiction over the offense under investigation or equivalent State warrant; or

(B) a court under title I or title VII of the Foreign Intelligence Surveillance Act of 1978 (50 U.S.C. 1801 et seq. and 1881 et seq.).

(2) Unless delayed notice is ordered under section 2705, not later than three days after a governmental entity receives contents of a communication under this subsection, the governmental entity shall notify the subscriber or customer concerned of the matters required in notices under, and by the means described in, paragraphs (4) and (5) of section 2705(a).[5]

HR 6339 contained provisions to require reporting related to the use of mobile tracking devices, and enhanced reporting of activities related to warrants compelling disclosure, including disclosure of cell tower data. Additionally, the bill included amendments to make suppression remedies the same for intercepted wire, oral, and electronic communications.

On March 20, 2013, S. 607: Electronic Communications Privacy Act Amendments Act of 2013 was introduced in the U.S. Senate. The bill included language nearly identical to HR 6339, and was referred to committee on May 7, 2013. It has not yet advanced out of the committee as of this writing.

Given the bourgeoning amounts of data in electronic storage and transmitted via e-mail, and the ongoing introduction of smartphones with feature sets unthinkable even a few years ago, Congress will eventually need to act to update the ECPA. There is currently a groundswell of awareness in the United States of electronic privacy issues, and while this focus may not be directly caused by weaknesses in the ECPA, it certainly would serve to provide political force supporting amendment of the law.

Notes

1. Acting Assistant Attorney General Elana Tyrangiel testimony before the U.S. House Judiciary Subcommittee on Crime, Terrorism, Homeland Security, and Investigations, March 19,2013.
2. 18 U.S.C. §2515.
3. *United States v. Kennedy,* 81 F. Supp. 2d 1103, 1109-11 (D. Kan. 2000).
4. *United States v. Charles,* 1998 WL 204696 (D. Mass. 1998).
5. HR 6339, Section 2.

CHAPTER 7

The Control Concept and Related Issues

Matthew P. Breuer and James P. Martin

A considerable amount of litigation has been spent on cloud computing-related issues as more and more companies have migrated their electronic communications and data storage to cloud-based solutions. In a cloud computing model, data storage and processing is performed by a third party service provider; production of data held by a third party provider is restricted by the Stored Communications Act (SCA). According to the SCA, one allowable avenue for production is to obtain the permission of the entity that controls the account to produce the data, however, the identity of the person or entity with that control is not always clear. To attempt to access data stored in the cloud, litigants have filed countless motions against companies and individuals to compel disclosure or force a party to consent to the production of what are perceived to be key documents. The basis for these arguments is usually centered on constitutional issues, a procedural aspect, or an overbroad subpoena. This has caused one of the major issues with cloud computing in civil litigation to be overlooked, which has been the question of *who has control of sought after documents?* In other words, ample litigation has taken place because parties cannot determine the correct individual or entity to subpoena when seeking production of sought after electronic communications.

The Application of Rule 34(a)

Courts have consistently struggled with the application of control under the Stored Communications Act (SCA) and the Federal Rules of Civil Procedure (FRCP) 34(a). These issues have plagued individuals and corporations in disputes and have put companies that have moved communications to cloud providers on notice. Electronic communications in litigation are governed by FRCP 34. Specifically, the rule states:

> A party may serve on any other party a request within the scope of Rule 26(b) . . . to produce and permit the requesting party or its representative to inspect, copy, test, or sample the following items in the responding party's possession, custody, or *control* . . . any designated documents or electronically stored information—including writings, drawings, graphs, charts, photographs, sound recordings, images, and other data or data compilations—stored in any medium from which information can be obtained either directly or, if necessary, after translation by the responding party into a reasonably usable form.[1]

Advances in technology have rapidly altered the landscape of discovery. Struggling to keep up with technological advancements has frequently been an issue for courts, and this has been particularly true in electronic discovery. The issue was finally addressed in 2006, with an amendment to the FRCP promulgated to define requirements for the production of "other data or data compilations stored in any medium from which information can be obtained".[2] Parties in litigation had always considered "documents" to include electronically stored information from a practical standpoint, but it was not until 2006 that stored data was specifically addressed in the FRCP.[3] It was apparent at the time that forms of electronically stored communications and other data would continue to become increasingly complex and voluminous in nature. The amendment aimed to ensure that electronically stored information would "stand on equal footing with the discovery of paper documents" and that the rule would "apply to information that is stored in a medium from which it can be retrieved and examined."[4] This language specifically encompassed the production of e-mail, one of the most pervasive types of electronically stored information.

In addition, by stating that discovery included "information stored in any medium," the amendment took into account future developments in computer technology.[5] The amendment intended to take a very broad approach to ensure it could maintain flexibility for future changes in technology, and also to ensure that a party could not move data out of the reach of production by simply storing it on another device. Courts have also consistently maintained that it is the moving party's responsibility and burden to establish that documents are within the other parties' control. Although the court's application has been inconsistent in determining control, courts all have the same approach. The definition of control is typically viewed as a functional one rather than a categorical one. Thus, it is a question of "whether an entity has actual, non-theoretical access to relevant documents in the physical possession of its parent or subsidiary."[6]

Rule 34(a) in Litigation

Thayer v. Chiczewski, No. 07 C 1290, 2009 WL 2957317 (N.D. Ill. Sept. 11, 2009) provides a good starting point in addressing the concept of control. On March 19, 2005, Thayer was arrested for participating in an anti-war march for which he was denied a permit. During discovery and in his deposition, Thayer admitted that he sent e-mails about the event, but claimed that the older e-mails had been subsequently deleted. On July 9, 2009, the city of Chicago issued a revised subpoena to AOL for messages from Thayer's account and eventually filed a motion to compel discovery. The court acknowledged that the Stored Communications Act (SCA) usually prohibited such disclosures of civil subpoenas against third parties.

However, because the plaintiff would have been forced to disclose the e-mails if he were in possession of them and AOL would have to produce them if the plaintiff requested, the e-mails were considered under the plaintiff's control for discovery purposes.[7] Because Thayer had already consented to the release of one e-mail, the court reasoned that he could not later object to the production of *all* of the e-mails. As *Thayer* demonstrated, the concept of control is not difficult when applied to the setting of a single individual's e-mail account. If a user opened the account containing electronically stored communications, then that user can be compelled to authorize disclosure and has control over the data.[8]

When extending beyond the individual account holder, the case law becomes much murkier, especially with respect to corporations. For example, how does the application of the SCA and the control concept vary, if at all, with respect to foreign corporations or entities that have their principal place of business abroad? What about successor companies to bankruptcy reorganizations? Does a subsidiary have control of its parent's third-party e-mail accounts? What about a parent having control of a subsidiary's e-mail? Unfortunately, case law does not provide that much guidance on the issue. There are few cases that have analyzed the control issue, if any, with respect to cloud computing in particular. Accordingly, the most instructive guides in regard to this issue have been those in which courts have analyzed under what circumstances entities have control of documents for discovery purposes.[9]

In re NTL, Inc. Securities Litigation involved the plaintiff filing suit on April 18, 2002, against NTL, Inc. ("Old NTL") alleging federal securities laws violations. Old NTL filed for Chapter 11 bankruptcy and emerged on September 5, 2002, with a "Second Amended Joint Reorganization Plan of NTL Incorporated and Certain Subsidiaries."[10] Pursuant to the plan, two main companies would emerge out of the bankruptcy: NTL Europe and NTL, Inc. NTL Europe was deemed to be the successor company, and the litigation commenced against this entity. New NTL was not named a party to the litigation; however, it took physical possession of the former company's records. The plaintiff sought discovery sanctions against defendant NTL Europe, claiming that they hindered discovery and allowed for key e-mails to be destroyed.[11]

With respect to who had control of the documents, defendant NTL Europe asserted that it did not have any control of the documents or electronically stored information that the plaintiffs sought because they were in New NTL's possession. Even though it was a party designated after bankruptcy to continue as the defendant, it still could not be responsible for the documents being destroyed or any actions taken since the case was filed. Quoting *Bank of New York v. Meridien Biao Bank Tanzania, Ltd.*, the court stated the rule for control pursuant to FRCP 34:

> Under Rule 34, control does not require that the party have legal ownership or actual physical possession of the documents at issue; rather, documents are considered to be under a party's control when that party has the right, authority, or practical ability to obtain the documents from a non-party to the action.[12]

Furthermore, some courts have clarified this approach by interpreting Rule 34 to require production "if the party has the practical ability to obtain documents from another, irrespective of his legal entitlement to the documents."[13] Applying this standard to the present case, the court determined that NTL Europe had the legal right and practical ability to obtain the relevant documents. Under the reorganization plan, New NTL was required to make available to defendant NTL Europe any documents it needed to comply with the securities litigation. In addition, prior case law has set precedent that allows treatment of both the assignor and assignee as parties in discovery when refusing to do so would frustrate discovery. The company also had a duty to initiate a litigation hold and preserve responsive documents and electronically stored information.

Because of these reasons, NTL had control of the documents and had a duty to preserve them prior to the litigation. From this case, the standard emerged that a party has control over documents if it has the practical ability, contractual right, or other legal right to do so. This enumerated standard was also important in what it did not include in the language. The fact that electronically stored information is not within an entity's physical possession or even within the United States does not allow a party to evade its obligations in discovery. *In re NTL* also showed that extending the analysis beyond the individual causes the courts to typically take a very fact-specific approach and scrutinize the relationships between the parties much more extensively to determine control. This sharply contrasts with the more bright-line approach courts have taken when determining control with individuals.

The control issue is also more complicated with respect to foreign entities. In *U.S. Intern. Trade Com'n v. ASAT, Inc.*, the U.S. International Trade Commission was investigating whether encapsulated integrated circuits by Carsem infringed three United States patents owned by Amkor Technology, Inc. An administrative law judge issued three subpoenas against non-parties, all of which allegedly had documents relative to Carsem's defenses. ASAT, Inc. was a California corporation with a principal office in Hong Kong. The entity was a wholly-owned subsidiary of ASAT Limited, a Hong Kong corporation with its principal office in Hong Kong, and ASAT Holdings Ltd., which was a Cayman Islands holding corporation with a principal office in Hong Kong as well. ASAT, Inc. claimed it did not have control of the documents and as a result moved to quash the subpoena.[14]

Unlike *In re NTL, Inc. Securities Litigation*, the court specifically listed five instances in which a subsidiary, like ASAT, Inc., has control of documents that are in a parent company's possession:

(1) the alter ego doctrine . . . warranted "piercing the corporate veil";

(2) the subsidiary was an agent of the parent in the transaction giving rise to the lawsuit;

(3) [t]he relationship is such that the agent-subsidiary can secure documents of the principal-parent to meet its own business needs and documents helpful for use in litigation;

(4) [t]here is access to documents when the need arises in the ordinary course of business; and

(5) [the] subsidiary was [a] marketer and servicer of the parent's product (aircraft) in the United States.[15]

The Commission attempted to rely on the fourth and fifth grounds arguing the close business relationship between the three entities and pointed out the principal activities ASAT, Inc. performed on behalf of its parent companies. The court was not persuaded by this argument. Applying a somewhat different standard, the court stated that control is defined as "the legal right, authority, or ability to obtain documents upon demand."[16] Carsem did not establish a lack of corporate separateness and failed to show a close business relationship between the three entities. The standard applied by the court was consistent with the concept that determining control is "more of a factual, practical inquiry than simple possession or corporate structure."[17] Accordingly, the court found that as a matter of law, ASAT, Inc. did not have control of the subpoenaed documents pursuant to FRCP 34, and the order enforcing the Commission's subpoena was reversed.

In *Zenith Electronics, LLC v. Vizio, Inc.*, Zenith alleged that defendant Westinghouse Digital Electronics, LLC was selling televisions with technology that infringed on Zenith's patents. The company also discovered a Samsung demodulator chip they believed infringed Zenith's patents, and as a result served a subpoena on Samsung America seeking documents and source code relating to the chipsets. The subpoena also included its foreign parent company, Samsung Electronics Corporation, a Korean corporation. Samsung America refused to produce any of the documents, claiming that it was only involved in the sales and marketing and that it did not develop any of the source code. Although Samsung America conceded that Samsung Korea may have the documents, it argued it was still not obligated to produce the documents because the two entities maintained separate records and archives to which Samsung America did not have access in the ordinary course of business.[18]

The court's inquiry was again a functional approach and focused on whether the corporation had access to the documents and the ability to obtain them as a practical matter.[19] *Zenith* was important in that it continued to stress that the party seeking the production bears the burden of establishing control. As a result of this principle, the court maintained that Zenith failed to establish that Samsung America had control over the Samsung Korea documents. The only evidence that Zenith was able to offer was the parent–subsidiary relationship and Samsung America's communications regarding an offer from the parent to provide documents if some claims were withdrawn by Zenith. The court held that this did not satisfy Zenith's burden. The court's inquiry did not look to specific factors or engage in lengthy discussion regarding the concept of control. Its approach was simple. It looked at whether Zenith had established its burden of showing that Samsung America had access to and the ability to obtain the documents. Ignoring corporate structure and the parent–subsidiary relationship, the court based its decision on what could have been an insufficient pleading.

Other cases involving parent–subsidiary entities have also been helpful in providing insight into the control aspect in civil litigation and how it would be applied to cloud computing. *In re Ski Train Fire of Nov. 11, 2000 Kaprun Austria* arose out of a fire that occurred on a ski train in Austria. Siemens AG Osterreich (Siemens Austria) was involved in the manufacture and/or installation of the electrical components on the car that caught fire, but was dismissed as a defendant in the action because of insufficient jurisdictional contacts with the district. However, the plaintiffs asserted that Siemens Germany (Siemens AG), the parent company of Siemens Austria, supplied the systems for installation and brought a motion against Siemens AG and Siemens Corporation, the New York subsidiary, seeking to compel Siemens AG to provide sought-after documents.[20]

The court elaborated on the control standard in a fair amount of detail stating that the control aspect means more than simple possession. "Control has been construed broadly by the court as the legal right, authority, or practical ability to obtain the materials sought upon demand."[21] The court also pointed out a trend that many other courts have adopted in finding that the parent of a wholly-owned subsidiary is usually required to produce documents that its subsidiary possesses. Whether this rule will always be adhered to is based on the degree of ownership and control exercised by the parent over its subsidiary, a showing that the two entities operate as one, a demonstration that documents are usually obtainable in the ordinary course of business, and looks at whether there is agency relationship.

In this instance, the court more or less tallied up each factor to determine whether Siemens AG should have been compelled to produce the documents. Given the fact that Siemens Austria was Siemens AG's largest subsidiary in Europe and was wholly owned by Siemens AG, the first factor tipped in the plaintiffs' favor. Because it had already been determined that the two companies do not operate as a single entity and the plaintiffs also failed to demonstrate that under Austrian law the owner of Siemens Austria is not entitled to give instructions to the managing board of Siemens Austria, the second factor came out in the defendants' favor. Moreover, the court found that the two entities regularly exchanged corporate documents. The court also failed to find an agency relationship for the fourth factor in their analysis.[22]

Reasoning that two factors favored the defendants and two factors favored the plaintiffs, the court went deeper and examined additional facts to make a final determination. The plaintiffs asserted that as the only shareholder of Siemens Austria, Siemens AG, elected Siemens Austria's Board of Directors, examined and approved reports and annual accounts, and adopted bylaws. In addition, if Siemens Austria attempted to undertake a new business venture outside of its normal course, it would need approval of a committee of Siemens AG Board. Several individuals also held positions in both companies. Because of these additional facts and the 100 percent ownership of Siemens Austria by Siemens AG, the court concluded that if Siemens AG needed assistance in a matter, it would receive such assistance. Therefore, assistance in the form of being provided documents in Siemens Austria's custody was easily obtainable by the parent company.

Accordingly, the parent company could not prevent production of those documents and was required to comply with the plaintiffs' request. *In re Ski Train Fire of Nov. 11, 2000 Kaprun Austria* demonstrated the extent to which the courts have examined the relationship between a parent and subsidiary for purposes of determining control pursuant to FRCP 34. It is an example of the fact that "regardless of whether the parent's documents are sought through the subsidiary or vice-versa, the inquiry is a factual-based one on what documents parties actually can access in practice."[23] The inquiry began with the court examining a basic rule, but then launched into looking at four factors. When this was not enough, the court actually looked into how extensively the two entities functioned with each other.

Flagg—A Modern Day Approach

With little guidance in the SCA, there is not ample case law that has addressed issues of subpoenas seeking to access e-mail accounts of a parent company when the subsidiary is a party to the litigation. However, as the existing case law has demonstrated, courts that have considered parent/subsidiary control issues have conducted their analysis from a functional standpoint.[24] Courts have refused to look simply at the high-level corporate structure. What becomes obvious though is that the interplay between FRCP 34 and the SCA is not entirely clear. The issue was addressed in *Flagg v. City of Detroit*. In the beginning of their analysis, the court explicitly denounced the sweeping proposition that the SCA "absolutely precludes the production of electronic communications in civil litigation."[25] Although it did not specifically discuss the parent–subsidiary relationship, in its dicta the court specifically referenced that a court "could order the production of documents in the possession of a defendant corporation's overseas affiliate." *Flagg* also discussed the distinct possibility that defendant corporations may have a duty under federal statutes to keep records that would be subject to discovery.[26]

Despite the minimal case law, several key principles can be extracted with respect to the SCA and Rule 34. The SCA was not meant to override FRCP 34 or preclude the discovery of electronic communications in discovery. Moreover, case law regarding parent and subsidiary companies for strict purposes of Rule 34 lead to the conclusion that any analysis pursuant to the SCA would look at the functionality of two entities. It looks to whether companies can readily access the documents in the ordinary course of business and take a practical approach. The burden will always be on the party seeking documents alleged to be in another party's control. Given the ruling in *Tomlinson*, courts may also find ways in the future to impose burdens on companies and require them to be able to produce documents in compliance with federal statutes.[27] Accordingly, this will force corporations to scrutinize relationships between affiliated parties in a more extensive manner when migrating electronic communications to the cloud.

With respect to the control issue, there are other considerations companies must take into account when storing electronic communications. Issues regarding relevance, undue cost, and invasion of privacy may preclude discovery of electronically stored information that is being stored in the cloud and is within the control of a party. For example, FRCP 26(b)(2)(B) specifically addresses electronically stored information, stating:

> A party need not provide discovery of electronically stored information from sources that the party identifies as not reasonably accessible because of undue burden or cost. On motion to compel discovery or for a protective order, the party from whom discovery is sought must show that the information is not reasonably accessible because of undue burden or cost. If that showing is made, the court may nonetheless order discovery from such sources if the requesting party shows good cause, considering the limitations of Rule 26(b)(2)(C). The court may specify conditions for the discovery.[28]

In *W. Holding Co., Inc. v. Chartis Ins. Co. of Puerto Rico*, the Federal Deposit Insurance Corporation (FDIC), as receiver for a failed bank, brought action under Financial Institutions Reform, Recovery, and Enforcement Act (FIRREA) against the bank's directors, officers, and their conjugal partnerships for negligence and other claims. The FDIC moved for an order establishing protocol for the bank's electronically stored information, and the court had to consider whether accessing information would create an undue burden. The case involved approximately 6.0 terabytes of data and 921,000 paper documents, which cost $2.1 million to upload and store in a database. The FDIC proposed using a different system even though transferring the data would cost an additional $2.7 million. Furthermore, they asserted that the data in the existing database were not reasonably accessible under Rule 26 and requested cost shifting.[29]

In determining whether it was reasonably accessible, the court stated that the party claiming that electronically stored information is not reasonably accessible must demonstrate an undue burden and the party cannot claim it is too expensive to produce because of volume. The FDIC needed to show that the cost must be associated with some technological feature that inhibits accessibility.[30] Reasoning that the FDIC did not show it was hindered by unique technological hurdles, the court concluded that it failed to trigger Rule 26(b)(2)(B). This case illustrates the extreme burden FRCP 26(b)(2)(B) carries with respect to showing electronically stored information not being reasonably accessible.[31]

Other examples of FRCP 26 issues with respect to electronically stored information include *Mackelprang v. Fidelity National Title Agency of Nevada, Inc.* and *United Century Bank v. Kanan Fashions*. In *Macklprang*, the court denied a motion to compel production of private messages sent on Myspace based on the relevance of the requested information. The court reasoned that Fidelity's ability to compel should be limited to messages relating *only* to Mackelprang's employment.[32] In *United Century Bank*, the court limited the scope of discovery to a period of five years because of the heavy costs associated with the full request and overall relevance.[33]

The final issue that companies migrating to the cloud need to keep in mind is the concept of spoliation. The most common case referenced with regards to spoliation has always been *Zubulake v. UBS Warburg, LLC*, which stands for the proposition that when litigation is reasonably anticipated, a litigation hold must be issued to prevent the spoliation of any potential evidence.[34] This concept of preservation is shadowed by great uncertainty. As one court noted:

> It remains unclear how courts will interpret and litigators will implement these preservation requirements given how cloud providers store and move data. It is also unclear how the collection and production of data from the cloud will affect the development of law regarding the production of metadata in response to discovery requests in litigation.[35]

Given the extreme amount of uncertainty, corporations should have clear procedures outlined with respect to data retention policies. If there is even a remote chance of litigation, companies should always err on the side of caution as well.

The control concept pursuant to FRCP 34 is not entirely consistent in its application to cloud computing issues beyond the individual. However, companies should keep in mind that the court's approach will always be a product of functionality and proceed accordingly. Case law will continue to define the scope and interplay between Rule 34 and the SCA, but companies need to have policies in place and heavily scrutinize their relationships with other entities. From a litigation standpoint, parties should keep these principles in mind when determining which party should be subpoenaed in a dispute. Knowing who has control of key documents could be the difference in conducting successful discovery and ultimately obtaining a favorable outcome in litigation.

Notes

1. FRCP 34(a).
2. See FED. R. CIV. P. 34 advisory committee's note (2006).
3. The Committee noted with respect to the 2006 Amendment that it would have been "obviously improper to allow a party to evade discovery obligations on the basis that the label had not kept pace with changes in information technology." See FED. R. CIV. P. 34 advisory committee's note (2006).
4. See *supra* note 2.

5. See *supra* note 2.
6. Wayne C. Matus, John L. Nicholson, and Shawn P. Thomas, "Taking Corporate Email to the Cloud: The Stored Communications Act and Control," Pillsbury Winthrop Shaw Pittman LLP white paper, March 17, 2011, p. 4.
7. *Thayer v. Chiczewski*, No. 07 C 1290, 2009 WL 2957317, 2 (N.D. Ill. Sept. 11, 2009).
8. Matus, Nicholson and Thomas, 3.
9. Matus, Nicholson and Thomas, 4.
10. *In re NTL, Inc. Securities Litigation*, 244 F.R.D. 179, 181(S.D.N.Y. 2007))
11. *Id.*
12. *Id.* at 195.
13. *Id.* quoting *Golden Trade, S.r.L. v. Lee Apparel Co.*, 143 F.R.D. 514, 525 (S.D.N.Y.1992). (The courts have "interpreted Rule 34 to require production if the party has the practical ability to obtain the documents from another, irrespective of his legal entitlement to the documents" [emphasis added].)
14. U.S. Intern. Trade Com'n v. ASAT, Inc., 411 F.3d 245, 247 (D.C. Cir. 2005).
15. *Id.* at 254.
16. *Id.*
17. Matus, Nicholson and Thomas, 4.
18. *Zenith Elec. v. Vizio, Inc.*, 2009 WL 3094889, at 2 (S.D.N.Y. Sept. 25, 2009).
19. *Id.*
20. *In re Ski Train Fire of Nov. 11, 2000 Kaprun Austria.* 2006 WL 1328259, at 1 (S.D.N.Y. May 16, 2006).
21. *Id.* at 5.
22. *Id.* at 6–7.
23. Matus, Nicholson and Thomas, 5.
24. Matus, Nicholson and Thomas, 6.
25. *Flagg v. City of Detroit*, 252 F.R.D. 346, 349 (E.D. Mich. 2008).
26. *Id.* at 354. Citing *Tomlinson v. El Paso Corp.*, 245 F.R.D. 474, 477 (D.Colo.2007). "In that case, defendant El Paso had a duty under the Employee Retirement Income Security Act of 1974 ("ERISA"), 29 U.S.C. §1001 et seq., and its implementing regulations to ensure that its employee benefit records were maintained in reasonable order and in a safe and accessible place, and in such manner as they may be readily inspected or examined . . . Although El Paso employed a third party, Mercer Human Resource Consulting, to administer its employee pension plan and maintain the electronic records associated with this plan, the court held that El Paso could not delegate its recordkeeping duties under ERISA to this third party. Rather, the court held that El Paso retained control over the pension plan data held by Mercer, and thus had the 'authority and ability to obtain' and produce the data requested by the plaintiff plan participants."
27. *"Tomlinson v. El Paso Corp.*, 245 F.R.D. 474, 477 (D.Colo. 2007)."
28. FRCP 26(b)(2)(C).
29. *W. Holding Co., Inc. v. Chartis Ins. Co. of Puerto Rico*, 293 F.R.D. 68, 68-69 (D.P.R. 2013).
30. *Id.* at 73.
31. *Id.*
32. See Ashish S. Prasad, "Cloud Computing and Social Media: Electronic Discovery Considerations and Best Practices," The Metropolitan Corporate Counsel (website), January 20, 2012, www.metrocorpcounsel.com/articles/17454/cloud-computing-and-social-media-electronic-discovery-considerations-and-best-practic citing Mackelprang v. Fidelity Nat. Title Agency of Nevada, Inc. 2007 WL 119149 (D. Nev. Jan. 9, 2007).
33. *United Century Bank v. Kanan Fashions*, 2012 WL 1409245 (N.D.Ill. Apr. 23, 2012).
34. *Zubulake v. UBS Warburg LLC*, 220 F.R.D. 212 (S.D.N.Y. 2003).
35. Allison C. Stanton and Andrew J. Victor, "What We See in the Clouds: A Practical Overview of Litigating Against and on Behalf of Organizations Using Cloud Computing," *E-Discovery* 59, no.3 (2001): 34–42, p. 37 citing Aguilar v. Immigration and Customs Enforcement Div. of the U.S. Dep't of Homeland Security, 255 F.R.D. 350 (S.D.N.Y. 2008).

CHAPTER 8

Current Issues in Cloud Data

*James P. Martin and
Matthew P. Breuer*

When the Electronic Communications Privacy Act (ECPA) was passed in 1986, cellular telephone was a fledgling industry. At the time, cellular telephones were mainly limited to car phones, due to the large batteries that powered the phone. Handheld models were extremely expensive, quite large by today's standards, and did little beyond the ability to make a call to a single person at a time. Very few people actually used the new technology due to the cost.

Today, cellular phone use is pervasive. Units are small enough to take everywhere, and many people now solely use a cell phone and no longer maintain a traditional wired home telephone. Additionally, phones have been joined by an array of devices that utilize the cellular data network connectivity, including portable computers, smartphones, tablets, and wireless hot spots. Hot spot devices connect to the cellular data network and provide wifi access to nearby digital devices.

Cell phones and smartphones are instances of new technologies that are the center of litigation that is being decided based on old laws; they are on the "bleeding edge" of litigation. Courts often interpret slight nuances in cases quite differently.

Cell Tower Data and Location Information

Cellular service is called *cellular* because a geographic area is broken into a number of overlapping *cells*; each cell is served by a cellular tower. A digital device connects to the cellular tower to obtain service, and as the digital device moves through the area (i.e., from cell to cell) the device connects to the tower in the new cell for service. The cellular communications companies maintain records of the devices that are served by each cell tower at any given time.

An emerging area is the use of data held by a third-party provider and resultant privacy issues in the area of cell tower dumps. Cell phones and other smart devices, when active, are in communication with nearby cellular towers. The towers include directional antennae that cannot pinpoint the location of the device but the towers and the cellular networks maintain histories of the connection records. A *tower dump* allows law enforcement to retrieve the connection records of all devices connected to a tower over an interval of time. Law enforcement uses tower dumps to obtain device connection histories from the areas where a crime was committed in the hopes that the perpetrator of a crime had a digital device, and that they can discern the identity of that device. Pragmatically, the dump also produces the connection logs for hundreds of thousands of devices that were not involved with the crime.

The data contained in a cell tower dump is data held by a third-party provider and is subject to the restrictions of the ECPA. However, there is debate about whether production of such data should require a search warrant or just a court order. Obtaining a court order for the production of data requires a far lower standard.

Cell tower data dumps have become a frequent and valuable tool for law enforcement. In the case of the High Country Bank Robbers, cell tower dumps lead to the capture and arrest of the perpetrators. On February 10, 2010, the Federal Bureau of Investigation (FBI) issued a wanted notice for two men described as "the High Country Bank Robbers" and described their method of operation as:

> The unknown male identified as suspect number one often enters the banks in rural locations near closing time and brandishes a black semi-automatic handgun. Suspect number one then demands all the money from the teller drawers. He obtains an undisclosed amount of money, puts it in a bag, orders everyone on the ground, then exits the banks with a second suspect. They have been seen leaving the banks on a green or maroon four-wheel ATV with suspect number two driving.[1]

The perpetrators wore hoodies and masks that made their identification difficult, despite surveillance photographs and videos. A witness to one of the robberies described a suspicious man hanging around the outside of the bank before the robbery occurred, and noted he was talking on a cellular telephone.

The FBI obtained a §2703(d) court order for a cell tower dump of the cell towers located near four of the robbery locations; the FBI stated they chose the four most remote locations to minimize the extraneous information obtained. Through the use of data analysis software, investigators correlated the device connection records and a single number was located in the tower data of all four locations. Analysis also showed a second phone number that was in contact with the first phone on the date of the robberies, and was identified on two of the cell towers. This was enough for the FBI to obtain additional information about the phone numbers, including the names and addresses of the owners. The suspects were identified as Joel Glore and Ronald Capito. Eventually, the FBI located the individuals, who were arrested for the robberies.

The extent of the data gathered through cell tower dumps is quite extensive, and allows a fairly detailed reconstruction of movements of a suspect. The FBI released a reconstruction of the events of a single day of a robbery:

> On 11/25/2009, both CAPITO's and GLORE's mobile telephones begin the day at 6:31 A.M. on the same cell tower in Show Low, Arizona, when CAPITO calls GLORE's mobile telephone. Both mobile telephones remain in Show Low until CAPITO's telephone uses a cell tower near Punkin Center, approximately 30 miles south of Payson, Arizona. By approximately 11:00 A.M., both CAPITO's and GLORE's phones are using the same cell tower in Star Valley, Arizona, approximately 5 miles east of Payson, Arizona, and likely covering areas of Payson, Arizona. By 11:50 A.M., both CAPITO's and GLORE's mobile telephones are using towers in Payson, Arizona, that are almost certainly within the coverage area of the Compass Bank located at 613 S. Beeline Highway, Payson, Arizona. GLORE's telephone remains on these Payson cell towers and last uses a Payson cell tower located only 1 mile from the Compass Bank at 3:27 P.M. when he receives a call from CAPITO's cell telephone.
>
> CAPITO's telephone continues to use the Star Valley and Payson towers through the 3:27 P.M. call, when CAPITO's telephone is using a cell tower located only 1.7 miles from the Compass Bank. At approximately 3:29 P.M., the High Country Bandits rob the Compass Bank, 613 S. Beeline Highway, Payson, Arizona. The next call on either GLORE or CAPITO's mobile telephones is at approximately 4:40 P.M. when they are contacting each other and both are using the cell tower near Punkin Center, approximately 30 miles south of Payson, Arizona. Both mobile telephones remain using that cell tower throughout the night and return to Show Low, Arizona, by 11:00 A.M. the next day.[2]

The breadth of information potentially revealed about innocent digital users through the acquisition of cell tower data is staggering. The FBI chose the four most rural locations for their search, and obtained records relating to over 150,000 registered cell phone numbers. Many civil libertarians are concerned that the government can access such large-scale information about the movements of individuals without a warrant. Cell tower information is covered by the restrictions of the ECPA. However, the information in the cell tower dumps is not believed to fall into the category of "contents" that would require a search warrant to access. Cell tower dumps are performed based on a court order.

Brian Owsley, a former federal magistrate and now a professor of law at Texas Tech University recently published a paper highlighting the concerns with cell tower dumps:

> Recently, the American Civil Liberties Union brought to light the popular use of government surveillance of cell phones, including the gathering of all cell phone numbers utilizing a specific cell site location. Known as a "cell tower dump," such procedures essentially obtain all of the telephone number records from a particular cell site tower for a given time period: "A tower dump allows police to request the phone numbers of all phones that connected to a specific tower within a given period of time." State and federal courts have barely addressed cell tower dumps. However, the actions by most of the largest cell phone providers, as well as personal experience and conversations with other magistrate judges, strongly suggest "that it has become a relatively routine investigative technique" for law enforcement officials.
>
> No federal statute directly addresses whether and how law enforcement officers may seek a cell tower dump from cellular telephone providers. Assistant United States Attorneys, with the encouragement of the United States Department of Justice, apply for court orders authorizing cell tower dumps pursuant to a provision in the Electronic Communications Privacy Act of 1986. The pertinent provision poses a procedural hurdle less stringent than a warrant based on probable cause, which in turn raises significant constitutional concerns.[3]

On May 12, 2012, U.S. Congressman Edward J. Markey (D-MA) sent a letter to the chairs of eight major cellular communications providers in the United States based on an article in the *New York Times* entitled "Police Are Using Phone Tracking as a Routine Tool." Markey requested data pertaining to the frequency of requests for phone data, and the amounts charged to provide such data.

On July 8, 2012, the *New York Times* reported on the results of Markey's request. Seven of the eight companies contacted replied with statistics of their level of data requests; T-Mobile declined to provide statistics. Combined, the companies responded to 1.3 million demands for subscriber information in 2011 alone. This total does not reflect the quantity of numbers released; a single demand for information could be a tower dump involving hundreds of thousands of records. The communications companies noted there was a lack of clarity regarding the proper procedures to authorize disclosure of the requested data, and indicated additional legislation might be helpful.[4]

In 2013, the U.S. Court of Appeals for the Fifth Circuit considered a case involving the required authorization for the production of cell data (*In re: Application of the United States of America for Historical Cell Site Data*):[5]

> In early October 2010, the United States filed three applications under §2703(d) of the Stored Communications Act ("SCA"), 18 U.S.C. §§2701-2712, seeking evidence relevant to three separate criminal investigations. Each application requested a court order to compel the cell phone service provider for a particular cell phone to produce sixty days of historical cell site data and other subscriber information for that phone. The Government requested the same cell site data in each application: "the antenna tower and sector to which the cell phone sends its signal." It requested this information for both the times when the phone sent a signal to a tower to obtain service for a call and the period when the phone was in an idle state. *In re Application of the United States for Historical Cell Site Data*, 747 F. Supp. 2d 827, 829 (S.D. Tex. 2010).

The magistrate judge assigned the case opined that the warrantless production of such data was unconstitutional; the United States appealed. On appeal, the district judge issued a single page opinion, noting:

> When the government requests records from cellular services, data disclosing the location of the telephone at the time of particular calls may be acquired only by a warrant issued on probable cause. The records would show the date, time called, number, and location of the telephone when the call was made. These data are constitutionally protected from this intrusion. The standard under the Stored Communications Act is below that required by the Constitution.

The United States appealed once again, and the case was reviewed by the Court of Appeals. The contention for the United States' appeal was that the cell tower data and connection records are records not gathered by the government, they are gathered as the business records of the communications companies.

The court's opinion was direct: "We are called on to decide whether court orders authorized by the Stored Communications Act to compel cell phone

service providers to produce the historical cell site information of their subscribers are per se unconstitutional. We hold that they are not."

The court agreed that the records sought were business records belonging to the communications company, not GPS or location records. This
differentiated the facts of the case from *United States v. Jones*, in which the
Supreme Court of the United States ruled that warrantless GPS tracking of a
suspect was unconstitutional:

> Under this framework, cell site information is clearly a business re-
> cord. The cell service provider collects and stores historical cell site
> data for its own business purposes, perhaps to monitor or optimize ser-
> vice on its network or to accurately bill its customers for the segments
> of its network that they use. The Government does not require ser-
> vice providers to record this information or store it. The providers
> control what they record and how long these records are retained.
> The Government has neither "required [n]or persuaded" providers
> to keep historical cell site records. Jones, 132 S. Ct. at 961 (Alito, J.,
> concurring in the judgment). In the case of such historical cell site
> information, the Government merely comes in after the fact and asks
> a provider to turn over records the provider has already created.[6]

The court also noted that subscribers understood they were providing
data to the cell tower, and that the use of cell phones was voluntary:

> A cell service subscriber, like a telephone user, understands that his cell
> phone must send a signal to a nearby cell tower in order to wirelessly
> connect his call. See United States v. Madison, No. 11-60285-CR,
> 2012 WL 3095357, at *8 (S.D. Fla. July 30, 2012) (unpublished)
> ("[C]ell-phone users have knowledge that when they place or receive
> calls, they, through their cell phones, are transmitting signals to the
> nearest cell tower, and, thus, to their communications service provid-
> ers."). Cell phone users recognize that, if their phone cannot pick up
> a signal (or "has no bars"), they are out of the range of their service
> provider's network of towers. And they realize that, if many customers
> in an area attempt to make calls at the same time, they may overload
> the network's local towers, and the calls may not go through.
>
> Because a cell phone user makes a choice to get a phone, to select a
> particular service provider, and to make a call, and because he knows that
> the call conveys cell site information, the provider retains this informa-
> tion, and the provider will turn it over to the police if they have a court
> order, he voluntarily conveys his cell site data each time he makes a call.[7]

Circuit Judge James L. Dennis, in a dissenting opinion, noted the issue was a statute issue, not a constitutional issue:

In my view, this appeal should be decided by adhering to the Supreme Court's constitutional question avoidance doctrine and construing the applicable ambiguous provisions of the Stored Communications Act to require that the government must obtain a warrant in order to secure an order requiring an electronic communications provider to disclose data potentially protected by the Fourth Amendment, such as the historical cell site location data sought in this case. Because the government did not apply for a warrant, but instead sought such data based only on a showing of reasonable suspicion, the district court reached the correct result in denying the government's request for an order for the provider to disclose that data. Accordingly, I would affirm the result reached by the district court, and I respectfully dissent from the majority opinion's contrary interpretation of the Stored Communications Act and its unnecessary interpretation of the Fourth Amendment as not affording individuals protection of their historical cell site location data.[8]

Privacy advocates are deeply disturbed by the government's use of cell tower dumps, and are concerned that their use constitutes something of a digital dragnet; it is not always clear what happens to the data that was gathered that was not related to the crime. For example, if a park bench was damaged at a Tea Party rally, or a window was broken at an Occupy movement site, law enforcement could obtain a court order for a cell tower dump for the day of the event. This would reveal the phone numbers and connection records for all the devices present during the event. This could potentially then be used for other purposes or tracking or correlated against other event data.

StingRay and Location Monitoring

Harris Manufacturing Company, a supplier of electronics for government and civil applications, has developed a device called the StingRay, or generically, an *International Mobile Subscriber Identifier* or *IMSI Catcher* that can accurately track the location of a suspect. The term *stingray* has become a generic term for devices of this type.

According to documents obtained by the Electronic Privacy Information Center (EPIC) in October 2013, the Department of Justice's policy on cellsite simulators is that their use is governed by the Pen Register device statute

(18 U.S.C. 3127(3));[9] much like a pen register, the StingRay collects signaling information. Notably, a cellsite simulator does cause a disruption in service; 18 U.S.C. 3124 requires that a pen register be implemented with a minimum of interference to services.

A StingRay is a portable device that when deployed acts like a cell tower. The StingRay sends out radio signals that make it appear as a cell tower to digital devices in the vicinity. These devices will connect to the StingRay thinking it is a tower on their provider's network. The devices will continue to operate as the StingRay passes the traffic through. The StingRay, however, can record the call information, much like a pen/trap device. Some devices can capture the packets that constitute contents of a connection. A StingRay can also identify the direction and distance of the connected device, which enables law enforcement to determine the location of the device with a good degree of accuracy. Investigators can take a distance reading, move the device, take another reading, and begin to triangulate the location.

It is believed a StingRay is typically deployed when a law enforcement agency has identified the subject of an investigation and wishes to monitor their communications behavior and their location. However, any digital device within the vicinity of the StingRay could connect to the StingRay, allowing their owners' communications behaviors and locations to also be monitored by the StingRay, even though they are not the subject of any investigation.

One of the first cases to test the legality of the use of a StingRay device is the case of *United States v. Daniel Rigmaiden*. Rigmaiden was indicted in 2010 on 74 counts of tax, mail, and wire fraud; he was accused of being a key member of a multistate scheme to obtain illegal tax returns. The FBI press release on the capture of Rigmaiden describes the pursuit and apprehension:

> Court documents, including the superseding indictment, and search and seizure warrant affidavits and returns, contain the following additional allegations and evidence. In May 2007, IRS-CI identified a Compass Bank account in Phoenix, Arizona, that was receiving fraudulently obtained tax refunds. From May 2007 through January 2008, the investigation was focused on Carter, who had opened the Compass Bank account under the name Carter Tax & Accounting, LLC. In January 2008, the investigation started to focus on an individual operating above Carter known only as the "Hacker" and another co-conspirator above Carter in the scheme. From January through April 15, 2008, an undercover operation was initiated that sought to identify and locate the Hacker and second co-conspirator. In the course of the operation, the investigators opened an undercover bank account in Arizona into which the Hacker unknowingly caused the deposit of numerous fraudulently obtained tax refunds. The fraudulent returns were filed via computers

and IP addresses not directly traceable to the Hacker. During this period, three $9,000 shipments of the tax refunds were made to the second co-conspirator in Utah. On April 15, 2008, the second co-conspirator was arrested. The co-conspirator's case is under seal.

From April through August 2008, investigators worked to identify and locate the Hacker. In May 2008, $68,000 in fraudulently obtained refunds were shipped to the Hacker, in the name of Patrick Stout, to Palo Alto, CA. The person who picked up the package was not apprehended. In July 2008, agents located the apartment in Santa Clara rented by the Hacker in the name of Steven Brawner. On July 23, 2008, a 50-count indictment was returned under seal against the Hacker (a.k.a Brawner and Stout). On August 3, 2008, the Hacker was arrested in Santa Clara after a foot and car chase. A key to the Hacker's apartment was found in his pocket during his arrest. On August 3 and 4, 2008, search warrants were executed in the Hacker's Santa Clara apartment and a storage unit in San Jose; investigators seized a laptop and multiple hard drives, $116,340 in cash, over $208,000 in gold coins, approximately $10,000 in silver coins, false identification documents, false identification manufacturing equipment, and surveillance equipment.[10]

The government eventually revealed that one of the "sources" in this investigation was a mobile tracking device deployed to monitor Rigmaiden's communications. Rigmaiden used a Verizon aircard (WiFi hotspot) as an Internet connection; the location and communications activities were monitored through the use of the mobile tracking device. The government stated during the case that the use of the equipment to communicate with Rigmaiden's aircard was authorized by a Rule 41 tracking warrant, application, and affidavit.[11]

Rigmaiden filed a motion to suppress the admission of any evidence gathered through the StingRay equipment. The American Civil Liberties Union (ACLU) filed an amicus brief asserting that the warrant was not valid because:

1. The StingRay equipment is intrusive; it sends radio signals out that permeate the house, pocket, or purse where a digital device is located.
2. The StingRay equipment gathers information from third parties that are not the subject of the investigation; this equates to a general warrant.
3. The investigators failed to reveal and describe the StingRay technology and the extent of the information gathered to the magistrate when they applied for the warrant.

The court ruled that the use of the equipment to locate the aircard did not violate Rigmaiden's Fourth Amendment right to privacy given the layers of false identities and fraudulent actions Rigmaiden employed to operate his scheme in the first place.[12]

The court noted that Verizon was clearly a provider of electronic communication services and was therefore subject to the ECPA. However, suppression is not an allowable remedy for ECPA violations.

BYOD Policies and Data Ownership

Bring Your Own Device (BYOD) is a trend in information technology that describes the practice of allowing employees to utilize their own computing devices to perform work for the organization; usually the devices are smartphones or tablet computers. A typical BYOD situation is an employee who purchases an iPad for home use, and then decides to access work e-mail through an application, or even brings the device to the workplace and uses it in place of the company computing asset. BYOD raises various legal issues for the organization, including potential ergonomic issues, compensation issues, and security issues. Relating to cloud computing and electronic discovery, the issue raised is one of data ownership and access.

Similarly, an employee may be provided with a device and access personal account information on that device, such as a Facebook account or personal e-mail account. Smartphones and tablets typically store the login information for applications; computers and laptops may store login information, but the verification to store the information is much more overt. The risk in storing login information on the device is that anyone who accesses the device can then, in turn, access the applications for which login information is stored.

Courts have considered cases where the ownership of the device is different than the ownership of the data contained on the device or accessible by the device. Given the relatively new nature of smartphones and tablets, this is an emerging area of law. Generally, however, courts will look to the identity of the subscriber to a service, the person with the relationship with the third-party provider. For a cloud application, such as a personal Gmail account, the subscriber would be the person that initiated the account with Gmail and that subscriber would be the only person authorized to access the account. Intentionally accessing data in the account without authorization would be prohibited by U.S.C. §2701.

In *Lazette v. Kulmatycki*,[13] the court held that a supervisor who had used a company BlackBerry device to access the personal e-mail account of the former employee to which the device had been assigned may have violated the Stored Communications Act.[14] The plaintiff had been an employee of Verizon, and had been issued a BlackBerry device by the company. During her employment, the plaintiff configured the device to allow her to access her personal Gmail account on the device. When the plaintiff left the company, she returned the device after she believed she had removed the Gmail information. She later learned that she had not removed the Gmail information; her former supervisor had been using the device to access the plaintiff's e-mail information and had shared the contents of the e-mail with others. The plaintiff claimed this access occurred over 18 months, and the supervisor read more than 48,000 personal e-mails.

The court ruled that the employer and supervisor did not have the authority to read the plaintiff's personal e-mail. The court held that the mere fact that the plaintiff used a company-owned device to access her personal e-mail account did not grant automatic access to her employer. Further, Verizon was held to be vicariously liable for the supervisor's actions in this case.

It is important to note that the supervisor had accessed the e-mail content on the Gmail server using the login credentials stored on the BlackBerry. The SCA prohibits accessing "a facility" without authorization; the Gmail server would be such a facility. In the case of *Garcia v. the City of Laredo, Texas*,[15] the court held that a cell phone is not a facility as defined by the SCA.

Fannie Garcia was a police dispatcher for the City of Laredo, Texas. She claimed the defendants (who included the City of Laredo, the deputy city manager, the chief of police, and several other police officials) accessed the contents of her cell phone without permission in violation of the SCA. On November 15, 2008, a police officer's wife removed Garcia's cell phone from an unlocked locker in a substation of the Laredo Police Department and accessed text messages and images found on Garcia's phone. Believing she had discovered evidence of violations of department policies, she set up a meeting with the deputy assistant city manager and the interim assistant police chief. At the meeting, she utilized Garcia's cell phone to access and to share the text messages sent from and received by the phone and the photographs stored on the phone.

Later, investigators successfully downloaded one video recording and 32 digital images from the cell phone; they were unable to download any of the text messages. A subsequent internal investigation concluded, based in whole or in part upon images and text messages retrieved from her cell phone, that Garcia had violated department policies. Garcia was terminated and filed suit.

The district court granted summary judgment for defendants and denied Garcia's motion for partial summary judgment on the SCA, finding that the statute did not apply to the defendants' actions in the case. The U.S. Court of Appeals for the Fifth District affirmed the lower court's decision.

The Court of Appeals, in a *de novo* review, likened a cell phone to a local drive on a computer to determine if it should be considered a *facility*:

> The Eleventh Circuit's decision in United States v. Steiger provides useful guidance. 318 F.3d 1039, 1049 (11th Cir. 2003). In Steiger, when a hacker accessed an individual's computer and obtained information saved to his hard drive, the court held such conduct was

beyond the reach of the SCA. The court found that "the SCA clearly applies . . . to information stored with a phone company, Internet Service Provider (ISP), or electronic bulletin board system," but does not, however, "appear to apply to the source's hacking into Steiger's computer to download images and identifying information stored on his hard drive.[16]

Even if Garcia's cell phone were somehow considered a facility, this stops short of demonstrating that storage of text messages and pictures on Garcia's cell phone fits within 18 U.S.C. §2510(17)'s definition of electronic storage. *Electronic storage* as defined encompasses only the information that has been stored by an electronic communication service provider.[17] Thus, information that an Internet provider stores to its servers or information stored with a telephone company—if such information is stored temporarily pending delivery or for purposes of backup protection—are examples of protected electronic storage under the statute. But information that an individual stores to his hard drive or cell phone is not in electronic storage under the statute.[18]

An individual's personal cell phone does not provide an electronic communication service just because the device enables use of electronic communication services, and there is no evidence here that the defendants ever obtained any information from the cellular company or network. Accordingly, the text messages and photos stored on Garcia's phone are not in electronic storage as defined by the SCA and are thus outside the scope of the statute.[19]

This concept is important for electronic discovery purposes as it removes local copies of documents or communications from the control of the SCA. While e-mails, pictures, documents, and voicemails are stored in the cloud, they are controlled by the restrictions of the SCA. If a user saves a local copy of an e-mail, picture, or document, or saves a voicemail file on a local hard drive, the restrictions on production placed by the SCA no longer apply to the files; they are subject to discovery as any other file on a local computer would be.

Notes

1. FBI Press Release, February 18, 2010, "Wanted: 'The High Country Bandits.'"
2. Criminal Complaint, *United States v. Capito*, No. 3:10-CR-08050-NVW (D. Ariz. Mar. 12, 2010).
3. Brian Owsley, "The Fourth Amendment Implications of the Government's Use of Cell Tower Dumps in Its Electronic Surveillance," *University of Pennsylvania Journal of Constitutional Law* 16 (2013). Available at SSRN: http://ssrn.com/abstract=2307525.
4. Eric Lichtblau, "More Demands on Cell Carriers in Surveillance," *New York Times* website, July 8, 2012. www.nytimes.com/2012/07/09/us/cell-carriers-see-uptick-in-requests-to-aid-surveillance.html?_r=0.

5. No. 11-20884, Filed July 30, 2013.
6. Decision, United States Court of Appeals, 5th Circuit, No. 11-20884, In re: Appl of USA for Hist Cell Site, p.18.
7. *Ibid.* 22
8. *Ibid.* 26
9. *EPIC v. FBI*, No. 12-667, October 2013 Production at 17.
10. U.S. Attorney's Office April 08, 2010, District of Arizona CASE NUMBER: CR-08-814-PHX-DGC. RELEASE NUMBER: 2010-060 (Rigmaiden et al.).
11. CR08–90330–MISC–RS.
12. Case 2:08-cr-00814-DGC Document 1009 Filed 05/08/13 at 14.
13. Case No. 3:12CV2416, 2013 U.S. Dist. LEXIS 81174 (N.D. Ohio June 5, 2013).
14. 18 U.S.C. §2701.
15. 2012 U.S. App. LEXIS 25370 (5th Cir. Tex. Dec. 12, 2012).
16. *Id.* at 6.
17. *Id.*
18. *Id.* at 8.
19. *Id.* at 8.

CHAPTER 9

The Rise of Social Media and Its Role in Litigation

Sarah Marmor and Deirdre Fox

Today, nearly everyone—individuals, employees, corporations, government entities—has a social media presence. Whether through Facebook, LinkedIn, Twitter, Instagram, Pinterest, Flickr, or YouTube, or any other means by which users create online communities to share information, ideas, personal messages, videos and other content, the ways that people and companies can communicate about themselves are ever expanding.[1] This revolution in communication—faster, broader, less mediated, and in many ways more impersonal than ever before—creates enormous opportunities and serious legal risks for organizations.

With social media so commonplace, parties in litigation have discovered and will continue to discover uses for the vast quantities of information that have been casually shared. This chapter focuses on the uses and pitfalls of social media in litigation, ranging from obligations to preserve social media evidence in prelitigation, to informal and formal discovery of such evidence before trial, to effectively using it at trial.[2]

Roots of Social Media

Precursors to social media trace back to the first e-mail, sent in 1971. In February 1978, the first dial-up computerized bulletin board system (CBBS) was launched, and electronic communication grew in popularity throughout the 1980s. October 1989 saw the birth of America Online, popularizing e-mail to the general public in the United States. And in 1993, students at the University of Illinois created the first graphical web browser, giving rise to what is now called Web 1.0, which enabled users to view websites but not contribute to content.

Soon, however, interaction with websites changed from viewing static web pages to allowing users to provide data and exercise some control over that data, starting with written information. Blogging became popular in the early 2000s. Wikipedia emerged in 2001. LinkedIn and MySpace appeared in 2003. User-created video became vastly easier to share when YouTube went online in 2005. Twitter created a new, instantaneous form of mass communication in 2006. And that same year, Facebook welcomed all users aged 13 and over, allowing users to share many kinds of data: photos, text, and video.

As with almost any innovation, litigation soon followed the rise of social media. The most common claims tied to social media use include defamation, copyright and trademark infringement, and invasion of privacy. Even when lawsuits are not specifically related to social media use, courts and litigants must grapple with this vast trove of potential discovery in claims involving employment discrimination, personal injury, divorce, and unfair competition.

Why, How, and When to Access Data on Social Media in Litigation

The tension between privacy rights and an organization's rights to protect itself comes into play in informal and formal discovery before and during litigation. Social media postings can be powerful, sometimes crucial, and increasingly collected and proffered as evidence in matters as diverse as criminal cases, employment cases, intellectual property matters, personal injury cases, and family law disputes.[3] Indeed, such postings can be significant evidence in any case in which intent, motives, state of mind, or physical or emotional condition are relevant.[4] But the notion of lawyers wading through the personal, password-protected musings of individuals likely will feel unseemly, at least, to judges—to some more than others. Certainly, lawyers should seek social media information about parties and witnesses only through legitimate channels, such as searching *public* portions of sites or using the formal discovery process provided by the applicable rules of civil procedure.[5]

Social media law generally vacillates between two poles: protecting the right to privacy and self-expression on the one hand, and mitigating risks to organizations and governments on the other. Both concerns are legitimate. In litigation, witnesses and parties may well feel aggrieved by efforts to obtain access to private social media pages, just as corporate entities may well argue that these sources of discovery are entirely legitimate and necessary. The ability to show that gathering and using another's social media data as evidence more properly falls on one end of the spectrum between these poles likely will dictate success or failure in obtaining and using it in litigation.

Obligations to Preserve Evidence

Difficulties with social media content as potential evidence begin with the obligation of a party to litigation to preserve relevant evidence and a lawyer's obligation to advise clients to do so. With social media, the user contributes and controls content that is hosted remotely; that content includes different data types and can be accessed through unique interfaces. Social media sites frequently are updated, and these dynamic and interactive sites may not have a good way to track or store changes. Also, multiple sources of relevant information, such as a corporation's social media communications, management personnel's personal social media communications, or other employees' personal social media communications, may be potentially relevant.

These difficulties and technical challenges do not change a litigant's duty to preserve relevant evidence, and the failure to do so can lead to legal sanctions, as *Gatto v. United Air Lines, Inc.*, illustrates. In *Gatto*, a personal injury plaintiff claimed permanent disablement, disability limits on physical and social activities, and an inability to work due to a workplace accident. The court ordered him to execute an authorization for the release of documents and information from his Facebook account, and he agreed to change his password to provide defense counsel access. Defense counsel accessed the account, which revealed comments and photographs (relating to trips and online business activities) that arguably contradicted the plaintiff's claims and testimony. When the defendant sent the plaintiff's authorization with a subpoena to Facebook, Facebook objected and recommended that the plaintiff as the account holder download the contents. The plaintiff agreed to do so and to certify that the data was not modified or edited. But the plaintiff deactivated the account, and its content was deleted. After finding that the plaintiff had legal control of his Facebook account because "he had authority to add, delete, or modify his account's content," the court sanctioned him for spoliation of evidence. In doing so, the court observed that litigants "have a duty to preserve relevant evidence that they know, or reasonably should know, will likely be requested in reasonably foreseeable litigation, and the court may impose sanctions on an offending party that has breached this duty."[6]

The lawyer's ethical duty to advise his client regarding preservation obligations likewise has not changed, and is particularly important where, as here, it can be so easy just to hit the delete button. Information from social media sources should be treated as any other potential source of discovery, and just as with any other relevant evidence, lawyers should counsel their clients to preserve social media information.[7]

Lester v. Allied Concrete Co. provides a dramatic example of the consequences when a lawyer and his client fail to preserve (and in this case, affirmatively destroy) social media evidence.[8] In *Lester*, a couple was in a terrible car accident, resulting in the death of the plaintiff's wife. After bringing a wrongful death action, the plaintiff was counseled by his attorney to remove a Facebook photograph that showed him holding a beer and wearing an "I [Heart] hot moms" T-shirt—an image, arguably, that could undermine the widower's claims in the case. The plaintiff's counsel e-mailed him "to 'clean up' his Facebook page because 'we do NOT want blow ups of other pics at trial so please, please clean up your facebook[*sic*] and myspace[*sic*]!'"[9] The plaintiff deleted his page, and then answered a discovery request, "I do not have a Facebook page on the date this is signed."[10] The defendant moved to compel, and the plaintiff reactivated his Facebook account.[11] After the plaintiff went on to testify that he never had deactivated his Facebook page, the defendant issued a subpoena to Facebook to verify that testimony and hired an expert, who determined that 16 pictures had been deleted. These pictures ultimately were produced to the defendant.[12] Although the defendant eventually obtained the desired evidence, the trial court issued a spoliation inference instruction and sanctioned the attorney in the amount of $542,000 and the widower plaintiff in the amount of $180,000.[13] The Virginia Supreme Court characterized the attorney's conduct as "patently unethical."[14] Indeed, published reports indicate the lawyer's license was suspended and he has ceased practicing law as a result of this case.[15]

The *Lester* case is a strong reminder that every lawyer should include social media preservation on a standard investigation checklist at the outset of litigation. And every lawyer should include social media in a litigation hold letter in anticipation of litigation.

Accessing Social Media

Evidence may be available on publicly viewable social media sites, such as Facebook or LinkedIn, and case investigations should include searches on these public sites.[16] Courts consistently have held that a reasonable expectation of privacy does not accompany *publicly* available social media content, although periodically, challenges are still made.[17]

However, users may have restricted access to the content of their social media sites through privacy settings, and relevant content may not be publicly viewable. While relevant nonpublic content generally may be accessed through formal discovery in litigation, when obtaining content from nonpublic portions of social networking websites, care must be exercised to comply with the law and avoid liability for improper access.

From Whom Is Social Media Discoverable?

Federal and state laws and the ethical obligations of lawyers restrict from whom nonpublic social media evidence can be obtained.

The Stored Communications Act

Organizations, investigators, and lawyers will not want to run afoul of the Stored Communications Act (SCA).[18] Congress passed the SCA in 1986, well before the rise of social media, "because the advent of the Internet presented a host of potential privacy breaches that the Fourth Amendment does not address."[19] Courts since have held that social media sites, such as Facebook, are electronic communication service (ECS) or remote computing service (RSC) providers, or both, and therefore are within the scope of the SCA's protections.[20] In short, the SCA prohibits providers from divulging the content of private, electronic communications to the government or to private parties.[21]

Critically, the SCA does not make an exception for civil discovery subpoenas.[22] Consequently, Facebook has taken the position that the SCA "prohibits Facebook from disclosing user content (such as messages, timeline posts, photos, etc.) in response to a civil subpoena."[23] Users of services subject to the SCA generally have standing to seek to quash subpoenas to third-party service providers when the subpoenas seek the users' electronic communications.[24]

Not only will subpoenas directed to social media sites likely fail to result in the desired discovery, such subpoenas may result in liability. With certain exceptions, the SCA prescribes criminal penalties and provides a private civil right of action against *anyone* who "(1) intentionally accesses without authorization a facility through which an electronic communication service is provided; or (2) intentionally exceeds an authorization to access that facility; and thereby obtains, alters, or prevents authorized access to a wire or electronic communication while it is in electronic storage in such system. . . ."[25] That "anyone" can include the lawyer issuing the subpoena, so caution in this area is crucial.

The SCA expressly allows a service provider to divulge contents of a communication if the service provider has the lawful consent of the originator or recipient of the communication.[26] This means that users (account holders) may voluntarily consent to disclose their social media content. Facebook content, for example can be downloaded by logging into a given Facebook account, selecting "account settings," clicking on a link entitled "download a copy of your Facebook data," and following the directions on the data download page.[27]

Of course, the one granting consent must be a "user." In *Konap v. Hawaiian Airlines, Inc.*, an employee gave certain coworkers authorization to access a secure website, and those coworkers agreed to allow management to access the secure site.[28] The court reversed summary judgment for the employer on an employee's SCA claim, concluding that the coworkers never actually "used" the website and therefore were not "users" within the meaning of the SCA's exception for consent authorized by a "user" of the service.[29]

A user's consent to disclose social media content must be voluntary and care must be taken not to exceed authorized access. Pressuring employees to provide access to private social media sites can violate SCA, as restaurant managers learned in *Pietrylo v. Hillstone Rest. Grp.*[30] In *Pietrylo*, employees of a chain restaurant set up a private, invitation-only MySpace group that existed to discuss work conditions at the restaurant where they worked. Two managers learned of the page and demanded the password from one of the employees. The managers continued to access the chat room even though they knew the employee had reservations about providing her password. The court found such access was unauthorized and violated the SCA, among other laws.[31]

State Laws Limiting Employer Access to Employee Social Media

Employers investigating employees for employee misconduct, to protect trade secrets, and to prevent workplace violence, in particular, must be mindful of the proliferation of written state laws that restrict asking employees to allow access to the private sections of their social media (outside of formal discovery in litigation).

Significant public attention was brought to bear on employers' use of social media after reports surfaced about employers asking candidates for passwords to applicant's Facebook accounts during the hiring process.[32] The resulting public outrage led 12 states to pass laws prohibiting employers from asking for or requiring an employee or applicant to disclose a user name or password for a personal social media account: Arkansas, California, Colorado, Illinois, Maryland, Michigan, Nevada, New Jersey, Oregon, Utah, Washington, and New Mexico.[33] More states are likely to follow suit.[34]

These laws vary in the scope of their restrictions on employers. Across the board, they preclude employers from requiring or requesting employees to disclose usernames and passwords to personal social media accounts. A few statutes stop there.[35] Others also ban employers from requiring or requesting employees or prospective employees to add an employee, supervisor, or administrator to contacts associated with his or her social media account.[36] Others preclude requiring or requesting an employee or applicant to access personal social media in presence of employer—that is, looming over the employee's shoulder[37]—or to change their privacy settings.[38] California broadly does not permit employers to require employees or applicants to "divulge any personal social media," unless a statutory exception applies.[39]

Many of these laws, to varying degrees, do carve out relatively narrow exception(s) that permit an employer to request or require social media content of an employee to comply with state and federal laws, rules, and regulations or to conduct a legitimate employment investigation to ensure compliance with applicable laws, regulatory requirements, or prohibitions against work-related employee misconduct *if* the employer has reason to believe, based on specific information, that content of an employee's personal online account or service is implicated or otherwise involved.[40] For example, New Jersey's new social media privacy law, which took effect on December 1, 2013, allows an employer, after receiving specific information, to investigate a violation of law, employee misconduct, or the unauthorized transfer of proprietary, confidential, or financial information via an employee's personal social media account.[41] Notably, these laws generally require the employee's personal social media account to be involved in the violation under investigation. Such exception(s), while allowing employers to request or require sharing of social media content, still may not allow employers to request or require passwords or to log on to the employee's account(s).[42] Importantly, not all such state employment social media privacy statutes expressly make exemptions for employers conducting investigations into workplace misconduct.[43] And only Arkansas expressly extends the exception to investigations of violations of employer policies.[44]

Although statutory language varies somewhat from state to state, the statutory restrictions generally do not apply to accounts opened at an employer's request, or provided or paid for by an employer, or set up on behalf of an employer,[45] or under some statutes, to accounts or services obtained "by virtue of" the employment relationship or used for the employer's "business purpose"—although there is variation in statutory language.[46] Arkansas' restrictions do not apply to an account set up to impersonate an employer through use of the employer's name, logos, or trademarks.[47] A few states make it clear an employer can view information that is publicly available on the Internet,[48] although there is no reason to think otherwise. Some specify that an employer is not liable for receiving an employee's personal social media account username or password through use of an electronic device the employer provided to the employee or a program that monitors the employer's network, but the employer may not use that information to access the employee's social media account.[49]

Attorney Ethical Limitations

It is unethical for attorneys, either themselves or through an agent, to use deceptive means to "friend" or cause another to "friend" a person to access social media postings that have a heightened privacy setting. The Philadelphia Bar Association Professional Guidance Committee has issued an advisory opinion, concluding that sending an anonymous friend request to a witness MySpace or Facebook account to gain access to nonpublic information would violate Rule 4.1, which prohibits knowingly "mak[ing] a false statement of material fact or law to a third person . . ." and Rule 8.4(c) of the Rules of Professional Conduct, which provides that it "is professional misconduct for a lawyer to . . . engage in conduct involving dishonesty, fraud, deceit, or misrepresentation."[50] The New York City Bar has issued a formal statement opining that a lawyer "may not attempt to gain access to a social networking website under false pretenses, either directly or through an agent."[51] Furthermore, in the case of a represented party, prior consent of counsel is required.[52]

Discoverability of Relevant Social Media

Once litigation is underway, the most effective way to obtain social media content is through the user of social media him or herself, oftentimes (but not always) a party to the litigation. Courts can and do permit discovery of social media sites, including content to which access is restricted by the user's privacy settings, from the social media user, but only if the party seeking the information can demonstrate that the social media content is relevant to the claims and defenses in the litigation.

A widely discussed case concerning the right to access social media evidence is *EEOC v. The Original Honeybaked Ham Company of Georgia Inc.*, a sexual harassment suit on behalf of a class of 22 women against a manager at the Honeybaked Ham Company.[53] The defendant sought social media evidence and text messages to dispute liability and damages claims, and the district court eventually sanctioned the EEOC for failing to provide social media discovery and for causing unnecessary delays in the eDiscovery process.[54]

Rejecting the EEOC's strenuous objections that such discovery violated the privacy rights of the plaintiff class members, the magistrate judge described the social media content as akin to a "file folder titled 'Everything About Me,' which [class members] have voluntarily shared with others."

> If there are documents in this folder that contain information that is relevant or may lead to the discovery of admissible evidence relating to [the] lawsuit, the presumption is that it should be produced. . . . Should the outcome be different because it is on one's Facebook account? There is a strong argument that storing such information on Facebook and making it accessible to others presents an even stronger case for production, at least as it concerns any privacy objection. It was the claimants (or at least some of them) who, by their own volition, created relevant communications and shared them with others.[55]

The court did not fully reject notions of privacy, however. The magistrate judge made the somewhat novel decision to have the social media information provided to a special master—a computer forensic company that was presumably well-versed in data mining in eDiscovery—and also provided that only relevant information would be turned over to the defense after an *in-camera* review. In November 2012, the magistrate court ordered all claimants to turn over to the special master social media communications and any cell phone used to send or receive text messages during a three-year period for a forensic collection and review, and to provide access to any e-mail account, website, or cloud-based storage location that they used to post communications or pictures.

Commentators have hailed this decision as evidence that the sometimes lopsided burdens of discovery between defendants and plaintiffs are being evened out—at least in employment cases. Indeed, given the burgeoning use of electronic media, and the consequent plethora of digital information to discover, the ability to seek such information in litigation is likely to become a significant aid to defendants in litigation. At least one other court in Pennsylvania has followed the example of *Honeybaked Ham*.[56]

However, other courts, concerned about the burden on judicial resources, have declined to appoint special masters or engage in such *in-camera* review. These courts instead rely on plaintiffs' counsel, in light of counsel's ethical obligations, to review plaintiffs' social media for documents response to document requests.[57] Some courts also have declined to require plaintiffs to provide passwords, relying instead on plaintiffs' counsel to turn over responsive social media.[58] Finally, a special master and/or *in-camera* process increases the expense of litigation, and those costs may well be split or borne by the party seeking the discovery.[59]

As with any other kind of evidence, courts will not allow a party to "conduct 'a fishing expedition' . . . on the mere hope of finding relevant evidence,"[60] and there is no "generalized right to rummage at will through information that Plaintiff has limited from public view."[61] Overly broad document requests are often denied; therefore requests are more likely to succeed if they are tailored to seek relevant categories of social media evidence.[62]

Not only must a lawyer ask the right person for social media evidence (the social media user), but the requesting party must demonstrate the relevance of the evidence sought. When social media evidence is sought, the threshold showing of relevance may be heightened by some courts and jurisdictions, in part out of concern over privacy concerns.[63] Other courts have rejected applying a heightened threshold to social media discovery, reasoning that it is no different from other forms of discovery.[64] It is prudent to be familiar with the articulation of the relevance predicate for a particular jurisdiction, court, and judge.

Process of Collecting Social Media Content

As with any other electronically stored information (ESI), planning, documenting and verifying the data collection process and results, which may be supported with affidavits or testimony, is key to withstanding either allegations of spoliation or challenges to later use of the social media content as evidence. The standards, principles, and protocols that have evolved for collection and preservation of ESI are applicable to social media content. However, because of its fluid nature, social media can present particular challenges when applying these standards, principles, and protocols.[65]

The best approach is to confer with opposing counsel and agree to reasonable steps for preservation and collection.[66] But such consultation may not be possible when the duty to preserve is triggered because the opposing party or counsel may not be identifiable then.[67]

Some court precedent permits the use and introduction of static images—screenshots and pdf images—collected from social media sites, which is economical, as a means of preserving relevant content of sites.[68] However, capturing social media content by static printing may not be complete and accurate, and may be challenging to authenticate if opposed. Such capture also will not properly collect nonstatic content like video content.

Another possible process—a video or interactive software demonstration of the collection of the content, thereby creating a record of navigating the site—may relay the dynamic information more accurately.[69] Any collection of the content of social media sites represents the site at the fixed time at which the content was collected; thus, periodic collections may be needed.[70] Additionally, a collection likely will have been captured without also collecting metadata and logging data that is useful to authenticating the data for uses as evidence and without the benefit of useful data that allows the content to be easily navigated and used.[71]

Consequently, tools for preserving and collecting social media content are being developed and rapidly are evolving—at least one eDiscovery software solution now exists that can instantly search and capture social media content in its native format, that is, the format of the social media application used to create and store it. This includes metadata, or "data about data" that is stored electronically and describes the characteristics of the social media content that can assist in establishing the chain of custody and authentication of the content and can facilitate more accurate and efficient data processing and review.[72] As each social media site is unique, tools used to preserve and collect content from one site may not work for another.[73]

Using Social Media in Litigation

Of course, social media evidence—like any other evidence—must be relevant, authentic, offered for a non-hearsay purpose or admissible under an exception to the hearsay rule, comply if necessary with the original writing or best evidence rule, and the probative value must outweigh any unfair prejudice. The discussion that follows focuses on authentication and hearsay hurdles because authenticity of social media evidence has presented a significant challenge in a number of cases, with courts reaching widely disparate conclusions depending on the court's preexisting sense of concern about potential abuse and manipulation of social networking, and because the immediacy and unmediated nature of social media evidence lends itself well to certain hearsay exceptions.[74]

Authenticity Has Presented a Significant but Undeserved Challenge

Courts have been suspicious of the "potential for abuse and manipulation of a social networking account by someone other than its purported creator or user."[75] Consequently, the most significant hurdle in using social media evidence in litigation is the authentication required for it to be admitted into evidence. It is worth remembering that inauthentic evidence is irrelevant because "'evidence cannot have a tendency to make the existence of a disputed fact more or less likely if the evidence is not that which its proponent claims.'"[76]

Concerns about social media—which often are speculative—include hacking, ease of creating fictitious accounts, and the fact that accounts on phones and computers are simply left open and unattended.[77] Such possibilities have led numerous courts to set a significantly, sometimes impossibly, higher bar for authenticating social media evidence—even absent any evidence of such hacking, fictitious accounts, or unattended computers or devices.[78] Such courts do not admit social media evidence unless the court definitively determines the evidence is authentic.[79]

Griffin v. State illustrates this "higher bar" approach. In *Griffin*, the state offered printouts from the MySpace page profile of the girlfriend of a defendant in a murder trial; the printouts included the statement, "Free Boozy [Defendant's nickname] Just Remember Snitches get stitches U Know who you are."[80] In the state's offer of proof of authenticity, the lead investigator stated that he knew the page was the girlfriend's page because of a photo of her and Boozy on front, references to Boozy, references to the girlfriend's children, and her birthdate on the printout.[81] The trial court admitted the printout, and on appeal, the appellate court also found that the state's circumstantial evidence of authenticity was sufficient.[82] However, the Court of Appeals reversed, concluding that (i) the picture, birthdate, and location of the girlfriend on the printout were not distinctive enough characteristics, (ii) that anyone could create the site and post photos and content, and (iii) that the account could be hacked or a fictitious account.[83] The Court of Appeals required, instead, either that the creator be asked if she created the profile and posts, or a showing that her computer was used to create the profile and to make the posts and that her Internet address and so forth were used to link to the profile.[84]

Unlike *Griffin* and similar cases, other courts have followed a "conditional relevance" approach to authentication that is consistent with the judge's and the fact finder's roles under Rules 104(a) and 104(b) of the Rules of Evidence, consistent with the admissibility standard for whether "the matter in question is what its proponent claims" under Rule 901(a), and consistent with the myriad of illustrative examples for authenticating evidence that are spelled out in Rule 901(b). In such cases, a court asks whether there is sufficient evidence of authenticity for a reasonable jury to conclude the evidence is authentic.[85] Preliminary determinations of admissibility of evidence are made by the judge under Rule 104(a) and may be made using inadmissible evidence.[86] If a question of fact must be resolved to determine admissibility, for example, by weighing circumstantial evidence that an account was created and maintained by a particular person and evidence that the account is fictitious, evidence may be conditionally admitted under Rule 104(b), and the trier of fact will resolve the factual issue based on admissible evidence.[87]

Tienda v. State illustrates the "conditional relevance" approach.[88] The state in *Tienda* offered MySpace pages from three MySpace accounts that allegedly belonged to the defendant.[89] Each account stated that it was "created by a 'Ron Mr. T'" or Tienda's well-known nickname, "Smiley-Face," and that the account owner lived in Dallas or D-Town, where Tienda lived.[90] The accounts were registered to e-mail addresses that included Tienda's name or nickname.[91] One account included a heading, "RIP [the victim]," above a link to a song played at the victim's funeral.[92] The accounts linked to photographs of someone who resembled Tienda. Instant messages between the owner of the account and others included details about the murder in question and said that the account owner was placed on electronic monitoring.[93] The sponsoring witness for the pages was the sister of the victim, who had directed the state to them, and a detective testified about typical gang usage of social media.[94] On the other hand, Tienda elicited testimony about the ease by which a person could create a MySpace page in someone else's name and send messages purportedly written by that person without their approval.[95] The *Tienda* trial court admitted the MySpace pages as evidence, and an intermediate appellate court concluded that the trial court did not err. The Court of Criminal Appeals of Texas agreed: There was "ample circumstantial evidence—taken as a whole with all of the individual, particular details considered in combination—to support a finding that the MySpace pages belonged to [Tienda] and that he created and maintained them," and whether the page had been fabricated was an "alternate scenario whose likelihood and weight the jury was entitled to assess."[96]

Indeed, the standard for whether "the matter in question is what its proponent claims" under Rule 901(a) is "quite low—even lower than a preponderance of the evidence." In *Lorraine v. Markel American Insurance Company*, Hon. Judge Paul Grimm noted:

> A party seeking to admit an exhibit need only make a *prima facie* showing that it is what he or she claims it to be. This is not a particularly high barrier to overcome. . . . 'The question for the court under Rule 901 is whether the proponent of the evidence has 'offered a foundation from which the jury could reasonably find that the evidence is what the proponent says it is. . . .' The Court need not find that the evidence is necessarily what the proponent claims, but only that there is sufficient evidence that the jury ultimately might do so.[97]

Because both the "higher bar" and the "conditional relevance" approach continue to coexist, it is prudent to research the positions of a particular jurisdiction, court, and judge; identify potential challenges to admitting the evidence, and have a plan (or more than one plan) for admitting the evidence from the beginning of investigating and developing a case; and to gather and document the collection of social media evidence with such plan(s) for admitting the evidence and using it.

As a practical matter, in many cases, the form of the social media evidence will be printouts or screen shots, and the authentication plan may be as simple and effective as a party admission or a stipulation from the opposing party on the foundation for the authenticity of the print outs or screen shots. A party admission can be obtained at deposition or through Rule 26(f) requests to admit. Production of documents by the opposing party in response to a well-tailored document request raises a presumption of genuineness. The content of social media also could be pleaded in a complaint, and thus potentially admitted in the answer.

Applying Rule 901(a)'s Illustrative Authentication Examples to Social Media

Rule 901(b) of the Rules of Evidence spells out illustrative examples of ways to sufficiently authenticate evidence. Some of these are particularly helpful for authenticating social media.

First, Rule 901(b)(1) allows evidence to be authenticated by testimony of a witness with knowledge "that a matter is what it claims to be." Circumstantial evidence may be used to infer that a person is the author of social media content. A witness with personal knowledge may testify that she knows the user name on the website of the person in question, that the evidence offered (e.g., printouts) accurately reflects the material on the person's page, and that some of the content from the page is unique or generally would be known only by the person in question or people closely associated with the person. Also, evidence from the hard drive of the person's computer may reflect that the user used the particular screen name associated with the postings.

Courts have assessed the authenticity of ESI using the testimony of a witness with "personal knowledge of how that type of exhibit is routinely made who provides 'factual specificity' about how the ESI is 'created, acquired, maintained, and preserved without alteration or change' or about how it was produced 'via a system or process that does so.'"[98] In *Dockery v. Dockery*, printouts of MySpace e-mails, in which a defendant asked his ex-wife's friend to ask her to call him, were authenticated by the ex-friend's testimony about the contents of the conversation between her and the defendant, her testimony that the printouts accurately reflected those conversations, and her testimony that she printed them directly from her computer.[99] A MySpace representative was not required to authenticate the MySpace e-mails.[100]

Second—and oft-used—Rule 901(b)(4) allows evidence to be authenticated by showing distinctive characteristics such as "[a]ppearance, contents, substance, or internal patterns . . . taken in conjunction with [the circumst]ances" to provide a basis for reasonably concluding that the evidence is what it purports to be." This rule has been a frequent way to authenticate e-mail content through distinctive characteristics in the content of the e-mail itself based on the identifying content of what the e-mail says.[101] The same approach can be applied to social media postings and messaging. Distinctive characteristics can include hash values and metadata, in addition to the content of the postings.

Third, Rule 901(b) (6) allows evidence from a telephone conversation to be authenticated by the reply doctrine or "circumstance, including self-identification, [that] shows the person answering to be the one that called,"[102] and identifying through responding to details that indicate he knew what the call recipient was talking about. This can be analogized to social networking conversations.

Fourth, Rule 901(b) (9) allows evidence about a process or system to be authenticated by evidence "showing that it produces an accurate result."[103] This will require a witness who has personal knowledge under 602 to explain how the social media evidence was created or an expert qualified under Rule 702 who can provide opinion testimony.

Hearsay and Social Media Evidence

As with authentication, lawyers should have a plan for overcoming hearsay objections to the use of social media as evidence. Hearsay issues are "pervasive when electronically stored and generated evidence is introduced."[104] Much of the content on social networking sites, however, probably is not hearsay, because it is not offered to prove the truth of the matter asserted—but rather is offered for the fact that it was said or posted—or because the content is posted by a party opponent and excluded from the definition of hearsay under Rule 801(d)(2) of the Rules of Evidence.

The content of social media also could fall within one or many of the exceptions to the hearsay rule. As Hon. Judge Grimm observed in *Lorraine*, "given the ubiquity of communications in electronic media (e-mail, text messages, chat rooms, Internet postings on servers like 'MySpace' or 'YouTube' or on blogs, voice mail, etc.), it is not surprising that many statements involving observations of events surrounding us, statements regarding how we feel, our plans and motives, and our feelings (emotional and physical) will be communicated in electronic medium. . . ."[105]

Rules 803 and 804 provide numerous exceptions for types of hearsay that are admissible because the statement has some degree of inherent trustworthiness. Hearsay exceptions dealing with perceptions, observations, state of mind, and sensation are particularly amenable to social media because of the immediate, interactive nature of social media: present sense impressions (803(1)); excited utterances (803(2)); then existing mental, emotional, or physical condition (803(3)).

First, Rule 803(1) provides an exception for statements that describe an event or condition while personally perceiving it or immediately thereafter. Through Twitter, Facebook, text messaging, and so on, users constantly are telling the world about events as the events occur.

Second, Rule 803(2) provides an exception for statements made under the stress and excitement of a startling event or condition that related to that event or condition—excited utterances. Statements made through Twitter, Facebook, text messaging, and the like, because of their typical immediacy, lend themselves to fitting within this exception. Practitioners should, of course, take care to lay a foundation that particular postings qualify under this exception.

Third, Rule 803(3) provides an exception for a statement of the "[t]hen existing state of mind, emotion, sensation, or physical condition (such as intent, plan, motive, design, mental feeling, pain, and bodily health)" of the declarant, but not a statement of memory or a belief to prove the fact remembered or believed (unless it related to a will). Rule 803(3) has been used to prove a variety of matters, including why a declarant would not deal with a particular supplier or dealer, motive, competency, lack of intent to defraud, willingness to engage in criminal conduct, confusion or secondary meaning in a trademark infringement case, and so forth.[106]

Of course, social media content proffered to prove the truth of a matter asserted, which is not an admission by a party opponent or which does not fall within an exception, will be excluded as inadmissible hearsay.[107]

Notes

1. Merriam-Webster defines *social media* as "forms of electronic communication (as websites for social networking and micro-blogging) through which users create online communities to share information, ideas, personal messages, and other content (such as videos)." "Social Media." Merriam-Webster.com. Last accessed October 25, 2013. www.merriam-webster .com/dictionary/social media.
2. This chapter concentrates on discovery and use of social media in civil litigation, and not criminal enforcement.
3. *See generally*, "Published Cases Involving Social Media Evidence (First Half 2012)", *X1 Discovery* website, www.x1discovery.com/social_media_cases.html (last visited November. 7, 2013) (collecting cases that involve social media by case type).
4. *See generally*, Hon. J. Grimm et al., "Keynote Address: Authentication of Social Media Evidence," *Am. J. Trial Advoc.* 36 (Spring 2013): 433, 437.
5. This chapter predominantly references the Federal Rules of Civil Procedure and the Federal Rules of Evidence; both have similar state counterparts.
6. 2013 U.S. Dist. LEXIS 41909, *8 (D.N.J. 2013). A specific request to reveal or produce evidence is not required for the duty to preserve to attach. See VOOM HD Holdings LLC v. EchoStar Satellite LLC, 93 A.D.3d 33, 939 N.Y.S.2d 321, 328 (1st Dept. 2012) ("Once a party reasonably anticipates litigation, it must, at a minimum, institute an appropriate litigation hold to prevent the routine destruction of electronic data").
7. A recent ethics opinion from the New York County Lawyers Association concluded that New York lawyers ethically may counsel civil clients about their use of social media, including how postings might be used for and against them in a civil case; indeed, an attorney's obligation to competently represent clients could in some circumstances give rise to an obligation (within legal and ethical requirements) to counsel on steps to mitigate adverse effects that a client's social media use could have on its legal position. (NYCLA Ethics Opinion 745, "Advising a Client Regarding Posts on Social Media Site", at 3

(July 2, 2013).) There is no ethical restraint on advising use of the highest level of privacy or security setting available, which will prevent direct access by adverse counsel to the contents of social media pages and require adverse counsel to request access through formal discovery channels. *Id.*, 2. New York Rule of Professional Conduct 3.4 prohibits lawyers from suppressing or concealing social media content that should be revealed. *Id.* While the Opinion goes on to opine that a lawyer in some circumstances may advise what may be "taken down" or removed from a social media site—provided there is no violation of the rules or substantive law pertaining to preservation or spoliation of evidence—the caveat warrants heavy emphasis: Keep in mind that the mere act of deleting social media content, even innocuous or irrelevant content, could appear suspicious, as it apparently did in *Gatto* to the plaintiff who deactivated his Facebook account.

8. 285 Va. 295 (Va. 2013).
9. *Id.* at 302.
10. *Id.*
11. *Id.* at 304.
12. *Id.*
13. *Id.*; *see also Lester v. Allied Concrete Co.*, 83 Va. Cir. 308 (Va. Cir. 2011).
14. 285 Va. at 307, n. 7 (finding the trial court did not err in denying Allied Concrete's motion for a new trial based on this misconduct).
15. Debra Cassens Weiss, "Lawyer Agrees to Five-Year Suspension for Advising Client to Clean Up His Facebook Photos," ABA Journal Law News Now (online), August 7, 2013, www .abajournal.com/news/article/lawyer_agrees_to_five-year_suspension_for_advising_client_ to_clean_up_his_f/ (last accessed April 27, 2014).
16. Recent legal ethics opinions have concluded that accessing a social media page open to all members of a public network is ethically permissible. New York State Bar Association Eth. Op. 843 (2010); Oregon State Bar Legal Ethics Comm. Op. 2005-164 at 453 (accessing opposing party's public website does not violate ethics rules limited communications with adverse parties: Accessing a public site conceptually is no different from reading a magazine article or buying a book written by that adverse party).
17. *See, e.g., EEOC v. The Original Honeybaked Ham Company of Georgia, Inc.*, 116 Fair Empl. Prac. Cas. (BNA) 743, *4-5 (D. Colo. 2012). In this same vein, the spate of recent state laws restricting employers from requesting personal social media passwords and user information from employees generally expressly do not preclude employers from reviewing publicly available information. See *infra* at II(B)(1)(b).
18. 18 U.S.C. §2701 *et seq.*
19. *Quon v. Arch Wireless Operating Co., Inc.*, 529 F.3d 892, 900 (9th Cir. 2008); *rev'd on other grounds sub nom. City of Ontario v. Quon*, 560 U.S. 746, 130 S.Ct. 2619, 177 L.E.2d 216, 210 (2010).
20. *Viacom International Inc. v. YouTube, Inc.*, 253 F.R.D 256, 264 (S.D.N.Y. 2008) (holding that YouTube is an RCS as it provides video storage services to its users and the SCA protects videos marked as "private"); *Pietrylo v. Hillstone Restaurant Group*, 2009 U.S. Dist. LEXIS 88702, *10-11 (D.N.J. Sept. 25, 2009) (holding that information on MySpace is protected by the SCA); *Crispin v. Christian Audigier, Inc.*, 717 F.Supp.2d 965, 989 (C.D. Cal. 2010) (holding that Facebook, MySpace, and Media Temple are both ESC providers, because they offered message delivery services, and RSC providers, because they offered message storage services, and quashing portions of subpoenas seeking private messages); *Ehling v. Monmouth-Ocean Hosp. Serv. Corp.*, 2013 U.S. Dist. LEXIS 117689, *24 (D.N.J. Aug. 20, 2013) (holding that an employee's Facebook wall posts, where the user had configured her privacy settings to restrict viewers of her wall postings to "friends," were protected by the SCA). Social media providers may fall into one or both categories depending on the message: As to the private messaging features of Facebook and MySpace, for unopened messages the entities are ECS providers providing temporary, intermediate storage, and for opened messages retained by the user, the entities are RCS providers providing storage services. *Crispin* at

988-990. Facebook and MySpace are both ECS and RCS providers as to wall posts and comments, and the SCA prohibits the services from divulging the contents of such wall posts and comments. *Id.*

21. The SCA prohibits an ECS provider, defined as "any service which provides to users thereof the ability to send or receive wire or electronic communications" from "knowingly divulg[ing] to any person or entity the contents of a communication while in electronic storage by that service." 18 U.S.C. §2510(15); 18 U.S.C. §2702(a)(1); 18 U.S.C. §2510 (17). That is, it prohibits an ECS provider from divulging the contents of communications that are either in temporary storage, such as messages that are waiting to be delivered, or that are kept for the purposes of backup protection. The SCA also prohibits a RCS provider, defined as "the provision to the public of computer storage or processing services by means of an electronic communications system," from "knowingly divulg[ing] to any person or entity the contents of any communication that is carried or maintained on that service." 18 U.S.C. §2711(2); 18 U.S.C. §2702(a)(2). The restrictions on an RCS provider are broader than those on an ECS provider, and are not limited to communications that are in temporary storage or that are kept for purposes of backup protection. Some courts have observed that logs of account usage, mailer header information (minus the subject line), a list of outgoing e-mail addresses sent from an account, and basic subscriber information are all considered to be non-content information. *See, e.g., People v. Harris*, 36 Misc.3d 868, 871, 949 N.Y.S.2d 590, 596 (Crim. Ct. N.Y. 2012), appeal dismissed, 39 Misc. 868, 949 N.Y.S.2d 590 (N.Y. Sup. App. Term. 2013).

22. *Crispin*, 717 F. Supp. 2d at 976 (rejecting the argument that the SCA permits the disclosure of the contents of communications pursuant to a civil discovery subpoena); *Flagg v. City of Detroit*, 252 F.R.D. 346, 350 (E.D. Mich. 2008) (observing, "as noted by the courts and commentators alike, that §2702 lacks any language that explicitly authorizes a service provider to divulge the contents of a communication pursuant to a subpoena or court order"); *Viacom*, 253 F.R.D. at 264 (S.D.N.Y. 2008) (holding that the SCA "contains no exception for disclosure of such communications pursuant to civil discovery requests"); *In re Subpoena Duces Tecum to AOL, LLC*, 550 F. Supp. 2d 606, 611 (E.D. Va. 2008) (reasoning that "[a]pplying the clear and unambiguous language of §2702 to this case, AOL, a corporation that provides electronic communication services to the public, may not divulge the contents of the Rigsbys' electronic communications to State Farm because the statutory language of the [SCA] does not include an exception for the disclosure of electronic communications pursuant to civil discovery subpoenas"); but see *Ledbetter v. Wal-Mart Stores, Inc.*, 939 N.Y.S.2d 331, *2 (D.Colo. Apr. 21, 2009) (denying plaintiff's motion for a protective order as to subpoenas issued to Facebook, MySpace, and Meetup.com—but without any discussion of the SCA). There is a key distinction between the government and a private entity: The government in a criminal matter may require an ECS provider to produce information relating to its users. 18 U.S.C. §2703.

23. See "May I Obtain Contents of a User's Account from Facebook Using a Civil Subpoena?," available at https://www.facebook.com/help/133221086752707/ (accessed October 19, 2013). Some commentators have noted that while *Crispin* supports Facebook's policy that subpoenas to social media sites generally are not enforceable to the extent they seek private user content, the court left the door open on whether subpoenas to social media sites are enforceable to the extent they seek public user content. See, e.g., Carole Levitt J.D., MLS & Mark Rosch, "Serving a Subpoena on a Social Media Site to Obtain Content of a User's Profile," available at www.techshow.com/2013/03/serving-a-civil-subpoena-on-a-social-media-site-to-obtain-content-of-a-users-profile (accessed October 19, 2013). In *People v. Harris*, 949 N.Y.S.2d at 591–592, when Twitter intervened to quash a prosecution subpoena seeking user information, including e-mail addresses and tweets posted from a defendant's account during a certain time period, the court rejected Twitter's motion, because Twitter's terms of service and privacy policy made clear that the subscriber lacked any privacy or property interest in his Twitter account data, and then required Twitter to disclose information

about the tweets. Twitter's appeal was denied in *People v. Harris*, 39 Misc. 3d 142, 2013 N.Y. Misc. 2039 (N.Y. Sup. App. Term 2013). As a practical matter, however, information most likely sought by subpoena would be private user content, as public user content would be readily accessible and, in fact, may have already been searched for in prelitigation investigation.

24. *See, e.g., Crispin* at 976.

25. 18 U.S.C. §2701(a) (prohibiting improper access); 18 U.S.C. §2701(b) (criminal penalties); 18 U.S.C. §2707(a) (private right of action). In 2004, for example, attorneys, who had issued subpoenas lacking time or subject matter limitations to the other parties' ISP seeking e-mail and who in response had been provided e-mail by the ISP, were sanctioned. *Theofel v. Farey-Jones*, 359 F.3d 1066, 1073 (9th Cir. 2004). Due to the SCA and the overbreadth of the subpoenas, the Ninth Circuit Court of Appeals found that the attorneys "transparently and egregiously" violated the Federal Rules of Civil Procedure and "acted in bad faith and with gross negligence in drafting and deploying the subpoena." Civil claims for violating the SCA could be maintained against the attorneys: "The subpoena's falsity transformed the access from a bona fide state-sanctioned inspection into private snooping." *Id.* at 1073.

26. 18 U.S.C. §2702(b)(3).

27. See https://www.facebook.com/help/131112897028467 (last accessed November 8, 2013); *In re White Tail Oilfield Servs., LLC*, 2012 U.S. Dist. LEXIS 146321, *8-9 (E.D. La 2012) (directing a party to download and produce Facebook information by following Facebook's "download a copy of your Facebook data" download process and forwarding content received by email to opposing counsel).

28. 302 F.3d 868, 880 (9th Cir. 2002).

29. *Id.*

30. 2009 U.S. Dist. LEXIS 88702 (D.N.J. Sept. 25, 2009).

31. *Id.; see also Van Alstyne v. Elec. Scriptorium Ltd.*, 560 F.3d 199, 204–205 (4th Cir. 2009) (finding that a plaintiff's manager, who accessed plaintiff's personal e-mail account without her permission and read her e-mails, violated SCA; the court vacated the jury award of statutory damages under the SCA because the plaintiff failed to show actual damages, but noted that punitive damages are available for SCA violations without actual damages); *Gates v. Wheeler*, 2010 Minn. App. Unpub. LEXIS 1136, *18–19 (Minn. Ct. App. Nov. 23, 2010) (affirming the issuance of a preliminary injunction that prohibited a party's use of an opposing party's private e-mails in litigation: A business co-owner's use of his access to the company's e-mail systems to route his opponent co-owner's e-mail, including all of his co-owner's personal e-mail sent using his work e-mail account, for use in the litigation violated the co-owner's reasonable expectation of privacy in his personal e-mails and likely violated the SCA and similar state law); *Ehling*, 872 F. Supp. 2d at 374 (denying employer's motion to dismiss where plaintiff's supervisor gained access to plaintiff's Facebook account by asking a coworker, who was friends with plaintiff on Facebook, to access the account at a work computer in the supervisor's presence, and the plaintiff was not Facebook friends with any management employees).

32. Similar concerns arose when universities and colleges asked students for their passwords to social media sites, and eight states have passed laws that prohibit colleges and universities from requiring students to disclose a user name or password for a personal social media account. Arkansas Code Annotated §6-60-104 (2013); Cal. Ed. Code §99121 (2013); Delaware Education Privacy Act, 14 Del. C. §8101 *et seq.* (2013); Michigan Internet Privacy Protection Act, MCLS §37.271 *et seq.* (2013); N.J. Stat. §18A:3-30 (2013); N.M. Stat. Ann. §21-1-46 (2013); Oregon SB 344, signed by governor June 13, 2013, effective January 1, 2014, and to be codified in Oregon Revised Statutes (ORS); Utah Internet Postsecondary Education Privacy Act, Utah Code Ann. §53B-25-101 *et seq.* (2013).

33. Arkansas Code Annotated §11-2-124 (2013); Cal. Lab. Code §980 (2013); Colorado Revised Statutes §8-2-127 (2013); Illinois Right to Privacy in the Workplace Act, 820 ILCS 55/1 et seq.; Md. LABOR AND EMPLOYMENT Code Ann. §3-712 (2013); Michigan

Internet Privacy Protection Act; MCLS §37.271 *et seq.* (2013); 2013 Nev. ALS 548 (to be codified in Nevada Revised Statutes, Chapter 613 (2013); N.J. Stat. §34:6B-6 (2013), effective December 1, 2013; Oregon Revised Statutes (ORS) - Chapter 659A, effective January 1, 2014; Utah Internet Employment Privacy Act, Utah Code Ann. §34-48-101 *et seq.* (2013); Rev. Code Wash. (ARCW) §49.44.250 (2013); N.M. S.B. 271 (2013) (signed by governor and limited to applicant login information).

34. So far, attempts to pass federal legislation have not been successful. The Social Networking Online Protection Act (SNOPA), which would prohibit employers from requiring a username, password, or other access to online content, was introduced in the United States House of Representatives in 2012 and 2013. But this bill died in committee in 2012 and is expected to do the same in 2013. In April 2013, the House of Representatives also voted down a proposed amendment to the Cyber Intelligence Sharing and Protection Act (CISPA) bill that would have barred employers from asking for passwords to social media sites.

35. N.J. Stat. §34:6B-6; 820 ILCS 55/10(b)(1); Md. LABOR AND EMPLOYMENT Code Ann. §3-712 (b); 2013 Nev. ALS 548 (to be codified in Nevada Revised Statutes, Chapter 613 (2013)); Utah Code Ann. §34-48-201.

36. See Ark. Code. Ann. 11-2-124(b)(1); Col. Rev. Stat. 8-2-127(2)(a) and (3); Or. Rev. Stat. (ORS)—Chapter 659A; Rev. Code Wash. (ARCW) §49.44.250 (2013).

37. See Cal. Lab. Code §980(b)(2); MCLS §37.273; Or. Rev. Statutes (ORS)—Chapter 659A; Rev. Code Wash. (ARCW) §49.44.250.

38. See Ark. Code. Ann. 11-2-124(b)(1)(C); Col. Rev. Stat. 8-2-127(2)(a); Rev. Code Wash. (ARCW) §49.44.250.

39. See Cal. Lab. Code §980(b)(3).

40. See Ark. Code Ann. 124(e) (employee social media account activity is reasonably believed to be relevant to a formal investigation or related proceeding by the employer of allegations of an employee's violation of federal, state, or local laws or regulations or of the employer's written policies); Cal. Lab. Code §980(e) (social media account activity is reasonably believed to be relevant to a formal investigation or related proceeding by the employer of allegations of an employee's violation of federal, state, or local laws or regulations); Md. LABOR AND EMPLOYMENT Code Ann. §3-712(e) (investigating to ensure compliance with applicable securities or financial law, or regulatory requirements, based on receipt of information about the use of an employee's personal website or web-based account or similar account for business purpose or employee's actions based on the receipt of information about unauthorized downloading of an employer's proprietary information or financial data to a personal website, web-based account, or similar account by an employee); Col. Rev. Stat. 8-2-127(4)(a) (similar); MCLS §37.275(5) (investigating or requiring an employee to cooperate in an investigation, if there is specific information about activity on the employee's personal Internet account, to ensure compliance with applicable laws, regulatory requirements, or prohibitions against work-related employee misconduct or if the employer has specific information about an unauthorized transfer of the employer's proprietary information, confidential information, or financial data to an employee's personal Internet account, or complying with a duty to screen employees or applicants before hiring or to monitor or retain employee communications that is established under federal law or by a self-regulatory organization, as defined in the Securities and Exchange Act of 1934); Utah Code Ann. §34-48-2-2(c, e) (similar); Oregon Revised Statutes (ORS)—Chapter 659A (similar); Rev. Code Wash. (ARCW) §49.44.250 (2) (may request or require employee to share content from a personal social networking account to make a factual determination in the course of an investigation undertaken in response to receipt of information about the employee's activity on that account if the purpose is to ensure compliance with applicable laws, regulatory requirements, or prohibitions against work-related employee misconduct or to investigate an allegation of unauthorized transfer of an employer's proprietary information, confidential information, or financial data to the employee's personal social networking account, and the employer does not request or require the employee to provide login information).

41. N.J. Stat. §34:6B-101.
42. Oregon Revised Statutes (ORS)—Chapter 659A; Rev. Code Wash. (ARCW) §49.44.250 (2)
43. See 2013 Nev. ALS 548 (does not provide express exceptions for investigations). Nevada's law does provide that the law may not be construed to prevent an employer from complying with other state or federal laws or with any rule of a self-regulatory organization. *Id.* Illinois, the second state to pass a law prohibiting employers from asking for information about an employee's, or prospective employee's, social media account, originally made no exemptions to this law. However, practical concerns about an employer's right to mitigate its social media risks led to an amendment, effective January 1, 2014. This amendment allows employers to access "professional" social media accounts where the employer has a duty to screen employees or applicants or monitor or retain employee communications under Illinois insurance law, federal law, or the rules of a self-regulatory organization, such as FINRA.
44. Ark. Code Ann. §11-2-124(e)(3) (social media account activity is reasonably believed to be relevant to a formal investigation or related proceeding by the employer of allegations of an employee's violation of federal, state, or local laws or regulations or of the employer's written policies). Colorado, Washington, and Illinois specify that the statutes do not prevent the employer from enforcing existing personnel policies that do not conflict with this statute. Col. Rev. Stat. 8-2-127(6); Rev. Code Wash. (ARCW) §49.44.250 (2013); 820 ILCS 55/10(b)(2).
45. See Ark. Code. Ann. 11-2-124(a)(B); Or. Rev. Stat. (ORS)—Chapter 659A; MCLS §37.275(1)(a); Utah Code Ann. §34-48-202(1); Rev. Code Wash. (ARCW) §49.44.250.
46. See MCLS §37.275(1)(a) (Michigan); Utah Code Ann. §34-48-202(1), §34-48-102(4); Rev. Code Wash. (ARCW) §49.44.250; N.J. Stat. §34:6B-5; Utah Code Ann. §34-48-102(4); see also MCLS §37.275(1)(e) and 820 ILCS 55/10(b)(2) (may monitor, review, or access data stored on an electronic communications device paid for the employer or traveling through or stored on an employer's network, in accordance with state and federal law); Cal. Lab. Code §980(d) and Md. LABOR AND EMPLOYMENT Code Ann. §3-712(b)(2) (may require or request disclosure of usernames or passwords used to access employer-issued electronic devices); Col. Rev. Stat. 8-2-127(2)(b) and Md. LABOR AND EMPLOYMENT Code Ann. §3-712(b)(2) (may require or request usernames of passwords to nonpersonal accounts or services that provide access to an employer's internal computer or information systems). New Jersey and Utah specifically limit protections to an account, service, or profile on a social networking website that is used by a current or prospective employee exclusively for personal communications unrelated to any business purposes of the employer. N.J. Stat. §34:6B-5; Utah Code Ann. §34-48-102(4). Arkansas, Oregon, and Washington immunize an employer from liability for inadvertently receiving an employee's username, password, or login information through use of an electronic device provided by the employer or a program that monitors an employer's network, but the employer may not use the information to gain access to an employee's social media account. Ark. Code. Ann. 11-2-124(b)(2); Or. Rev. Stat. (ORS)—Chapter 659A; Rev. Code Wash. (ARCW) §49.44.250.
47. Ark. Code. Ann. 11-2-124(a)(B).
48. Ark. Code. Ann. 11-2-124(d); MCLS 375(3); N.J. C.34:6B-10(d); Or. Rev. Stat. (ORS)—Chapter 659A; Utah Code Ann. §34-48-202(4); 820 ILCS 55/10(b)(3).
49. Ark. Code Ann. §11-2-124(b)(2).
50. Philadelphia Bar Association Professional Guidance Committee, Opinion 2009-2 (March 2009).
51. New York City Bar Formal Opinion 2010-2 (September 2010). The Committee, acknowledging the New York Court of Appeals policy favoring informal discovery as promoting expeditious resolution of disputes, concluded that an attorney or her agent "may use her real name and profile to send a 'friend request' to obtain information from an unrepresented person's social networking website without also disclosing the reasons for making the request." However, such a request must comport with other ethical obligations: "While there are ethical boundaries to such 'friending' . . . they are not crossed when an attorney or investigator uses

only truthful information to obtain access to a website, subject to compliance with all other ethical requirements," such as Professional Rule of Conduct 4.2, which prohibits communications with parties, including witnesses, potential witnesses, and others with an interest or right at stake, who are known to be represented by counsel unless the prior consent of the party's lawyer is obtained or the conduct is authorized by law. *Id.*

52. See NYCBA Eth. Op. 2010-2 (2012) NYSBA Eth. Op. 843 (Rule of Professional Conduct 4.2).
53. 2013 U.S. Dist. LEXIS 26887 (D. Colo. Feb. 27, 2013).
54. *Id.*
55. *EEOC v. The Original Honeybaked Ham Company of Georgia Inc.*, 116 Fair Empl. Prac. Cas. (BNA) 743, 2012 U.S. Dist. LEXIS 160285, *4–5 (D. Colo. Nov. 7, 2012); see also *EEOC v. Simply Storage Management LLC*, 270 F.R.D. 430, 434 (S.D. Ind. 2010) (noting that privacy settings were not a discovery shield," [a]lthough privacy concerns may be germane to the question of whether requested discovery is burdensome or oppressive and whether it has been sought for a proper purpose in litigation," and that a protective order would address privacy concerns); *Romano v. Steelcase, Inc.*, 30 Misc. 3d 426, 434; 907 N.Y.S.2d 650, 656; 2010 N.Y. Misc. LEXIS 4538, *15 (Sup. Ct. N.Y. 2010) (observing that neither Facebook nor MySpace guarantee complete privacy and plaintiff has no legitimate reasonable expectation of privacy).
56. See *Perrone v. Rose City HMA LLC*, No. CI-11-14933, May 3, 2013 (available at https://docs.google.com/file/d/0B83Pxa3TYcXMX3Fuelh1Ujl6UDQ) (ordering an examination of plaintiff's Facebook account by a neutral computer forensics examiner).
57. See *Fawcett v. Altieri*, 38 Misc. 3d 1022, 1028, 960 N.Y.S.2d 592, 598 (N.Y. Sup. Ct. 2013) ("[Asking courts to review hundreds of transmissions 'in-camera' should not be the all-purpose solution . . . [c]ourts do not have the time or resources to be the researchers for advocates seeking some tidbit of information that may be relevant in a tort claim); *Giacchetto v. Patchogue-Medford Union Free Sch. Dist.*, 293 F.R.D. 112, 2013 U.S. Dist. LEXIS 83341, *15–16 (E.D.N.Y. 2013) (seeing no reason to have a third-party provider access and review the plaintiff's social networking postings when the plaintiff has access to this information herself; it is a reasonable approach for the plaintiff's counsel to review the plaintiff's postings for relevance and to make a determination regarding the relevance of the postings, keeping in mind the broad scope of discovery contemplated by Rule 26).
58. *Howell v. The Buckeye Ranch, Inc.*, 2012 U.S. Dist. LEXIS 141368, *3 (S.D. Ohio 2012) (ordering the plaintiff's counsel to access the plaintiff's social media accounts and produce responsive information, as opposed to having the plaintiff provide the defendant with her usernames and passwords); *Anthony v. Atlantic Gr. Inc.*, 2012 U.S. Dist. LEXIS 129639, *9–10 (D.S.C. 2012) (directing the plaintiff to access and produce social networking postings directly as opposed to having the defendant seek the information from the service providers, where social networking data, electronically stored information, and electronic mail relating to the employees' residences or receipt of per diem amounts in wrongful employment termination case were relevant because the requested information related to the employer's contention that employees had claimed per diem amounts to which they were not entitled); *In re Air Crash Near Clarence Ctr, New York*, 2011 U.S. Dist. LEXIS 146551 (W.D. N.Y. 2011) (denying a request for consent authorizations subject to renewal if plaintiff's production was insufficient).
59. See *Fawcett*, 960 N.Y.S.2d at 598 (observing in dicta that fees to be paid to special masters for "in camera" review should be paid by the party seeking such discovery in a tort case, but may be shared by the parties in a commercial or matrimonial matter). In the *Honey Baked Ham* case, the fees were split between the parties.
60. *Salvato v. Miley*, 2013 U.S. Dist. LEXIS 81784, *7 (M.D. Fla. June 11, 2013) (denying plaintiff's motion to compel discovery of social media evidence because "the mere hope that [defendant's] private text-messages, e-mails, and electronic communication might include an admission against interest, without more, is not a sufficient reason to require Brown to

provide Plaintiff open access to his private communications with third parties").

61. *Tompkins v. Detroit Metro. Airport*, 278 F.R.D. 387, 388-389 (E.D. Mi. 2012) (finding that surveillance footage and the plaintiff's public Facebook postings of photographs showing the plaintiff holding a small dog and smiling and standing at a birthday party were not inconsistent with the plaintiff's claim of injury or with the medical information that she had provided as she did not claim she was bedridden or incapable of leaving her house or of participating in modest social activities, and, thus, the footage and public postings did not show relevance of private postings); see also *Potts v. Dollar Tree Stores, Inc.*, 2013 U.S. Dist. LEXIS 38795, *7,8 (M.D, Tenn. 2013) (finding on a motion to compel in a Title VII action, that absent a threshold relevancy showing from public portions of the plaintiff's Facebook page of the need for the private information on the plaintiff's Facebook account, the requests were akin to "fishing expeditions" and not a calculated request that would lead to relevant information); *McCann v. Harleysville Ins. Co. of N.Y.*, 78 A.D.3d 1524, 1525, 910 N.Y.S.2d 614, 615 (N.Y. App. Div. 2010) (affirming denial of motion to compel production of photos and authorization for the plaintiff's Facebook account information because the defendant failed to establish a factual predicate as to the relevancy of the evidence on the Facebook page, essentially seeking permission to conduct a fishing expedition).

62. See *Kregg v. Maldonado*, 98 A.D.3d 1289, 1290, 951 N.Y.S.2d 301, 302 (App. Div. N.Y, Sup. Ct. 2012) (holding that "proper means by which to obtain disclosure of any relevant information contained in the social media accounts is a narrowly-tailored discovery request seeking only that social-media-based information that relates to the claimed injuries arising from the accident," and that disclosure of the "entire contents" of Facebook and MySpace accounts set up by family members of an injured party and Internet postings made on his behalf on those accounts was overbroad and a "fishing expedition"); *Keller v. Nat'l Farmers Union Property & Casualty Co.*, 2013 U.S. Dist. LEXIS 452, *12 (D. Mont. 2013) (denying a motion to compel full printouts from a litany of the plaintiff's social media sites, subject to reconsideration upon a showing of relevance, as defendant was not entitled to "delve carte blanche into the nonpublic sections" of the plaintiff's social media accounts); *Howell*, 2012 U.S. Dist. LEXIS 141368 at *3 (in a sexual harassment action, denying broad access to the plaintiff's social networking websites, but permitting defendant to serve requests for production of information on those websites tailored to the claims and defenses in the lawsuit); *Giacchetto* at *14 (requiring the plaintiff to produce any social networking postings that refer or relate to any of the events alleged in the Amended Complaint, but noting the defendant's discovery request was overbroad in requesting the plaintiff's username and password, as that would provide access to all information in private sections of social media accounts, relevant and irrelevant alike); *Schubart v. Horizon Wind Energy*, 2012 U.S. Dist. LEXIS 175063, *5–6 (C.D. Ill. 2012) (request for all social media information related to the sex discrimination plaintiff's mental state was overly broad; it lacked time limitations and a connection to the events of the case); *Mailhoit v. Home Depot USA, Inc.*, 285 F.R.D. 566, 571 (C.D. Cal. 2013) (holding that the majority of the defendant's document requests for plaintiff's social media were not described with sufficient particularity and thus not reasonably calculated to lead to discovery of admissible evidence); *Muniz v. United Parcel Service, Inc.*, 2011 U,.S. Dist. LEXIS 11219, *13 (N.D. Cal. 2011) (quashing a third-party subpoena that sought social media information from the Facebook page of the plaintiff's counsel that described the "work" or "efforts" of the plaintiff's counsel and/or case "events" as vague and overbroad and calling for irrelevant information when the only issue in the case was the reasonableness of fees).

63. See, *e.g.*, *Tapp v. N.Y.S. Urban Dev. Corp.*, 102 A.D.3d 620, 958 N.Y.S.2d 392 (1st Dept. 2013) (the defendant's contention that Facebook activities "may reveal daily activities that contradict or conflict with the plaintiff's" claim fell short: "Mere possession and utilization of a Facebook account is an insufficient basis to compel a plaintiff to provide access to the account or to have the court conduct an in-camera inspection . . . [D]efendants must establish a factual predicate for their request by identifying relevant information in the plaintiff's

Facebook account—that is, information that 'contradicts or conflicts with plaintiff's alleged restrictions, disabilities and losses, and other claims'").

64. *Giacchetto*, 2013 U.S. Dist. LEXIS 83341,*5 n.1 (adopting a "traditional relevance analysis" rather than requiring a threshold evidentiary showing, because taking the approach that the private section of a Facebook account is only discoverable if the party seeking the information can make a "threshold evidentiary showing that the plaintiff's public Facebook profile contains information that undermines the plaintiff's claims" can lead to "results that are both too broad and too narrow": a plaintiff should not be required to turn over the private section Facebook postings that may or may not contain relevant information "merely because the public section undermines the plaintiff's claims" but "should be required to review the private section and produce any relevant information, regardless of what is reflected in the public section," and the threshold evidentiary showing "approach improperly shields from discovery the information of Facebook users who do not share any information publicly").

65. The Sedona Conference, *Primer on Social Media*, October 2012, at 37.

66. *Id.* at 38.

67. *Id.*

68. See *infra* at 12–16.

69. Sedona *Primer* at 38.

70. *Id.* at 39.

71. *Id.*

72. See Federal Law Enforcement Training Center, "Justification and Approval Notice," issued Sept. 23, 2013, discussing X1 Social Discovery software, available at https://www.fbo.gov/index?s=opportunity&mode=form&id=8a343106726515f83b0114effd2a3aec&tab=core&_cview=0 (last accessed April 27, 2014).

73. Sedona *Primer* at 38. Social media sites may publish rules and specifications that allow application programming interfaces (APIs) to interact with the site to capture data automatically, and products may be developed that can collect available metadata fields for individual social media sites and generate MD5 hash tag values during collection. Known as a *digital fingerprint* in litigation support and computer forensics, an MD5 hash is a computer algorithm that takes the bits of a file as input and outputs a practically unique text string; if any deletion is made from the text, the MD5 hash is completely different; the hash will be the same when the file is accurately copied, even if the file name is changed. *Id.* at 39.

74. *Lorraine v. Markel American Insurance Co.*, 241 F.R.D. 534 (D. Md. 2007), a seminal case on each of these admissibility factors applied to electronically stored information, is instructive for social media evidence as well. See Hon. J. Paul Grimm et al., "Keynote Address: Authentication of Social Media Evidence," 36 *Am. J. Trial Advoc.* 433, (Spring 2013).

75. *Griffin v. State*, 19 A.3d 415, 423–424 (Md. 2011); see also Grimm et al., "Keynote Address," 444.

76. Grimm et al., "Keynote Address," 459–460, quoting *Lorraine*, 241 F.R.D. at 539.

77. *State v. Eleck*, 99 A. 3d 818, 821-25 (Conn. App. Ct. 2011), *Griffin* at 421; Grimm et al., 447–448.

78. Grimm et al., 455.

79. *Id.*

80. *Griffin* at 418.

81. *Id.*

82. *Id.* at 417, 419.

83. *Id.* at 424.

84. *Id.* at 427–428.

85. Grimm et al., 447.

86. Grimm et al., 459–460, *citing* Fed. Rule of Civ. Proc. 104(a).

87. *Id.*, citing *Lorraine* at 539. Under Rule 104(b), the trial court must determine whether the proponent of the evidence has offered a satisfactory foundation from which the jury could reasonably find that the evidence is authentic." *Id.* If the judge finds the evidence is clearly authentic or clearly inauthentic, and determines that a reasonable jury could not find to the contrary, the judge "withdraws the matter" from the jury's consideration. *Id.*, citing Fed. Rule Evid. Adv. Comm. Note to 104(b). If, after all the evidence, the jury could reasonably find the evidence to be authentic, the evidence goes to the jury for it to "ultimately resolve[] whether evidence admitted . . . is that which the proponent claims. *Id.*, citing *Lorraine* at 539–540.
88. 358 S.W.3d 633, 647 (Tex. Crim. App. 2012).
89. *Id.* at 634–635.
90. *Id.*
91. *Id.*
92. *Id.*
93. *Id.* at 635–636.
94. *Id.*
95. *Id.*
96. *Id.* at 645–646; *see also State v. Bell*, 145 Ohio Misc. 2d 55, 882 N.E.2d 502, at ¶34 (Ct. Com. Pl. 2008) (viewing the defendant's complaints "that the [social media] communications at issue are incomplete, easily altered, or possibly from an unidentified third party using his account information as akin to issues involving chain-of-custody disputes" which touch upon concerns regarding the weight of given evidence and not its authenticity.)
97. 241 F.R.D. at 542.
98. 2009 Tenn. App. LEXIS 717, *16–18 (Ct. App. 2009).
99. *Id.*
100. *Id.*
101. *Lorraine*, 241 F.R.D. at 546.
102. Federal Rules of Evidence, Rule 901 (b) (6) (a).
103. Federal Rules of Evidence, Rule 901 (b) (9).
104. *Id.* at 562.
105. *Lorraine*, 241 F.R.D. at 568–569.
106. *Id.* at 570.
107. *See, e.g., Miles v. Raycom Media, Inc.*, 2010 U.S. Dist. LEXIS 122712, 7–9, n.1 (S.D. Miss. Nov. 18, 2010) (finding that Facebook messages proffered to prove the truth of the matter asserted were inadmissible hearsay).

SECTION THREE
Relevant Cases

CHAPTER 10

Modern Case Analysis Shaping Litigation

*Matthew P. Breuer and
James P. Martin*

A s the deployment of cloud computing solutions has become more prevalent in today's society, courts have struggled with the application of the Fourth Amendment and federal statutes such as the Electronic Communications Privacy Act (ECPA) and Title II of the ECPA, the Stored Communications Act (SCA). Issues pertaining to the production of electronic communications in discovery have been ripe for litigation, especially when dealing with data stored by a third-party service provider, as is the case when a cloud solution is utilized. However, the treatment of cloud computing–related issues in court has not been entirely consistent, and further legislation may be necessary to bring clarity in litigation. As one court noted, "In light of rapid changes in computing technology since the enactment of the SCA, courts have struggled to analyze problems involving modern technology within the confines of this statutory framework, often with unsatisfactory results."[1]

O'Grady v. Superior Court, 139 Cal.App.4th 1423 (2006)

Apple Computer, Inc. filed an action against a group of unidentified individuals for wrongful publication of trade secret information regarding an unreleased Apple product. Petitioner O'Grady owned and operated *O'Grady's PowerPage*, an online news magazine covering news and information about Apple computers. *PowerPage* and another online news source published information regarding the upcoming product that Apple was developing. Apple obtained authority to issue civil subpoenas to the publishers of the websites where the information appeared and to the e-mail service provider for *PowerPage*. In response, the publishers moved for a protective order to prevent discovery. The trial court denied the motion on the ground that the publisher had involved itself in the unlawful misappropriation of a trade secret. Petitioner appealed, bringing an action seeking the trial court to set aside its denial of the motion for the protective order.

The court began by considering whether the trial court should have quashed or granted the subpoenas served on Nfox, the e-mail service provider for petitioner, and its owner Karl Kraft. The issue became whether or not the subpoena for certain e-mails was prohibited by the ECPA, and specifically Title II, the SCA. Petitioner argued that 18 U.S.C. §2702(a)(1) and 18 U.S.C. §2702(a)(2) invalidated the subpoena under the Supremacy Clause. As a preliminary matter, Apple did not dispute that the basic components for application of the SCA were present. Nfox was an entity providing electronic communication service to the public, and the contents of the e-mail account were communications in electronic storage.

The court's analysis shifted to Apple's assertion that the sought-after disclosures fell within one of the exceptions of the SCA and that the SCA should not apply to civil discovery. The SCA specifically lists several exceptions to the rule that service providers may not disclose the content of stored messages. These exceptions include disclosures:

- To an addressee or intended recipient of such communication or an agent of such addressee or intended recipient;
- As otherwise authorized in section 2517, 2511(2)(a), or 2703 of this title;
- With the lawful consent of the originator or an addressee or intended recipient of such communication, or the subscriber in the case of remote computing service;
- To a person employed or authorized or whose facilities are used to forward such communication to its destination;
- As may be necessary to incident to the rendition of the service or the protection of the rights or property of the provider of that service;
- To the National Center for Missing and Exploited Children, in connection with a report submitted thereto under section 2258A;
- To a law enforcement agency
  - If the contents
    - Were inadvertently obtained by the service provider; and
    - Appear to pertain to the commission of a crime.
- To a government entity, if the provider, in good faith, believes that an emergency involving danger of death or serious physical injury to any person requires disclosure without delay of communications relating to the emergency.

Apple argued that compliance was necessary for the protection of the provider because noncompliance would subject the service provider to contempt.

The court rejected this circular argument because it assumed that noncompliance of the subpoena could support legal sanctions.

Apple's main contention was that Congress did not intend to preempt civil discovery of stored communications and there was an implied exception of the Act for civil discovery. The court found no such exception supporting this argument or any ambiguity in the statute. Apple also failed to make an argument that refusal of civil discovery under the SCA would be contradictory to any legislative policy. Moreover, the court also discussed applying these protections to telephone calls and written letters. In those methods of communication, discovery must be directed at the parties involved in the communication. Accordingly, the court did not wish to "unnecessarily discourage potential customers from using innovative communications" and "discourage American businesses from developing innovative forms of telecommunications and computer technology."[2]

The court also affirmed the idea that the SCA prohibits the disclosure of contents of a communication. However, it does explicitly permit a service provider to disclose a record or other information pertaining to a subscriber or customer of such a service. Apple argued that the SCA was not violated because they sought the disclosure of the identity of the author of a communication and this was permissible under the Act. The court was not persuaded by this argument. Apple's subpoena sought more than the identity of the author or authors; it sought "documents relating to the identity of any person or entity who supplied information regarding an unreleased Apple product. . . ."[3]

In this instance, the disclosure of the identification of any of those senders would likely disclose the contents of the messages written by the senders. "By seeking to identify the sender of communications to the subscriber, or the addressee of communications from the subscriber, Apple steps well outside the statutory authorization."[4] The sought-after disclosures were not the identity of anyone who posted anything on *PowerPage*, or a subscriber who posted on the website. Apple was actually seeking the identities of the sources of content posted by *PowerPage*, which were contained in messages in the *PowerPage* e-mail account. If such a disclosure was permitted, it would have violated the SCA and the subpoenas were unenforceable as a result.

The court's analysis was a relatively straightforward approach in applying the SCA and the enumerated exceptions that Apple advocated. Despite Apple's assertion, the disclosure did not fall within one of the several enumerated exceptions under 18 U.S.C. §2702(b). Apple also challenged the validity of the SCA as it applied to civil discovery, but this argument was unsuccessful. In their opinion, the court very clearly pointed out that the SCA did not have any ambiguity or confusion and did not violate any public policy that would mandate for them to make an exception in civil discovery.

Many critics of the SCA disagree with the analysis of the *O'Grady* court, as the SCA has come under scrutiny for being confusing and difficult to apply. Senator Patrick J. Leahy, chairman of Senate Judiciary Committee, noted that:

> It is more complicated than it needs to be. It has sections that are redundant and merely confusing. The absence of a statutory suppression remedy has created significant uncertainty about how the statute works. The SCA also offers surprisingly low privacy protections when the government seeks to compel the contents other than unretrieved communications held pending transmission for 180 days or less.[5]

The Act has also come under fire for failing to define key terms, such as *consent* and others that are crucial in its application.[6] This criticism has even prompted legislative proposals to be introduced in the 112th and 113th Congresses to clarify the provisions of the SCA. Clearly, the *O'Grady* court does not reflect the sentiments of numerous legislators and other government officials in the ease of applicability of the SCA to litigation.

The content/noncontent distinction also surfaced in *O'Grady*.[7] However, in this case, it was not entirely black or white in regard to the information sought after and whether it would fall under the definition of content pursuant to the SCA. This was especially true when Apple sought "all communications from or to any disclosing person(s) relating to the product."[8] Apple argued that it only sought the identity of the authors of the e-mails; however, the court concluded that this would still violate the SCA. By asking for such a disclosure, the identification of the senders concerning the products would also likely disclose the contents of the message. In addition, the court reasoned that the SCA only authorizes the disclosure of a record of information pertaining to the subscriber, not the identity. The court attempted to bring clarity to the content/noncontent distinction and did not allow Apple to circumvent the provisions of the SCA by being creative with the wording of their subpoena request. However, future challenges to the content/noncontent distinction are likely.

Krinsky v. Doe 6, 72 Cal.Rptr.3d 231 (2008)

In January 2006, plaintiff Lisa Krinsky sued 10 "Doe" defendants alleging that the defendants had made defamatory comments on a Yahoo! finance message board and other websites, using pseudonyms to conceal their identities. In her complaint, the plaintiff sought damages and an injunction after accusing the defendants of intentional interference with a "contractual and/or business employment relationship" between the plaintiff and SFBC International, Inc.

One of the defendants, Doe 6, was referred to as "Senor-Pinche-Wey," the screen name he had used while posting on the Yahoo! message board. During the litigation, the plaintiff attempted to discover the identity of the 10 anonymous posters by serving a subpoena on the message-board host. Yahoo! moved to quash the subpoena and the trial court denied the motion. Doe 6 appealed the ruling, contending that he had a First Amendment right to speak anonymously on the Internet.

The majority of the comments on the message board were actually directed at Jerry Lew Seifer, whom Doe 6 referred to as a "mega scum bag and cockroach" and other derogatory names.[9] However, Doe 6 went on to criticize the whole management team (which included Krinsky) as being incompetent. He further stated that Krinsky had a "fake medical degree" and made several obscene comments regarding her personal hygiene. Krinsky served a subpoena on the custodian of records at Yahoo! in Sunnyvale, California, to obtain the identity of the anonymous posters. In response, Yahoo! informed Doe 6 that it would comply with the subpoena unless a motion to quash or other legal objection was filed. Doe 6 then moved to quash the subpoena. However, the trial court denied the motion, and Doe 6 appealed the ruling.

A significant amount of the majority's opinion in *Krinsky* was devoted to the discussion of the First Amendment and speech on the Internet. This contrasted to prior case law that involved e-mails, text messages, and other forms of communication. The Internet offers an opportunity for an individual to express his or her views through the forum online message board to a very broad audience, and this message can also be disseminated to other networks of recipients. This mass communication can also be done under anonymity. Consequently, as the court noted, "the relative anonymity afforded by the Internet forum promotes a looser, more relaxed communication style."[10] This was something that was critical in the court's analysis.

The court also began to discuss when the scope of the First Amendment protection was exceeded. Despite the court's long standing tradition of recognizing the constitutional right to publish under the cloak of anonymity, when criticism reaches to the level of defamation, constitutional protection is no longer afforded to that speech. The court also made special note of the fact that this criticism could be related to the economic viability of SFBC and its management team. Citing *Reno v. American Civil Liberties Union*, the court noted, "Through the use of chat rooms, any person with a phone line can become a town crier with a voice that resonates farther than it could from any soapbox. . . . [O]ur cases provide no basis for qualifying the level of First Amendment scrutiny that should be applied to this medium."[11] Therefore, the court reasoned that criticism on the Internet that is done in a harmful and reckless manner extends beyond the rules of what is covered by oral communication, especially in the financial sector.

Both the plaintiff and defendant agreed that the general approach of the viability of the subpoena was to weigh Doe 6's First Amendment rights to speak anonymously against the plaintiff's interest in discovering his identity. The plaintiff advocated for the application of three court decisions, but the court was not persuaded with this argument. The court did engage in extensive discussion, however, regarding the applicability of *O'Grady*.[12] In *O'Grady*, the court held that the SCA prohibited disclosure of certain information pertaining to documents relating to the identities of the defendants and communications regarding Apple's new product. Specifically, the court stressed that SCA did not "authorize the disclosure of the identity of the *author* of a stored message; it authorizes the disclosure of a record or other information pertaining to a subscriber to or customer of such service."[13] Based on the facts of the present case, the court was able to distinguish *O'Grady* because the plaintiff here sought only the identity of the detractor, not the content.

Despite reaching this conclusion and distinguishing the case from *O'Grady*, the court ruled that the subpoena should be quashed because the plaintiff stated no viable cause of action that overcame Doe 6's First Amendment right to speak anonymously. The plaintiff had never made a prima facie showing for the elements of the libel claim asserted. The order denying Doe 6's motion to quash the subpoena was reversed, and the trial court was ordered to quash any part of the subpoena ordering Yahoo! to disclose the identity of "Senor-Pinche-Wey."

The critical factor in the court's analysis was again the content/non-content distinction. If Krinsky would have sought the contents of communications, the court would have likely ruled differently before addressing the other merits of the case. This was the reason that the *O'Grady* court reached the opposite result in this aspect. The court also stressed the fact that the postings were made anonymously on a Yahoo! message board. The test adopted by the court also made it necessary for a plaintiff to make a prima facie showing regarding the elements of libel to overcome a defendant's motion to quash a subpoena. If there is an actual and legal basis for believing libel could have occurred, then the author is not afforded First Amendment protection. The language in this case was simply crude and satirical comments that did not amount to libel; therefore, the plaintiff did not state a viable cause of action.

Flagg v. City of Detroit, 252 F.R.D. 346 (E.D. Mich 2008)

On April 30, 2003, Tamara Greene was murdered in a drive-by shooting in Detroit, Michigan. The shooting gained national notoriety after allegations surfaced that the mayor of Detroit at the time, Kwame Kilpatrick, had connections to Greene's murder. Greene's minor children brought an action seeking an award of damages under 42 U.S.C. §1983 against Detroit and Kilpatrick, alleging that the defendants deliberately obstructed the Detroit Police Department investigation into Greene's murder. The plaintiffs contended that but for this obstruction, they could have brought a state court wrongful death action against the individual(s) who murdered their mother and successfully recovered an award to compensate for their loss.[14]

Prior to the commencement of litigation in the present case, the defendant city of Detroit entered into an agreement with SkyTel, Inc. for text messaging services. SkyTel was a non-party service provider of text messaging devices and corresponding services to several city officials and employees, including some of the defendants. Despite the fact that the city of Detroit discontinued their service, SkyTel allegedly maintained copies of several of the text messages received by the officials during the relevant period of the case.

Accordingly, the plaintiffs issued two subpoenas to SkyTel in February 2008 seeking the disclosure of several items, including: "(i) all text messages sent or received by 34 named individuals, including the individual Defendants, during a number of time periods spanning over five years, and (ii) all text messages sent or received by any city official or employee during a four-hour time period in the early morning hours of April 30, 2003, the date that Plaintiff's mother was killed."[15] The defendants contended that these communications, regardless of their content, did not satisfy the standard for discovery pursuant to Federal Rules of Civil Procedure 26(b)(1) and as a result moved to quash the subpoenas. The court rejected the defendants' motion and ordered two magistrate judges to conduct a review of the sought-after communications. During this time, the defendant city and Christine Beatty filed motions asserting that the SCA prevented the plaintiffs from obtaining the text messages remaining in SkyTel's possession. Defendants argued that the SCA absolutely precluded the production of electronic communications in civil litigation.

The court began by looking at the prohibitions in the SCA. Pursuant to 18 U.S.C. §2702(a)(1), "a person or entity providing an electronic communication service to the public shall not knowingly divulge to any person or entity the contents of a communication while in electronic storage by that service."[16] It further prohibits—again, subject to certain exceptions—a "person or entity providing remote computing service to the public" from "knowingly divulg[ing] to any person or entity the contents of any communication that is carried or maintained on that service."[17] As the court noted, §2702 lacks any language that explicitly authorizes a service provider to divulge the contents of a communication pursuant to a subpoena or court order. Consequently, the defendants argued that the lack of statutory authorization would not permit a court to compel the production of the documents.

Furthermore, the defendants relied on *Quon v. Arch Wireless Operating Co.*, 529 F.3d 892, 903-09 (9th Cir. 2008), claiming that an employee's reasonable expectation of privacy in his or her personal communications was not subject to discovery due to the immunity of the Fourth Amendment. The court ultimately rejected the defendants' arguments premised on privacy and privilege, reasoning that the defendants did not show that the SCA prohibits either (a) the submission of SkyTel text messages to the court for in-camera review or (b) the production to plaintiffs of the communications determined by the court to be discoverable under the Federal Rules of Civil Procedure, namely FRCP 26(b)(1).[18]

The court then moved onto a lengthy discussion regarding the concept of "control" and whether or not the defendants had control over the communications. Applying FRCP 34(a)(1) and case law, the court opined that the defendant, the city of Detroit, had control over the text messages preserved by the third party based on its contractual relationship with Skytel.[19] Moreover, in the city's motion, the defendant admitted it had the ability to consent to Skytel's production of the text messages but that it was unwilling to do so. Therefore, if the city could block the disclosure of text messages by withholding its consent, it could also permit the disclosure by giving its consent. This ability to consent "qualified as a 'legal right to obtain' within the meaning of Rule 34(a)(1)" and thus satisfied the definition of control.[20]

Furthermore, the court ruled that the SCA did not override the defendants' obligations to produce relevant, nonprivileged electronic communications within their control. According to the defendants, while the SCA recognized various exceptions to the rule of nondisclosure, the defendants claimed that the only exception relevant to this case was "with lawful consent." The court noted that of key importance to this case was the fact that the plaintiff sought production of the text messages under a Rule 34 document request directed at the defendant instead of a third-party subpoena at Skytel. Accordingly, any documents would have to pass through an intermediary, which would be obligated under Rule 34 to produce the documents. This would not qualify as "divulging" pursuant to §2702 if SkyTel was merely fulfilling a request to a customer.

The court also spent ample time analyzing the case in light of the ruling in *Quon*. In Quon, the defendant was a municipality, the city of Ontario, California, and the plaintiffs were a police officer and several of the other employees. The defendant entered into a contract with a service provider, Arch Wireless, that provided text-messaging and wireless communication services. The city ordered an audit of the text messages sent and received by several officers to determine to what extent the phones were being used for personal rather than work-related purposes. When the audit launched an investigation by internal affairs, the officers brought suit asserting federal claims under the SCA and 42 U.S.C. §1983, as well as claims under California law.

Arch Wireless filed a motion for summary disposition claiming that the service it provided was an RCS and that the city, by requesting disclosure of the texts, had provided the necessary subscriber consent to permit the disclosure. The district court considered the factors that differentiate an ECS and RCS. Because the text messages that Arch had retrieved from storage had been transmitted and read in the past, their continued storage "could not be construed as 'temporary' or 'incidental' to their transmission."[21] Thus, the district court then turned to whether the messages been stored "for purposes of backup protection," which the court concluded was not the case.[22] Reasoning that messages are stored for backup purposes only if it is the sole place where a user stores messages, the court found the services provided by Arch Wireless to be an RCS. As a result, consent of the subscriber would be needed for disclosure.

The Ninth Circuit had recently reversed the district court's holding in *Quon* and found that Arch Wireless was actually an ECS. While conceding that Arch Wireless did archive text messages on its server, it opined that both ECSs and RCSs "entail some form of 'storage,' and it found that Arch Wireless did not provide the 'virtual filing cabinet' function that was cited in the legislative history of the SCA that is characteristic of an RCS."[23] Moreover, the Ninth Circuit also found the district court erroneously relied on *Theofel v. Farey–Jones*, 359 F.3d 1066, 1077 (9th Cir.2004). In *Theofel*, the Ninth Circuit held that a user who does not delete messages from their e-mail account is in essence leaving those messages on the server for purposes of backup protection. The user could access the hosted copy in the event the user needed to access it again. Because it was stored on the ISP server after delivery for purposes of backup protection, the *Quon* court held that the ISP was an ECS.

Despite the appellate court's ruling, the court in *Flagg* was more inclined to the position of the lower court's finding in *Quon*. The court reasoned with the view of the district court in *Quon* that "Congress took a middle course" in enacting the SCA, under which a provider such as SkyTel may be both an ECS with respect to some communications and an RCS with respect to some communications to the same customer.[24] However, for purposes of this analysis, the court needed to determine the nature of the service SkyTel was currently providing to the city with respect to the sought-after communications. In other words, the service that SkyTel provided to the city at the time the company was being called to retrieve the text messages from the archive during the litigation. To make this determination, the court had to examine whether the SkyTel maintained the archive "for purposes of backup protection."[25] This would enable the court to choose whether the contents were held in electronic storage by an ECS pursuant to 18 U.S.C. 2702(a) (1) or whether the archive was computer storage under an RCS pursuant to 18 U.S.C. 2711(2).

The Flagg court then performed a detailed analysis of the defendant city's relationship with SkyTel. At the time of the trial, SkyTel was no longer providing text messaging services to the city of Detroit. The city had admitted in earlier pleadings that it had discontinued the service in 2004, and that the text message devices provided by SkyTel were no longer in use. Accordingly, the archive text messages that SkyTel had in its possession were the only available record of these communications and could not serve as a backup copy of communications stored elsewhere. As the *Theofel* court pointed out, a service provider that "kept permanent copies of temporary message could not fairly be described as 'backing up' those messages," and that "messages are not stored for backup purposes if a computer repository is 'the only place' where they are stored."[26]

As a result, the court held that the services provided by SkyTel could be properly characterized as a virtual filing cabinet and thus SkyTel could be properly characterized as an RCS pursuant to the SCA. Because the city had "control" of the text messages pursuant to Rule 34, the city could give consent to SkyTel to retrieve the communications. The court concluded, "were it otherwise, a party could readily avoid its discovery obligations by warehousing in documents with a third party under strict instructions to release them only with the party's consent."[27]

Flagg was a major victory for parties seeking to compel disclosure in civil litigation. It established that a party has the duty to take the steps necessary to exercise control and obtain requested documents. Despite being a victory, it showed the difficulty of applying the SCA in civil litigation. Both *Quon* and *Flagg* demonstrate that the application of the SCA is not entirely clear. The court in *Flagg* opted to adhere to the lower court's ruling in *Quon*, and the justices from the two different jurisdictions disagreed with others' reasoning in several aspects.

An important aspect of the court's decision was the mechanism through which the documents were requested. The plaintiffs served subpoenas not on the text message service providers, but on the defendants themselves. Through FRCP 34(a)(1), the plaintiffs were able to enforce the subpoena. This ultimately rested on the concept of control. Because the defendants could have consented to the blocking of the message by withholding consent, they could also permit the disclosure by giving consent. This constituted control according to the court's definition of Rule 34(a)(1).

The court also discussed *Theofel* in detail. In *Theofel*, defendant Farey-Jones sought the disclosure of e-mails from the plaintiffs' ISP. The attorney for the defendant ordered the production of "all copies of emails sent or received by anyone" at ICA. The plaintiffs challenged the subpoenas with a motion to quash, claiming the subpoenas were overboard and violated the FRCP. The motion was granted and sanctions were levied against the defendants. The plaintiffs also filed a civil suit against Farey-Jones, claiming they violated the SCA and other federal statutes. The district court held that none of the federal statutes applied, and the plaintiffs appealed.

The defendants argued that the messages accessed were not in electronic storage and fell outside the scope of the SCA. The court concluded that the within the ordinary meaning of *stored* for purposes of backup protection, the services provided by the plaintiffs' e-mail hosts were in "electronic storage" regardless of whether they have been previously accessed. The court did not dispute that once opened, the message was no longer in temporary storage. Because the messages functioned as backup for the user, the e-mail messages did indeed fall within the backup portion of the definition of electronic storage. This interpretation was a split between the original definition of electronic storage under §2510(17)(A) and set a higher standard to obtain open e-mail content in rejecting the narrow definition of electronic storage. The Ninth Circuit is the only jurisdiction that follows this precedent, and many courts have explicitly rejected this approach.

The *Flagg* court discussed *Theofel* as resting "on a unitary approach" where service providers either provided ECS or RCS services, but not both.[28] However, the *Flagg* court was not inclined to follow this position. Instead, the court reasoned that the services provided by SkyTel with respect to different communications could be both an ECS and RCS and focused on what type of services SkyTel was presently providing to the city for the particular sought-after communications. *Flagg* was not the only case that refused to follow *Theofel* in some aspect, and the *Theofel* has not been followed for the most part beyond the Ninth Circuit. These discrepancies in the characterization of e-mails are also problematic because a "single e-mail could be subject to as many as four different levels of privacy protections under ECPA, depending on where it is stored and when it is sent."[29] The lack of unity in the interpretation by courts and the slightly varying nature of e-mails led to varying results in different jurisdictions that produce inconsistencies when applying SCA in litigation.

Warshak v. United States, 631 F.3d 266 (6th Circ. 2010)

Warshak, the president of Berkeley Premium Nutraceuticals, Inc., was being investigated for mail and wire fraud, money laundering, and other federal offenses. Pursuant to the SCA, which required ISPs to disclose the contents of electronic communications under certain instances, such as a subpoena, the government obtained two ex parte court orders compelling Warshak's ISP to preserve his e-mails. In January 2005, the government obtained a subpoena ordering the ISP to turn over the e-mails it had been preserving. Upon discovering the government's actions, Warshak filed a declaratory judgment seeking to invalidate §2703(d) under the Fourth Amendment. Warshak sought to enjoin the federal government from conducting further ex parte e-mail searches. The Southern District of Ohio granted the motion and enjoined the government from seeking the contents.

The government was permitted access to approximately 27,000 e-mails. Based on the evidence obtained from the ex parte search, Warshak was indicted on September 20, 2006, by a federal grand jury. Warshak argued that the governmental action constituted an unreasonable search and seizure under the Fourth Amendment. The government countered that even if they violated the Fourth, they relied in good faith on the SCA and that the hypothetical violation was harmless.

The court proceeded in their analysis under *Katz*. In his majority opinion, Justice Boggs reasoned that Warshak reasonably believed that his e-mails would be free from outside scrutiny. Looking at the nature of the e-mails, the court noted that his entire business and personal life was contained in the e-mails, which warranted a finding that he had a reasonable expectation of privacy. Under the second prong, the court also found that it was an expectation of privacy that society was willing to accept due to the sensitive and intimate information conveyed in e-mails. Most importantly, in their discussion the court noted, "the Fourth Amendment must keep pace with the inexorable march of technological progress, or its guarantees will wither and perish."[30]

The court also discussed *Jacobsen* and *Ex Parte Jackson*, explaining that letters in the mail receive protection from government intrusion. Moreover, the court stated that trusting an intermediary with a letter did not defeat a reasonable expectation of privacy. The analysis then focused on whether or not from a fundamental standpoint this reasoning should be applied to e-mails. Given the similarities, the court reasoned that it would defy common sense to not afford the same protection to e-mails. If e-mails were not given that protection, the Fourth Amendment would not effectively guard private communication. The ISP is the equivalent of a post office or telephone company. Consequently, under *Jacobsen*, if the governmental authorities compel an ISP to surrender e-mails, a Fourth Amendment search has been conducted and a warrant is required.

Recognizing a potential conflict, the court went on to address *U.S. v. Miller*, which held that a bank depositor does not have a reasonable expectation of privacy over the records that the bank maintains relative to a customer's bank account. The court distinguished Miller based on the fact that the present case involved confidential information and not the business records maintained by the ISP. The information was also used in the ordinary course of business. The ISP in this case was an intermediary, not the intended recipient of the communications. Based on these facts, the court found an actual reasonable expectation of privacy did exist unlike *Miller*. The court held because the government did not obtain a warrant, and obtained records that should be considered confidential, it violated the Fourth Amendment as an unlawful search.

Despite reaching this conclusion, the court concluded that the e-mails were not subject to the exclusion rule because the officers relied in good faith on the SCA to obtain them. Warshak argued that the provisions of the SCA were unconstitutional. The court stated that the SCA had never been subject to any successful Fourth Amendment challenges and that on its face it was not plain or obvious that it was unconstitutional when it was passed. Warshak also argued that the government failed to inform him of either the subpoena or order for over a year. The government conceded this point, but claimed it was irrelevant to the issue of reasonable reliance in obtaining the contents. The court agreed with this assertion and also rejected his argument that a factual basis was never provided on the order.

Although the government violated the Fourth Amendment, the exclusionary rule did not apply because the government relied in good faith on §2703(b) and §2703(d). The court in *Warshak* recognized the need to keep up with technology and logically compared e-mails to earlier decisions giving similar protection to traditional methods of communication. "Given the fundamental similarities between email and traditional forms of communication, it would defy common sense to afford emails lesser Fourth Amendment protection."[31] The court recognized the vital role e-mails play in everyday business, and they made it clear that the protections afforded to traditional methods of communication would be extended.

Warshak was also important because it affirmed that an individual has a reasonable expectation of privacy in the contents of their e-mail stored through a commercial ISP. Applying *Katz*, the court ensured that federal authorities would obtain search warrants in the course of their investigations. *Warshak* has also been construed as authority that if the government seeks noncontent information, such as subscriber information, the to/from line, or IP addresses of Web sites visited, federal authorities can obtain such information through a subpoena.[32] These rules would likely apply to any e-mail service provided, whether cloud-based or the traditional client-based e-mail.[33]

Warshak also criticized the approach in *Theofel*. *Warshak* argued that the government's definition of electronic storage conflicted with *Theofel*, which held that prior access was irrelevant. The court stated that the Ninth Circuit ruling was not binding and also cited criticism of *Theofel*, noting that it was "quite implausible and hard to square with statutory test."[34] However, it is still also evidence that the interpretation of the SCA has led to varying conclusions. *Warshak* also highlights another problematic area in the SCA, in that it fails to take into account constitutional safeguards. Specifically, there is no suppression remedy available for disclosures in violation of the SCA.[35] The court had to discuss the exclusionary rule from a constitutional perspective in finding that the government relied in good faith on several provisions of the SCA. The SCA fails to cover the intermingling of constitutional protections with the discovery procedures outlined in the SCA.

Ehling v. Monmouth-Ocean Hospital, 872 F.Supp.2d 369 (D.N.J. 2012)

Plaintiff Deborah Ehling was a registered nurse and paramedic, who was hired by the defendant Monmouth-Ocean Hospital Service Corporation (MONOC). In 2008, the plaintiff assumed the position of acting president of the local union for Professional Emergency Medical Services Association in New Jersey. The plaintiff alleged that as a result of her position with the union, the defendant engaged in retaliatory practices and terminated her employment in July 2011.

During the time of the alleged misconduct, the plaintiff maintained a Facebook account. Many of the plaintiff's coworkers were her friends on Facebook and had access to her page, but she did not invite any members of MONOC management. Ehling claimed that MONOC management summoned one of the employees, who was her Facebook friend, and threatened the employee to give management access to the plaintiff's page to view her postings. The plaintiff had made several comments regarding a shooting in Washington, D.C., and criticized the paramedics that arrived on the scene. Consequently, MONOC sent letters regarding the Facebook post to the New Jersey Nursing Board and the New Jersey Department of Health, Office of Emergency Medical Services. According to Ehling, this was done to damage her reputation and future employment opportunities and to risk her losing her license and certification.

The plaintiff alleged the defendant violated the New Jersey Wiretapping and Electronic Surveillance Control Act by "accessing without permission and improperly monitoring the electronic communications being stored on Plaintiff's Facebook account."[36] An individual is guilty of such a crime if they knowingly access a facility through which electronic communication service is provided without consent. Under the NJ Wiretap Act, electronic storage is defined as: "(1) any temporary, intermediate storage of a wire or electronic communication incidental to the electronic transmission thereof; and (2) any storage of such communication by an electronic communication service for purpose of backup protection of the communication."[37]

Pursuant to this definition, the court followed New Jersey precedent and held that the Act only protects electronic communications that are in the course of transmission or used as backup. In *White v. White*, the court refused to hold that the Act applied to communications received by the recipient that were placed in posttransmission storage and then accessed by another unauthorized individual. The reasoning behind this conclusion was that an individual loses the expectation of privacy once the message is sent. When it reached posttransmission storage, it fell outside of the scope of the Act. As a result, the court found that Ehling had failed to state a valid claim under the NJ Wiretap Act.

The plaintiff also alleged a common law invasion of privacy count. Courts had not yet developed a uniform approach in regard to privacy in social networking, and it was an underdeveloped area of case law at the time. The plaintiff argued that she had a reasonable expectation of privacy because her posts were only disclosed to a limited number of people that she personally invited to be her friends. On the other hand, the defendants argued that the posts were disclosed to potentially hundreds of people, and, as a result, the plaintiff could not possibly have a reasonable expectation of privacy. The court refused to dismiss this count because of the "open-ended nature of the case law" and the fact that the issues regarding this count could not be properly resolved on a motion to dismiss.[38] As a result, the motion to dismiss was granted in part and denied in part.

Ehling was another case in a very murky area of social media and discovery of electronically stored material. The court focused heavily on the fact that Ehling had her privacy settings modified, and that only her friends that she invited to be friends or accepted an invite from could view her posts. It is likely that the result may have been different had her privacy settings not been modified. This outcome was very critical in Fourth Amendment jurisprudence establishing that forms of social media, particularly Facebook posts, can possibly be subject to the SCA. Issues regarding the SCA and social media would also surface in *Juror Number One v. California*, and this case would attempt to shed more light on the courts' treatment of social media under the SCA.

Juror Number One v. California, 206 Cal.App. 4th 854 (2012)

The plaintiff was a jury foreperson in a trial in Sacramento County Superior Court. During the criminal trial, he posted several comments on his Facebook page regarding the trial, including his opinions on the potential guilt of the defendant in the trial. Another juror who became Facebook friends with Juror Number One and saw the posts contacted the defense counsel after a verdict of guilty was reached. The judge in the original case questioned Juror Number One under penalties of perjury regarding his online activities during the case, and he denied such actions. The criminal defendants issued a subpoena to Facebook requesting copies of Juror Number One's page contents pursuant to the SCA. The judge quashed the subpoena but issued an order for the plaintiff to sign a consent form allowing Facebook to disclose Juror Number One's postings.

The plaintiff moved for a temporary restraining order and injunction to enforce the order. The plaintiff argued that signing a consent form would be a violation of the Fourth Amendment right to privacy, Fifth Amendment right against self-incrimination, and the ECPA. He claimed that the order compelled him to waive his Fifth Amendment rights because his own comments could later be used in a subsequent proceeding for perjury. In regard to the Fourth Amendment, he also argued that he had a reasonable expectation of privacy in what he posted on Facebook. Instead of addressing the merits of the plaintiff's argument, the court engaged in an abstention analysis to determine if the hearing was proper and denied the temporary restraining order.

On February 10, 2011, an appellate court in California denied the request for stay. However, on March 30, 2011, the California Supreme Court granted review and transferred the matter back to the Court of Appeals for further consideration. Respondents, the Superior Court of Sacramento County, and other related parties, argued that under *Moreno v. Hanford Sentinel* the information posted was provided for others to read and as a result lost its privacy. The court distinguished the posting in *Moreno* because it occurred on MySpace, and this was visible to the entire forum and not to just a few select friends. As the court noted, "a party does not forfeit SCA protection by making his communications available to a closed group, i.e., a private bulletin board."[39]

Juror Number One argued that Facebook has been recognized as a provider of electronic communication services pursuant to the SCA. Citing *Crispin v. Christian Audigier, Inc.*, the court concluded that Facebook and MySpace qualified as ECSs. The court then also examined whether the messages were in electronic storage pursuant to the SCA. It concluded that the messages were not in immediate storage awaiting delivery to the recipient. The communications were stored on a Facebook "wall" and this was not the final destination for the messages. However, the messages were also held for backup purposes once posted and could qualify as being an RCS. However, even if *Crispin* was the correct citation, "the case did not establish as a matter of law that Facebook is either an ECS or an RCS or that the postings are protected by the SCA" because the result of *Crispin* was based on evidence presented by the parties.[40] In this instance, Juror Number One provided the court with nothing regarding the specific operations of Facebook. Therefore, the court concluded that they were unable to determine to what extent the SCA was applicable.

Despite reaching this decision, the court still went on to discuss the hypothetical outcome if the postings were encompassed by the SCA. The court concluded that the SCA "applies only as to attempts by the court or real parties in interest to compel Facebook to disclose the requested information."[41] The compulsion in this instance was on Juror Number One, not Facebook. Citing *Flagg*, the court discussed materials being in the actual possession of the party. "A party's disinclination to exercise this control is immaterial, just as it is immaterial whether a party might prefer not to produce documents in its possession or custody."[42] Under FRCP 34(a)(1), a party has a duty to produce documents under his control when requested to do so by another party. If Juror Number One could be compelled to produce documents, then the court could compel Juror Number One to consent to the disclosure by Facebook.

Juror Number One argued that he had a reasonable expectation of privacy in the information requested and any disclosure would violate the Fourth Amendment. This argument was rejected by the court, but only because Juror Number One failed to provide any legal support for this assertion. The court further reasoned that even if he had privacy interest in his Facebook posts, these rights would still need to be balanced against the rights of the parties in interest to ensure a fair trial. The court concluded that these privacy interests were insubordinate to the importance of the constitutional right to a fair trial, and as a result rejected Juror Number One's argument.

The court also was unpersuaded by Juror Number One's Fifth Amendment argument that producing the communications would violate his right against self-incrimination. Because his constitutional rights had not been violated and the SCA protects against disclosure by third parties (not the posting party), the trial court was within its power to inquire into whether Juror Number One had engaged in juror misconduct. Accordingly, Juror Number One would be compelled to consent to the production of the communications.

Despite reaching the conclusion that Juror Number One did not establish enough evidence regarding the specific operations of Facebook, the court still attempted to bring more clarity under the SCA and engaged in analysis under the hypothetical that the postings were subject to the SCA. In this instance, the court concluded that the compulsion to consent to the production of documents was on Juror Number One, not on Facebook. This was an important component of the court's analysis because the court went on to rely on *Flagg*. Specifically, the court cited the control component pursuant to FRCP 34(a)(1). Because Juror Number One could consent to the disclosure, the postings were within his control and thus discoverable. Even though the facts of this case were distinguishable from *Flagg*, the court still proceeded under the same analysis and the control aspect turned out to be the decisive factor.

The court also engaged in a *Katz* analysis. Reasoning that Juror Number One did not have a reasonable expectation of privacy, the court opined that even if he did have an expectation, this expectation would still need to be balanced against the rights of the other parties. This was somewhat of a variation from the original two prong test. If a reasonable expectation of privacy was recognized, the court in this instance would have had to then determine and balance the rights of all the interested parties. Many of the prior decisions that utilized a *Katz* analysis did not discuss a balancing interest with respect to the right to a fair trial or any potential constitutional violations. This is a sharp contrast with the reasoning of some of the prior decisions.

The application of the SCA in modern day litigation has not always produced results that seem to be congruent. Rapid advancements in technology for individuals and businesses have also compounded the problem and put more strain on courts to keep pace with new technology. Despite the ECPA being useful in governmental law enforcement, it still has been "hampered by conflicting standards that cause confusion for law enforcement, the business community, and American consumers alike."[43] Issues such as the correct interpretation of electronic storage pursuant to §2510(17)(A) have produced mixed results in different jurisdictions. Courts have also struggled with balancing constitutional protections in litigation and discovery phases. *Katz* at the very least set a threshold for protection, but the safeguards against intrusion by the government recognized in *Katz* need to be reconciled with the SCA. This has prompted demand for the SCA to be amended, but whether such reform is implemented remains to be seen.

Summary of Cases

Table 10.1 shows a summary of modern-day cloud computing cases discussed in this chapter.

Table 10.1 Modern-Day Cloud Computing Cases

Case	Case Summary	Warrant/Subpoena	Outcome	Basis
O'Grady v. Superior Court	Apple sued several defendants alleging misappropriation of trade secrets after anonymous individuals posted on an online blog.	Subpoenas were served on the websites' e-mail host.	Outstanding subpoenas could not be enforced without compelling the email hosts to violate the SCA.	The court explicitly rejected the concept that Congress preempted civil discovery of stored communications. The SCA also did not authorize contents of a stored message to be disclosed, just records pertaining to a subscriber.
Krinsky v. Doe 6	The plaintiff attempted to discover the identity of the several individuals who made alleged defamatory comments on a Yahoo! message board.	A subpoena was served on the custodian of records at Yahoo!	The order denying Doe 6's motion to quash the subpoena was reversed. Yahoo! was not required to disclose the identity of the author.	Because only the identity of Doe 6 and the others was sought, the case was distinguishable from O'Grady. The content was not at issue. However, because Krinsky did not state a viable cause of action, the subpoena was quashed.
Flagg v. City of Detroit	Plaintiffs sought text messages from city officials after alleging the defendants deliberately interfered with a police investigation.	Two subpoenas were issued on the defendants' service provider for text messaging services.	Services provided could be characterized as an RCS pursuant to the SCA, and the defendants were compelled to produce electronic communications.	Because the city had "control" of the text messages pursuant to Rule 34, the city could give consent to SkyTel to retrieve the communications. This was required for an RCS provider.
Warshak v. U.S.	Warshak was being investigated for mail and wire fraud and the government sought his e-mails.	Two ex parte orders were obtained compelling preservation and a subpoena was issued to obtain the preserved e-mails.	The e-mails were not excluded from evidence, and Warshak's Fourth Amendment rights had not been violated.	Warshak did have a reasonable expectation of privacy in his e-mails. However, because the government relied on the subpoenas in good faith, the exclusionary rule did not apply in this instance.

(continued)

Table 10.1 (*Continued*)

Case	Case Summary	Warrant/Subpoena	Outcome	Basis
Ehling v. Monmouth-Ocean Hospital	Defendants obtained copies of the plaintiff's Facebook posts and disseminated them to allegedly damage her reputation and get her nursing license revoked.	Defendants coerced a coworker into accessing the plaintiff's Facebook page on their behalf so they could view the posts.	Plaintiff had failed to state a claim under the NJ Wiretap Act. Therefore, the Facebook posts were admissible in court.	The court reasoned that only electronic communications that were in the course of transmission or used as a backup were protected. An individual loses privacy once the message is sent.
Juror Number One v. California	An individual serving on a jury during a criminal trial was accused of misconduct and the defense counsel sought Facebook posts he made regarding the trial.	Subpoena was issued originally requesting the Facebook posts. The judge also issued an order compelling Juror Number One to sign a consent form to disclose the posts.	The SCA did not apply because Juror Number One failed to state the specific operations of Facebook, so the court was unable to determine to what extent the SCA was applicable.	Juror Number One failed to demonstrate how the SCA would be applicable. Even if the SCA did apply, the compulsion was on Juror Number One, not on Facebook. He could be compelled to consent to the disclosure. The court also rejected Juror Number One's Fourth and Fifth Amendment arguments.

Notes

1. Juror Number One v. Superior Court, 2011 WL 567356 (2011)
2. O'Grady v. Superior Court, 139 Cal.App.4th 1423, 1445 (2006).
3. *Id.* at 1447.
4. *Id.* at 1448.
5. Richard M. Thompson II, "Cloud Computing: Constitutional and Statutory Privacy Protection," CRS Report for Contress, March 22, 2013, 16.
6. Thompson, 18.
7. Pursuant to 18 U.S. §2510, content includes "any information concerning the substance, purport, or meaning of that communication."
8. *Id.* at 1437.
9. *Krinsky v. Doe 6*, 72 Cal.Rptr.3d 231, 235 (2008).
10. *Id.* at 232.
11. *Id.* at 238.
12. See discussion of *O'Grady*.
13. *Doe 6*, 72 Cal.Rptr at 233.
14. *Flagg v. City of Detroit*, 827 F. Supp.2d 765 (E.D. Mich 2011).
15. *Flagg v. City of Detroit*, 252 F.R.D. 346, 348 (E.D. Mich 2008).
16. 18 U.S.C. §2702 (a)(1).
17. 18 U.S.C. §2702 (a)(2).
18. FRCP 26(b)(1) states "Unless otherwise limited by court order, the scope of discovery is as follows: Parties may obtain discovery regarding any nonprivileged matter that is relevant to any party's claim or defense—including the existence, description, nature, custody, condition, and location of any documents or other tangible things and the identity and location of persons who know of any discoverable matter. For good cause, the court may order discovery of any matter relevant to the subject matter involved in the action. Relevant information need not be admissible at the trial if the discovery appears reasonably calculated to lead to the discovery of admissible evidence. All discovery is subject to the limitations imposed by Rule 26(b)(2)(C)."
19. FRCP 34(a)(1) states that "a party may serve on any other party a request within the scope of Rule 26(b): (1) to produce and permit the requesting party or its representative to inspect, copy, test, or sample the following items in the responding party's possession, custody, or control. . . ."
20. *Flagg*, 252 F.R.D. at 348.
21. *Id.* at 361.
22. *Id.*
23. *Id.* at 362
24. *Id.*
25. *Id.* at 363.
26. *Id.*
27. *Id.*
28. *Id.*
29. Thompson, 16.
30. U.S. v. Warshak, 631 F.3d 266, 285 (6th Circ. 2010).
31. *Id.* at 285-286.
32. Thompson, 9.
33. Thompson, 19.
34. *Warshak* at 291.
35. Thompson, 15.
36. *Ehling v. Monmouth-Ocean Hosp. Service Corp.*, 872 F. Supp.2d 369, 371 (D.N.J. 2012)
37. *Id.* at 372.

38. *Id.* at 375.
39. *Juror Number One v. California,* 206 Cal.App. 4th 854, 862 (2012).
40. *Id.*
41. *Id.* at 863.
42. *Id.* at 864.
43. Thompson, 16.

CHAPTER 11

Cloud Computing and Reasonable Expectations of Privacy: Fourth Amendment Concerns

*Matthew P. Breuer and
James P. Martin*

Despite the growing complexity of cloud computing as an issue in litigation and discovery, much of the ideology that has driven the Supreme Court's treatment can be traced back to basic, fundamental constitutional principles.

The Fourth Amendment states:

> The right of the people to be secure in their persons, houses, papers, and effects, against unreasonable searches and seizures, shall not be violated, and no Warrants shall issue, but upon probable cause, supported by Oath or affirmation, and particularly describing the place to be searched, and the persons or things to be seized.[1]

When the government obtains information by physically intruding on a constitutionally protected area, a "search" within the original meaning of Fourth Amendment has occurred.[2] This occurs when an "expectation of privacy that society is prepared to consider reasonable is infringed."[3] Pursuant to the Fourth Amendment, a "seizure" of property occurs "not when there is a trespass, but when there is some meaningful interference with an individual's possessory interests in that property."[4] Evidence obtained from these types of intrusions is inadmissible in court.[5] Until 1961, the Fourth

Amendment did not apply to states until the Supreme Court held in *Mapp v. Ohio* that evidence obtained by illegal searches and seizures were inadmissible in a state court.[6]

Endless litigation has been spent on whether or not the protections of the Fourth Amendment should be afforded to individuals during government investigations. This can be attributed to two major factors. The very nature and importance of the Fourth Amendment as one of the fundamental values of the U.S. Constitution has given rise to ample litigation. Given that importance, it has also been difficult to apply this amendment in a consistent and uniform manner to new issues that have come before the court that could have never been contemplated by the original framers of the Constitution.

Case law regarding Fourth Amendment issues has covered a variety of issues that have come before the court, including anything from searches and seizures of personal letters and packages to wireless communications and e-mail. The foundational case law analysis traces several of the earliest Supreme Court rulings regarding this subject matter to more recent case law, which, as the analysis demonstrates, has evolved over time to coincide with technological advances and has also been evident in present-day litigation regarding cloud computing issues.

Ex Parte Jackson, 96 U.S. 727 (1877)

Congress had passed an act to prohibit publications in the mail related to illegal lotteries, gift concerts, enterprises offering prizes, or other publications concerning schemes to defraud the public for the purpose of obtaining money through false pretenses. The petitioner was indicted under this law in the Southern District of New York. The issue before the court was whether or not Congress had the authority to exclude materials it deemed to be obscene from the U.S. postal system.

Although the central issue in this case was whether or not Congress had the authority to regulate the postal system in such a manner, the court engaged in a discussion regarding searches and seizures of packages. The court noted in its dicta that packages and envelopes were allowed to be examined, but any examination could only be superficial by looking at the form and weight of a package. The court extended the constitutional protection of the Fourth Amendment to one's papers regardless of whether they were in an individual's domicile or the possession of the U.S. postal system.

This protection, however, could be overcome if a party obtained a warrant under oath that particularly describes the item to be seized. It was imperative for the court to uphold the principle that officials connected to the postal service (or other government officials) would be prohibited to invade the privacy of letters and sealed packages in the mail. As the court noted, "all regulations adopted as to mail matter of this kind must be in subordination to the great principle embodied in the Fourth Amendment of the Constitution."[7]

Despite its older roots, *Ex Parte Jackson* still merits discussion because of several of the foundational principles that emerged from the Justice Field's opinion. One important aspect of the court's decision is the fact that the justices wanted to ensure that the protections against unreasonable searches and seizures extended beyond one's own domicile. Despite the fact that an individual's personal papers may be in the possession of a government entity, i.e. the post office in this instance, this did not permit the government to invade the privacy of the owner of the effects. *Ex Parte Jackson* established that individuals would be guaranteed a certain level of privacy in their written communications.

Moreover, a key principle still embodied in case law today emerged from the court's discussion. In their reasoning, the court discussed a dichotomy between examining the package itself and the actual contents. The court permitted superficial searches, such as examining the weight and/or form. However, the court refused to allow a government official to look at the actual contents of a package by opening a sealed package. This concept is incorporated into the Stored Communications Act (SCA), as the prohibitions state that "a person or entity providing an electronic communication service to the public shall not knowingly divulge to any person or entity the *contents* of a communication while in electronic storage by that service."[8]

Under the SCA, information is stored in three categories: (1) basic subscriber and session information; (2) noncontent records and other information pertaining to the customer; and (3) contents. Content encompasses actual files stored in an account, e-mail text, voicemails, subject lines of an e-mail, and the like. What constitutes content can also vary depending on the jurisdiction and whether the content is held by an electronic communication service (ECS) or remote computing service (RCS). The *Jackson* case was decided back in the 1800s, but the court was already making a content/ noncontent distinction. Moreover, information that could be observed on the outside of the package, such as the routing information, was not subject to Fourth Amendment restrictions.

The court in *Ex Parte Jackson* was one of the earliest examples of the court recognizing the idea that the contents of a package are subject to a higher level scrutiny and ultimately are afforded more protection. The importance of this distinction is still evident today in the SCA, other legislation pertaining to wireless communications, and recent case law.

Olmstead v. United States, 277 U.S. 438 (1928)

The petitioners were involved in a conspiracy to import, possess and sell liquor unlawfully during Prohibition. Olmstead was convicted in the District Court for the Western District of Washington for conspiracy to violate the National Prohibition Act along with 72 other individuals. Olmstead was the leading conspirator and general manager of the business. Without judicial approval, wiretaps were installed in Olmstead's building by federal agents, and he was convicted based on evidence obtained from the intercepted messages. Petitioners challenged the conviction arguing that evidence of private telephone conversations intercepted through wiretapping violated their Fourth and Fifth Amendments.

The court concluded that the petitioner's Fourth and Fifth Amendment rights had not been violated. Because there was no evidence of compulsion to induce the defendants into talking and they voluntarily transacted business without knowledge of the interception, the court's focus shifted solely onto the Fourth Amendment issue. In deciding that the wiretapping was not a search and seizure, the court noted that the Fourth Amendment did not apply to an individual's conversation—it applied to a physical examination of one's person, papers, tangible materials, effects, or home. These types of communications were not protected under the Fourth Amendment. Therefore, the Supreme Court upheld the conviction of the petitioners, ruling that the wiretappings were not searches and seizures pursuant to the Fourth Amendment.

This case was eventually overturned, but it was significant in that it was one of the first cases to address wireless communications with respect to the Fourth Amendment. Until this point, the court had never had to make any decisions regarding Fourth Amendment issues and wireless communications because the eavesdropping technology simply did not exist. The case itself was unchartered waters for the court, which had previously dealt with physical trespass or intrusion into one's personal effects. Moreover, the Federal Communications Act was not passed for another six years after *Olmstead* in 1934. This would eventually address the issues brought forth in *Olmstead* and the Act intended to limit the government's ability to wiretap, so the court in this instance had very little guidance.

The court took a very literal interpretation of the Constitution, holding that wireless communications were not encompassed by the Fourth Amendment, and that it applied to only one's persons, papers, tangible material effects, or home. The court's analysis was very straightforward and engaged in a policy decision to not expand the safeguards afforded by the Fourth Amendment. This could be attributed to the fact that the court was not ready to embrace the technology at the time and as a result did not wish to expand the scope of protection under the Fourth Amendment.

Katz v. United States, **88 S.Ct. 507 (1967)**

The petitioner, Charles Katz, was convicted of transmitting wagering information over state telephone lines in violation of federal law. At his trial, the government sought to introduce evidence of the petitioner's end of telephone conversations over Katz's objection. The phone calls on Katz's end were intercepted by FBI agents, who had attached an electronic recording device to the outside of a public telephone booth that he had used to make the phone calls. The Court of Appeals affirmed his conviction, reasoning that there was no actual, physical entrance into the phone booth or the area occupied by the petitioner.

On appeal, the petitioner raised two fundamental issues:[9]

1. Whether a public telephone booth is a constitutionally protected area so that evidence obtained by attaching an electronic listening recording device to the top of such a booth is obtained in violation of the right to privacy of the user of the booth.
2. Whether the physical penetration of a constitutionally protected area is necessary before a search and seizure can be said to be violative of the Fourth Amendment to the U.S. Constitution.

The court's analysis stressed the nature of the telephone booth from which the call was made. The Fourth Amendment does not protect what a person knowingly exposes to the public, even in his own home or office. Despite the government's focus on the booth being glass and the high visibility of petitioner's activities, the court's focus was premised on the fact that the petitioner did not want anyone to listen in on his conversation. The court opined that an individual who occupies a phone booth shuts the door, pays the toll for the call and assumes his conversation will not be broadcasted to the public.

Consequently, the government's activities of electronically listening to the petitioner's words violated the privacy that Katz justifiably relied upon when using the phone booth. The government in this instance never obtained a valid warrant to justify the search. In addition, the court also maintained that the Fourth Amendment protections are attached to a person, not the place. This constituted a search and seizure under the Fourth Amendment. The court also disregarded the fact that an electronic device did not physically penetrate the wall of the phone booth.

An important aspect of this case is the fact that the court recognized that the Fourth Amendment protects people and not just places. This continued to expand the protection of the Fourth Amendment outside the realm of just a physical location or one's own dwelling. Moreover, in his concurring opinion, Justin Harlan introduced the idea of a "reasonable ex-pectation of privacy" when discussing what protection it affords to people. Harlan's understanding of the rule is twofold. The first part of the inquiry is to examine whether the person exhibited an actual (subjective) expecta-tion of privacy, and, second, whether or not society would accept the ex-pectation as reasonable. The critical factor, according to Justice Harlan, is that the phone booth is a private place where occupants have expectations against intrusion.

From a foundational aspect, this case addressed the issue of communi-cations via telephone and was one of the first cases in which the Supreme Court decided that these communications fall within the scope of the Fourth Amendment. The court's focus here was a simplistic approach into an individ-ual's reasonable expectation of privacy, and this approach would ultimately be used going forward. As the court noted, one who speaks into the mouthpiece in a closed telephone booth can correctly assume that what he says will not be broadcast to the entire world. It was irrelevant that there no was physical intrusion into the booth by the government.

This idea of a reasonable expectation of privacy has found its way into present day litigation pertaining to cloud computing. Several courts have addressed the issue of whether or not an individual storing information on a cloud has a subjective expectation of privacy and whether that expectation is one society is fully prepared to recognize as reasonable. For example, in *Warshak v. United States*, officials obtained 27,000 e-mails from the defendant's Internet service provider (ISP) without a warrant, and the court proceeded with the *Katz* analysis in the majority opinion. *Warshak* demonstrated that this reasonable expectation of privacy test could be expanded to the Internet.[10] Perhaps most importantly as well, this case reversed the holding in *Olmstead*, which would open the door for subsequent litigation.

United States v. Miller, 425 U.S. 435 (1976)

Miller was convicted of possession of an unregistered still, conducting a dis-tiller without giving bond, and intent to defraud the government of taxes owed. Prior to the trial, two of Miller's banks were subpoenaed for records of his accounts. The banks complied and the evidence was used to convict Miller at his trial. He subsequently appealed alleging that his Fourth Amendment rights had been violated.

After receiving a tip from an informant and then discovering a warehouse full of nontax-paid whiskey and paraphernalia, the Bureau of Alcohol, Tobacco, and Firearms (ATF) issued a subpoena to produce "all records of accounts, i.e. savings, checking, loan, or otherwise, in the name of Mitch Miller . . . from

October 1972 through the present date ... in the case of Citizens & Southern National Bank of Warner Robins."[11] These records were required to be kept pursuant to the Bank Secrecy Act of 1970. Miller never received any notice from the banks that his accounts had been subpoenaed. Agents were shown microfilm records at each branch and were provided with copies of checks, deposit slips, financial statements, and monthly statements. The evidence obtained from the subpoenas was used at a federal grand jury proceeding and also introduced at Miller's trial.

Miller's grounds for appeal were premised upon the fact that the subpoena was defective because it was issued by the U.S. Attorney rather than a court, no return was made to a court, and the subpoenas were returnable on a day when a grand jury was not in session. The Court of Appeals agreed with Miller, reasoning that the subpoenas did not adhere to the proper legal process. The government claimed that the Court of Appeals erred in deciding that the respondent had the Fourth Amendment interest "necessary to entitle him to challenge the validity of the subpoenas duces tecum through his motion to suppress."[12] The government appealed, arguing his Fourth Amendment rights had not been violated and that the warrant was not defective.

In Justice Powell's opinion, the court distinguished the present case from *Boyd*.[13] Miller could not possibly claim ownership or possession over the documents subpoenaed. The documents sought after by the government were business records of the bank. The records of the respondent were related to transactions in which the bank itself was a party, and the bank was not merely a neutral third party. Because the banks were actual parties to the transaction, a subpoena to the institutions was comparable to subpoenaing a normal business for their records.

Miller further argued that as a result of the Bank Secrecy Act, the government could circumvent the requirements of the Fourth Amendment. Because of the recordkeeping requirements of the Act and by allowing the government to directly subpoena a financial institution, the government can obtain a depositor's records without following the legal requirements that would be required if it subpoenaed Miller directly. In addition, Miller urged the court to adhere to the ruling in *Katz* by finding that Miller had a reasonable expectation of privacy in the documents he sought to be protected.

The court disagreed. The court reasoned that the checks "are not confidential information but negotiable instruments to be used in commercial transactions."[14] This information was also voluntarily given to the banks when Miller chose them as his financial institutions. Moreover, the lack of legitimate privacy was contemplated by Congress when enacting the Bank Secrecy Act. One of its purposes was to require records to be maintained so they "have a high degree of usefulness in criminal tax, and regulatory investigations and proceedings."[15] It is the depositor that assumes the risk by revealing his financial affairs to another who could in turn convey that information to the government.

Because no Fourth Amendment interests of the depositor were affected, the court adhered to the rule that an issuance of a subpoena to a third party does not violate the rights of the defendant. Accordingly, the court held that the District Court properly denied the respondent's motion to suppress the evidence, since no Fourth Amendment rights were implicated.

Miller was a landmark case in constitutional litigation and specifically with respect to the Fourth Amendment. *Miller* elaborated on the concept of a reasonable expectation by carving out documents and data considered to be the business records of the service provider which, by definition, do not belong to the individual and the individual could have no claim of privacy. The distinction of business records of the service provider vs records and data of an individual has become a key issue in litigation involving cloud data. The category of business records of the service provider now includes data such as cell tower logs and communication connection records.

In what was a very important decision, the court refused to extend the reasonable expectation of privacy doctrine to records created by a service provider regarding a customer's activities. The court appeared to have reasoned in such a manner based on the second prong of *Katz*: The court did not believe society would find a reasonable expectation of personal privacy in the business records of a third party. In addition, the court opined that Miller had voluntarily conveyed his information, and should have realized that the bank would need to create and maintain business records with regard to his account, and the reasonable expectation of privacy became extinguished as a result. Consequently, *Miller* reaffirmed the concept that an individual's expectation could be voluntarily waived, an issue courts have addressed when deciding if an individual has voluntarily given up his information to service providers.

Miller also prompted the federal government to enact the Right to Financial Privacy Act. This Act intended to provide financial institution customers a reasonable amount of privacy from intrusion by the federal government. The Act establishes specific procedures that government authorities are mandated to follow when requesting a customer's financial records from a bank or other financial institution.[16] For example, the government is required to give written notice to the customer, explain the purpose for which the documents are sought, and include a statement describing the procedures a customer could follow if he or she did not wish for those documents to be made available. The holding in *Miller* would also be limited by *Hancock v. Marshall*, 86 F.R.D.

209 (1980). This would be one of the first of many examples of the government legislature enacting guidance on discovery procedures for communication being stored by a third-party.

United States v. Jacobsen, 466 U.S. 109 (1984)

United States v. Jacobsen addressed the issue of warrantless searches of letters and other sealed packages. Employees of a private freight carrier observed a white powdery substance emerge from a box that had been damaged by a forklift while being moved. The employees then contacted federal authorities, who removed a sample and later determined it was cocaine after a chemical test.

Consistent with all Fourth Amendment cases, the justices' decision rested on the specific details of the search and the manner in which it was conducted. The package containing the cocaine was an ordinary cardboard box wrapped in brown paper. Inside the box was a 10-inch tube with five or six crumpled newspapers covering the tube. The tube contained a series of four plastic zip-top bags. The outermost bag enclosed the other three bags, while the innermost contained approximately six and a half ounces of white powder. The employees of the carrier cut the tube open and notified the Drug Enforcement Agency. Before federal authorities arrived, the employees replaced the plastic bags in the tube and put all of the contents back inside the box.

When the first DEA agent arrived, the box was still wrapped in brown paper, but had a hole punched in its side and was open at the top. The agent removed the four plastic bags from the tube and observed the white powder. After removing traces with his knife blade, a field test confirmed that the white powder was cocaine. A warrant was executed to search the place to which the package was addressed, and the respondents were arrested and charged with possessing an illegal substance with intent to distribute. The respondents attempted to file a motion to suppress the evidence as a result of an illegal search and seizure, but they were denied. After being convicted, the respondents appealed and the court of Appeals overturned their conviction. The Supreme Court granted cert due to the fact that the lower court's decision conflicted with another decision and the role that field tests play in the enforcement of narcotics.

The court's analysis first determined whether or not the item in question fell under the definition of an "effect" pursuant to the Fourth Amendment. The court noted that "letters and other sealed packages are in the general class of effects in which the public at large has a legitimate expectation of privacy; warrantless searches of such effects are presumptively unreasonable."[17]

However, in his majority opinion, Justice Stevens pointed noted that the first search was conducted by the employees of the private freight carrier. Because the Fourth Amendment protects individuals from searches and seizures by government officials, it was not applicable to the first search of the container performed by the freight company employees. Therefore, the first search of the container performed was not in violation of the Fourth Amendment.

The issue then became whether the subsequent search by the government violated the Fourth Amendment. The court pointed out that "it is well-settled that when an individual reveals private information to another, he assumes the risk that his confidant will reveal that information to the authorities."[18] Consequently, in those types of instances, the Fourth Amendment does not prohibit use of that information. Once the original expectation of privacy has been extinguished, the government is free to use the nonprivate information. The court went on to cite *United States v. Miller* in holding that the Fourth Amendment does not preclude the obtaining of information revealed "to a third party and conveyed by him to Government authorities, even if the information is revealed on the assumption that it will be used only for a limited purpose and the confidence placed in a third party will not be betrayed."[19]

Justice Stevens' opinion then dissected the individual actions taken by the DEA when they removed the tube and plastic bags from the box and then performed a field test. The respondents did not have a privacy interest since the package remained unsealed and the employees had just examined the package. The employees simply invited the federal agents for the purpose of viewing the contents. This viewing of what a private party had made freely available to the agent for his inspection did not violate the Fourth Amendment. Removing the items did not allow the agent to learn anything new that had not been discovered in the private search, and therefore it was not a search pursuant to the Fourth Amendment. Due to the fact that it was open and unsealed, the court also held that it was a not a seizure pursuant to the Fourth Amendment.

The court also upheld the validity of the chemical test based on the fact that it did not compromise any legitimate interest in privacy; the court held that it was both a seizure and search. Because the federal agents did not infringe any constitutionally protected interest that had not already been infringed by the private action, there was no violation of the Fourth Amendment. Moreover, any infringement was deemed to be "de minimis and constitutionally reasonable."[20] The Court of Appeals holding was overturned as a result.

Jacobsen had significant implications on Fourth Amendment searches and seizures with packages and letters. It also bolstered several concepts discussed in *Miller. Jacobsen* was important in that it maintained that a private party was not subject to the Fourth Amendment restrictions. The employees of the private freight company clearly were not government officials. The court went on to extend this idea by reasoning that once the contents of the package had become nonprivate, the government is free to search and the Fourth Amendment is not implicated.

However, the court did maintain that warrantless searches of an individual's effects are presumptively unconstitutional. This is an important starting point when examining government investigations. This presumption strengthens the Fourth Amendment protections given to individuals and places the burden on the government to prove justification for a search conducted during an investigation.

United States v. Jones, 132 S.Ct. 945 (2012)

The most recent prominent case regarding Fourth Amendment issues involved the use of a global positioning system (GPS) tracking device on a vehicle. Antoine Jones was suspected of trafficking narcotics. After being investigated by the FBI, the government applied in the U.S. District Court for the District of Columbia for a warrant authorizing the use of an electronic tracking device on his vehicle. The warrant authorized a 10-day window, but the device was not installed until the eleventh day. Based off the extensive information discovered by the tracking device, the respondent was convicted for conspiracy to distribute and possession with intent to distribute cocaine. His motion to suppress the evidence was denied and he was ultimately convicted. The U.S. Court of Appeals reversed the conviction, and the Supreme Court granted certiorari.

The court held that this constituted an unlawful search under the Fourth Amendment. A critical factor for the court in their analysis was the fact that the government physically occupied private property for the purpose of obtaining information when they planted the tracking device on his vehicle. The word *property* is not included in the text of the Fourth Amendment; however, the court had no issue extending the scope in this instance. The government argued for the *Katz* standard, asserting that a person does not have a reasonable expectation of privacy when they drive on public roads, since the roads are visible to all. The court did not agree with this argument.

Instead, the court opined the present case should not be analyzed exclusively under the *Katz* formulation. Prior to that case, Fourth Amendment issues were decided based on common-law trespass to one's property or tangible things, such as the *Olmstead* case. The decision in *Katz* did not involve an intrusion of property and later decisions departed from the property-based approach. As the court noted, "the reasonable expectation of privacy test added to, not substituted for, the common-law trespassory test"[21] to ensure that the analysis would protect people and not just places. The court's focus was on the fact that an individual's property was physically occupied for the purpose of gathering information. Although not analyzed under *Katz*, it did not conflict or repudiate its holding.

Justice Sotomayor's concurring opinion urged the court to adopt a strict *Katz* analysis. She asserted that this would be particularly important in an era where surveillance could be accomplished without physical intrusion. Another concurring opinion was written in which Justice Alito agreed with the outcome, but disagreed with framing the issue in terms of trespass to property. The court concluded that it was an unlawful search and seizure, and the judgment of the Court of Appeals was upheld.

Jones is one of the most recent cases concerning Fourth Amendment and violations of the reasonable expectation of privacy. The court made a departure from its earlier way of analysis in Fourth Amendment cases. In *Olmstead*, the court was reluctant to expand the scope of the Fourth Amendment by reasoning that telephone conversations were not encompassed under the protections of the Fourth Amendment. In *Miller*, the court would not expand the safeguards of the Fourth Amendment to bank records, finding that these were expected business records of a service provider. *Jones* took the opposite approach. *Jones* affirmed the idea that a vehicle, although not specifically enumerated in the Fourth Amendment, still would be afforded protection.

The case also calls into question the future direction of Fourth Amendment litigation. The majority, while not repudiating *Katz*, refused to follow the two-prong approach originally adopted. While noting the transition in Fourth Amendment jurisprudence from common-law trespassory to the reasonable expectation of privacy, the court basically considered *Katz* a supplementary case to modern-day constitutional litigation. This was a point of contention with the other justices, particularly Justice Sotomayor, who believed treating the issue as a trespass of property in an age where physical intrusions occur less infrequently was illogical. Whether the courts will proceed under the *Katz* analysis in Fourth Amendment litigation in the future remains to be seen.

Summary of Cases

Table 11.1 provides a summary of the cases discussed in this chapter.

Table 11.1 Fourth Amendment Foundational Case Analysis Summary

Case	Nature of Search	Warrant/ Subpoena	Outcome	Basis
Ex Parte Jackson	The issue was centered around the ability of Congress to regulate the postal system, but the court engaged in a discussion of a physical inspection of a package sent through the mail.	No	The ability of Congress to regulate the postal system is valid; however, they do not have the right under the Fourth Amendment to open sealed packages or letters without a search warrant.	The Fourth Amendment protects an individual's papers and effects against unreasonable searches and seizures. Regulations adopted as to mail must be subordinate to the principles embodied in the Fourth Amendment.
Olmstead v. U.S.	Wiretaps were installed in the petitioner's building.	No	The conviction was upheld based on the information obtained from the wiretaps. The Fourth Amendment did not apply to an individual's conversation.	The Fourth Amendment does not apply to an individual's conversation. The court took a very strict interpretation of the Constitution and applied it to an examination of one's person, papers, effects, or home.
Katz v. U.S.	Phone calls of petitioner were intercepted by an electronic recording device attached to the outside of a public telephone booth.	No	Petitioner's Fourth Amendment rights were violated by the government without having obtained a warrant.	The Fourth Amendment Protections are attached to a person, not places. An individual shuts the glass door and does not expect his conversation to be broadcast to the world. Justice Harlan also introduced the reasonable expectation of privacy in his concurrence.
U.S. v. Miller	Authorities subpoenaed Miller's bank without giving him notice.	Yes	The Government did not violate the Fourth Amendment when they obtained Miller's banks records through his financial institutions.	Miller could not claim a reasonable expectation of privacy. He voluntarily conveyed his financial information to his bank and the information was not confidential information. These records were considered typical business records and Miller's rights were not circumvented as a result.

(continued)

Table 11.1 (*Continued*)

Case	Nature of Search	Warrant/ Subpoena	Outcome	Basis
U.S. v. Jacobsen	DEA agents searched a package that had been damaged by a forklift after private freight carriers had already examined it.	No	The DEA search did not violate the respondents' Fourth Amendment rights despite not having obtained a search warrant.	Removing the items from the package did not yield any new information that had not been discovered in the private search. The employees were not government agents, and information obtained from them could be used in the investigation.
U.S. v. Jones	A GPS tracking device was placed on Jones' vehicle.	Issued, but not valid	The GPS device without a properly executed warrant being attached to a vehicle was an unlawful search pursuant to the Fourth Amendment.	The court focused on the fact that there was a physical intrusion onto an individual's property for the purpose of obtaining information. The Katz analysis was not used and the court's discussion focused on the evolution of the common-law trespassory analysis when analyzing rights under the Fourth Amendment.

Notes

1. U.S. Const. amend. IV.
2. U.S. Const. amend. IV.
3. *U.S. v. Jacobsen*, 466 U.S. 109, 113 (1984).
4. U.S. Const. amend. IV.
5. This is subject to certain exceptions, such as the consent exception or plain view doctrine.
6. *Mapp v. Ohio*, 367 U.S. 643 (1961).
7. Ex Parte Jackson, 96 U.S. 727, 733 (1877).
8. 18 U.S. Code §2702(a).
9. *Katz v. U.S.*, 389 U.S. 347, 349 (1967).
10. See discussion on *Warshak* in Chapter 11.
11. *U.S. v. Miller*, 425 U.S. 435, 438 (1976).
12. *Id.* at 439.
13. *Boyd v. United States*, 116 U.S. 616, 622, 6 S.Ct. 524, 528, 29 L.Ed. 746, 748, (1886).
14. *U.S. v. Miller*, 442.
15. *Id.* at 443.
16. Right to Financial Privacy Act, *Customer Compliance Handbook*, 1.
17. *U.S. v. Jacobsen*, 466 U.S. 109, 114 (1984).
18. *Id.* at 116.
19. *Id.* at 117.
20. *Id.* at 126.
21. *U.S v. Jones*, 132 S.Ct. 945, 951 (2012).

CHAPTER 12

Compelled Production of Cloud Computing Data: Fifth Amendment Concerns

*Matthew P. Breuer and
James P. Martin*

Technological advancements frequently create situations that are not easily addressed by the historical interpretations of basic constitutional law. One of the many undesired consequences of this incompatibility is the fact that inconsistent rulings can be rendered in various jurisdictions with regard to Fifth Amendment rights, which states that:

> No person shall be held to answer for a capital, or otherwise infamous crime, unless on a presentment or indictment of a Grand Jury, except in cases arising in the land or naval forces, or in the Militia, when in actual service in time of War or public danger; nor shall any person be subject for the same offense to be twice put in jeopardy of life or limb; nor shall be compelled in any criminal case to be a witness against himself, nor be deprived of life, liberty, or property, without due process of law; nor shall private property be taken for public use, without just compensation.[1]

Courts have been charged with the task of finding the correct balance between supporting an individual's Fifth Amendment rights and allowing government investigations to proceed for the common good. This has proved to be quite challenging. For example, courts have struggled with the challenge of the application of concepts such as the "foregone conclusion" doctrine, which was originally intended for act-of-production issues for paper documents.[2]

Even more perplexing for the court has been interpreting the standard of the reasonable particularity requirement of subpoenas and defining a precise scope with regard to the definition of testimonial acts.

Prior chapters discuss instances in which a party to litigation has been compelled to authorize a cloud computing (third-party) provider to produce data as a way to circumvent the restrictions of the Stored Communication Act (SCA). The SCA states that permission of the account holder will allow the provider to produce data to a third party, however, it does not directly address the matter from a litigation perspective. In many cases, the sought-after documents are potentially incriminating to a defendant in a criminal proceeding. Requiring a defendant to consent to the production of potentially incriminating documents has invoked constitutional concerns and has also prompted criminal defendants to claim violations of their Fifth Amendment rights. The following cases are frequently cited in Fifth Amendment jurisprudence with respect to compelled disclosure of data held in a cloud computing solution.

United States v. Doe, 465 U.S. 605 (1984)

The respondent, the owner of several sole proprietorships, was being investigated by a federal grand jury after he was accused of corruption in the awarding of county and municipal contracts. The grand jury served several subpoenas on the defendant, who filed a motion seeking to have them quashed. The District Court of New Jersey granted the motion, except with respect to the documents that were required by law to be kept or disclosed to a public agency. The government appealed this ruling.

Affirming the District Court's ruling, the Third Circuit considered whether the documents being sought were privileged. In *Fisher v. United States*, the court opined that contents of business records are ordinarily not privileged because they are created voluntarily and free of any compulsion. However, the Court of Appeals found that the business records at issue here were privileged, reasoning that a sole proprietorship's records are no different than an owner's records despite the holdings in *Fisher* and other Third Circuit precedent. In addition, turning the papers over would in itself admit the documents' existence and authenticity. Thus, the subpoenaed records would have "communicative aspects of [their] own,"[3] and the respondent was able to succeed in asserting his Fifth Amendment privilege. The U.S. Supreme Court granted certiorari to resolve the conflict between the holding of the Court of Appeals and the underlying reasoning in *Fisher*.

In *Fisher*, the contents being sought after were the accountant's work papers that were in the possession of the defendant taxpayers' lawyers. These documents were related to the taxpayer's individual returns and were deemed to be personal even though they were in the possession of a third party. Holding for the IRS, the court formulated the foregone conclusion doctrine and held that the act of producing papers would not involve testimonial self-incrimination. Pursuant to this doctrine, the court found that the government "can compel production when the existence and location of documents are a foregone conclusion and the defendant adds little or nothing to the sum total of the Government's information by conceding that he in fact has the papers."[4] Despite addressing these facts and rationale, the court failed to decide the issue of whether the Fifth Amendment privilege protects the *contents* on an individual's tax records in his possession (or his counsel).[5]

However, the court still found the rationale in *Fisher* to be persuasive, as the Fifth Amendment "protects the person asserting the privilege only from *compelled* self-incrimination."[6] The court opined that the preparation of business documents is a voluntary act and therefore has no compulsion involved. The subpoena in this instance did not seek oral testimony or attempt to compel the taxpayer to affirm the truth of the contents of the documents sought. In addition, the taxpayer cannot avoid compliance with the subpoena by arguing that the documents he is required to produce contain incriminating writing. Because the respondent did not contend that he prepared the documents involuntarily or the subpoena would force him to testify to the truth of their contents, the contents were not privileged. The court also stated that the fact that the records were in the respondent's possession was irrelevant to the determination as to whether the creation of the documents was compelled.

The court's analysis then shifted to the act of producing the documents. Although the contents may not have been privileged, it was possible that the act itself of producing the documents could have an incriminating effect. Under *Fisher*, this analysis would always depend on the facts and circumstances of the present case. The key difference in *Fisher* was the act of producing the documents; its effect on the taxpayer would have only minimal testimonial value and would not incriminate the defendant. In the present case, the District Court found that the act of producing the documents would involve testimonial self-incrimination. Stating that they would not overturn the finding unless there was support in the record, the court did not wish to disturb the ruling of the lower courts who both reached the same result. Moreover, the court refused to grant any immunity in the absence of a formal request.

Accordingly, the court concluded that the contents of the subpoenaed documents were privileged under the Fifth Amendment and the act of producing the documents could not be compelled without a grant of immunity. The judgment of the Appeals Court was therefore affirmed in part and reversed in part.

The court's analysis was largely drawn from *Fisher*, which was very important in that it formulated the "foregone conclusion" doctrine. This issue would surface in later Fifth Amendment jurisprudence and would ultimately be used to decide whether the government can compel production of certain subpoenaed documents. The holding in *Fisher* that "the existence and location of the papers are a foregone conclusion and the taxpayer adds little or nothing to the sum total of the government's information by conceding that he in fact has the papers" has been cited frequently in later cases.[7] In addition, *Fisher* stresses the idea of possession as one of the most important concepts.[8]

Doe also introduces another key concept in Fifth Amendment jurisprudence. In determining whether a defendant's rights have been infringed, a court must look at the production of the contents *and* the act of producing the documents. As later discussed, the court's analysis in many Fifth Amendment cases actually centers on the act of production itself. In *Doe*, the court stressed that they did not wish to disturb the lower court's ruling, which determined that that the act of producing documents involved testimonial self-incrimination. The court would have only overturned this decision if there was a factual basis to do so in the record. The rationale in *Fisher* was crucial to the court's analysis, but even more imperative may have been the court's desire to not disturb the prior holdings of the lower courts.

Doe v. United States, 487 U.S. 201 (1988)

The petitioner was being investigated by a federal grand jury stemming from allegations of fraudulent manipulation of oil cargoes and failing to report income. He was ordered to produce documents relating to transactions in accounts at three banks in the Cayman Islands and Bermuda. Although he complied with the subpoena, he testified that no additional records responsive to the subpoena were in his possession or control. When the grand jury attempted to question him about additional records that Doe claimed were not in his possession, he invoked the Fifth Amendment privilege against self-incrimination. Moreover, the three banks were subpoenaed to produce account records, but all of them refused to comply with the requests citing bank-secrecy laws.

The government then filed a motion to compel Doe to sign forms consenting to the production of the documents. These forms contained the account numbers of foreign banking institutions and described documents that the government requested the banks to produce. Accordingly, the motion was denied by the U.S. District Court for the Southern District of Texas. The court reasoned that that the consent forms would constitute "an admission that Doe exercised signatory authority over such accounts."[9] The Court of Appeals for the Fifth Circuit reversed, finding that the form did not have testimonial significance, and on remand Doe was ordered to comply with the court's order. Doe refused and was held in contempt.

The U.S. Supreme Court granted certiorari to determine whether compelling Doe to consent to the disclosure of the foreign bank records violated his Fifth Amendment rights. Before beginning their analysis, the court stated that foreign bank records sought by the government were not privileged under the Fifth Amendment. Instead, the focus of the analysis was whether compelling the petitioner to sign the consent forms was inconsistent with the Fifth Amendment. Doe argued that consenting to the disclosure was testimonial in nature, because it was a declarative statement of consent made by the petitioner to the foreign banks and would be used by the government to produce account records that would be incriminating to the jury. The government countered by asserting that signing the consent forms would not be testimonial unless it related to a factual assertion and Doe's execution of the form would not disclose any facts or information.

The government's view relied on *Fisher*, which had been accepted by the Court of Appeals, and concluded that the act of producing the documents could constitute protected testimonial communication because "it might entail implicit statements by fact: by producing documents in compliance with a subpoena, the witness would admit the papers existed, were in his possession or control, and were authentic."[10] The court concluded that the Fifth Amendment applies to acts that imply assertions of fact. Essentially, the main point of contention was the meaning of "testimonial," and the court was more inclined to the government's argument.

In rejecting Doe's argument of the production being testimonial in nature, the court stressed that in order to be testimonial, an accused's communication must relate a factual assertion or actually disclose information. It is at this time in which a person is then compelled to be a witness against himself. In an attempt to provide more clarity, the court compared this to instances in which suspects are required to furnish a blood sample or provide a handwriting sample among other things. These instances all have one thing in common and that is the suspect is required to "disclose any knowledge he might have or to speak his guilt."[11]

Once the definition had been established, the court then applied the facts and circumstances of the present case and ultimately sided with the Court of Appeals in holding that neither its form nor its execution was testimonial. Specifically, the court noted that it was drafted so that it did not reference a specific amount and did not acknowledge that an account in a foreign financial institution is in existence or that it is actually controlled by Doe. The form also did not even identify the specific bank. Moreover, the court stressed that the government would have to locate the evidence by the "independent labor of its officers" and the government would not be relying on "truthtelling" of Doe's directive to show the existence of the records.[12]

Doe also would not make any statement regarding the existence of the account by signing the form. His signature on the consent forms would also not admit the authenticity. It was crucial in the court's analysis that the directive would not offer any view on the issue and any statement by Doe would not establish the records as genuine. The form also did not state that Doe consented to the release of the records, but merely stated that the directive shall be construed as consent with respect to several of the banking laws. Consequently, signing the form was a nontestimonial act and did not violate Doe's Fifth Amendment privilege against self-incrimination.

In reaching the opposite result of *U.S. v. Doe*, 465 U.S. 605 (1984), the Court again used *Fisher* in their rationale. The analysis in this case turned on whether the act of producing the documents implied assertions of fact and the definition of testimonial. If Doe's production of the documents would have communicated or implied a factual assertion, then by definition it would be a testimonial act. Examining the very writing of the subpoena, it did not reference a specific amount or a financial institution. This was crucial to the court. In signing the disclosure form, Doe would not offer any view on the issue nor establish authenticity of the records. As the court pointed out, this was more similar to providing a blood sample or handwriting exemplar, which has been upheld in past Fifth Amendment jurisprudence. Because of the way the subpoena was crafted, Doe's consent to the form was not considered a testimonial act by the court.

United States v. Hubbell, 530 U.S. 27 (2000)

The respondent, Webster Hubbell, was being investigated for tax evasion and related crimes in a prosecution initiated by independent counsel relating to the Whitewater Development Corporation. In 1994, he pleaded guilty to charges of mail fraud and tax evasion arising out of his billing practices as a member of his law firm and was sentenced to 21 months in prison. Pursuant to his plea agreement, Hubbell was required to provide the independent counsel with complete and accurate information relating to the Whitewater investigation. While incarcerated, he appeared before a grand jury after being served with a subpoena requesting production of 11 categories of documents. Hubbell invoked his Fifth Amendment privilege against self-incrimination and refused to state whether the named documents were within his possession or control.

The respondent produced the documents pursuant to §18 U.S.C. 6000(a), which directed him to respond to the subpoena and granted him immunity to the "extent allowed by law."[13] In addition, the respondent also answered questions that proved that all of the documents were in his custody.[14] He was subsequently charged in a 10-count indictment alleging tax-related crimes and mail and wire fraud. However, the indictment was eventually dismissed, as the subpoenaed documents violated §6002 because "all of the evidence he would offer against respondent at trial derived either directly or indirectly from testimonial aspects of respondent's immunized act of producing those documents."[15] The District Court went as far as to characterize the subpoena as "the quintessential fishing expedition."[16] This judgment was vacated by the Court of Appeals and remanded. The matter was eventually heard by the U.S. Supreme Court to examine the "reasonable particularity" requirement and determine the scope of the grant of immunity.

In his majority opinion, Justice Stevens discussed prior cases such as *Fisher* and *Doe* as a basis that the Fifth Amendment protects prosecutor's use of incriminating information derived directly or indirectly from compelled testimony. The court first focused on the scope of a grant of immunity. Under §6002, a safeguard is given to an accused, and a defendant that is given a grant of immunity does not have the burden of proving that his testimony was incorrectly used. The burden is on the prosecution to prove that evidence has not been tainted due to prior testimony and show that evidence is derived "from a legitimate source wholly independent of the compelled testimony."[17] Instead, the court stated that the disagreement between the parties came down to the significance of the testimonial aspect, and similar to prior cases this was dependent not on the contents of the documents produced but by the act of producing the documents.

The court was not concerned with whether the subpoena may be introduced at trial, which would be a prohibited use of the immunized act production. Its interest focused instead on whether the government *already* made derivative use of the testimonial act in obtaining the indictment against Hubbell. The critical piece in the court's analysis was the extent and broadness of the 11-category request, which sought "any and all documents reflecting, referring, or relating to any direct or indirect sources of money or other things of value received" to individuals or members of his family during a three-year span.[18] Providing a catalog of documents relating to the 11 categories of documents would surely provide a prosecutor with a lead to incriminating evidence or at least "a link in the chain of evidence needed to prosecute."[19]

The documents were produced as a result of the grand jury in an effort to assist the independent counsel's attempt to determine whether Hubbell had violated his first plea agreement. These documents that were produced directly led to his second indictment. The testimonial aspect of respondent's act of producing the documents was the beginning and one of the first steps in a chain that led to his subsequent prosecution. The documents were a product and were only produced after the respondent asserted his privilege and received immunity. As the court noted, "it was only through respondent's truthful reply to the subpoena that the government received the incriminating documents of which it made substantial use ... in the investigation that led to the indictment."[20] Because his act of production had a testimonial aspect, Hubbell could not be compelled to produce those documents unless he received immunity under §6003.

One of the major takeaways of the court's analysis was the fact that the justices did not find the government's argument to be encompassed by foregone conclusion doctrine. Instead, the court distinguished *Fisher*. The government claimed general knowledge that businessmen usually possess business records, but this did not fall within the scope of the doctrine. The court essentially failed to define the scope of the foregone conclusion standard.[21] In *Fisher*, the government already knew the documents were in the attorney's possession and could independently confirm their existence. The government could make no such claim in this instance. The government never proved that they could confirm the existence, custody, and authenticity of the documents nor any prior knowledge of their whereabouts.

In re Boucher, 2009 WL 424718 (D. Vt. 2009)

Boucher was accused of knowingly transporting child pornography in interstate or foreign commerce in violation of 18 U.S.C. §2252(a)(1). His computer was seized after customs and border protection agents conducted a secondary inspection while he was trying to cross the Canadian border. The government subsequently applied for a search warrant of his laptop computer that was seized from his vehicle; however, the contents were stored on an encrypted drive and were unintelligible without the proper password. The forensic expert was unable to conduct a search or analysis of the drive due to the enctyption. The grand jury issued a subpoena to Boucher for any password associated with the laptop, and Boucher moved to quash the subpoena, asserting that the act of production of the information would violate his Fifth Amendment privilege against self-incrimination. The language in the subpoena requested Boucher to:

> Provide all documents, whether in electronic or paper form, reflecting any passwords used or associated with the Alienware Notebook Computer, Model D9T, Serial No. NKD900TA5L00859, seized from Boucher at the Port of Entry at Derby Line, Vermont, on December 17, 2006.[22]

Originally, the government stated that it only sought the password for the encrypted drive and that it needed Boucher to open the drive before the grand jury, but also later requested that it only needed Boucher to provide an unencrypted version of the drive to the grand jury. The U.S. magistrate judge granted Boucher's motion to quash the subpoena, and the government appealed the ruling.

Consistent with past jurisprudence in this subject matter, the beginning of the court's analysis began with discussing the fact that even though the contents of a document may not be privileged, the act of producing such documents may violate a defendant's Fifth Amendment rights. Thus, the issue became whether compelling Boucher to produce an unencrypted version of the drive would constitute compelled testimonial communication. The court stated that there are two situations in which the act of producing documents can communicate incriminating facts, which the court described as: "(1) if the existence and location of the subpoenaed papers are unknown to the government; or (2) where production would implicitly authenticate the documents."[23]

Citing *Fisher*, the court stated there are no constitutional rights infringed when the existence and location of documents are previously known to the government and the foregone conclusion doctrine is triggered. The magistrate judge had ruled that this doctrine did not apply because the government had not viewed the actual files and could not determine if they were incriminating. This determination was inconsistent with Second Circuit jurisprudence; a party only has to fulfill the reasonable particularity requirement and know the existence and location of the documents. Government agents viewed the contents of some of the drive when Boucher was originally apprehended, and as a result the government knew of the existence and location of the files.

In regard to the second instance of authentication, the court concluded that Boucher's act of producing the drive would not be necessary for its authentication. The government submitted that it could link Boucher to the files without him producing the drive and stated it would not use the act of production of evidence. Consequently, Boucher's motion to quash the subpoena was denied. He was directed to produce an unencrypted version of the drive with the instruction that the government was not allowed to use his act of production to authenticate the drive or its contents before the grand jury.

The justices in *Boucher* again focused on the act of production. Consistent with past jurisprudence, they also focused whether production of documents would imply assertions of fact. *Boucher* is important in this line of cases because it discussed the idea of the reasonable particularity requirement. In dismissing the magistrate judge's holding, the court found that a party only has to know the existence and location of documents. This sets a lower threshold for authorities in federal investigations. In *Hubbell*, the Supreme Court did not adopt the exact wording of the D.C. Circuit, which upheld the reasonable particularity requirement. Instead, the Supreme Court left *Hubbell* with the broader "existence, control, and authenticity standard, declining to adopt the proposed standard of reasonable particularity."[24] However, *Boucher* trended back to the reasonable particularity requirement that the D.C. Circuit court originally employed.

In re Grand Jury Subpoena Duces Tecum, March 25, 2011, 670 F.3d 1335 (11th Circ. 2011)

During the course of a child pornography investigation, authorities seized several pieces of digital media and began investigating an individual YouTube .com account that the government suspected of sharing child pornography. In October 2010, authorities tracked Doe to a hotel in California and applied for a search warrant to search his room for all digital media and encryption devices or codes necessary to access such media. The officers seized several laptops and external hard drives, but forensic examiners were unable to access certain portions of the hard drives. A grand jury issued a subpoena requiring Doe to produce the unencrypted contents of the digital media. Doe stated to the U.S. Attorney that following the subpoena would violate his Fifth Amendment, and he was granted the limited act-of-production immunity.

If Doe was indicted for child pornography in violation of 18 U.S.C. §2252, the issue became whether the Fifth Amendment would prohibit the government from establishing that the decrypted contents were actually Doe's because the hard drive belonged to him and contained child pornography. Doe argued that the establishment of the second prong would constitute the derivative use of his immunized testimony to the grand jury. Specifically, he asserted that by decrypting the contents, Doe as opposed to any other individual could be identified as the one who put the contents on the hard drive and could retrieve them at will.

The court's analysis focused on the testimony of the forensic examiner, who testified that he cloned more than 5 TB of data from the various digital devices. Moreover, he opined that the data had been encrypted, which could potentially make the data inaccessible. The examiner stated that he believed the sought-after data existed on the encrypted parts of the hard drive, and the government introduced an exhibit showing "nonsensical characters and numbers," which it argued revealed the encrypted form of data in question.[25] However, on cross-examination the examiner did admit that it was possible the encrypted hard drives did not contain anything. The District Court concluded that Doe's decryption and production of the drives would not constitute "testimony" and held Doe in contempt when he refused to produce the unencrypted contents.

The major issue in dispute again centered on whether the government sought testimony within the meaning of the Fifth Amendment. Like the preceding cases, the court's analysis looked into whether the act of production was testimonial in nature, which can be established when the production of documents "explicitly or implicitly conveys some statement of fact." Using both *Fisher* and *Hubbell* as starting points, the Court reaffirmed the principle that an act of production can be testimonial if it conveys some statement of fact that certain materials exist, are within the possession or control of the individual, or are authentic. "The touchstone of whether an act of production is testimonial is whether the government compels the individual to use the 'contents of his own mind' to explicitly or implicitly communicate some statement of fact."[26] The Fifth Amendment will not be triggered if the government is compelling a physical act.[27] In addition, the Fifth Amendment is not infringed if the government can show with reasonable particularity that it already knew of the materials making the testimonial aspect a foregone conclusion.

Applying this framework to the present case, the court concluded that the decryption and production of the drives would require the use of the contents of Doe's mind, not merely a physical act. His ability to identify the location of the files, his possession, and his capability to decrypt the files would amount to more than just a physical act. The court stated that the government never sought the "key" or "combination" in *Fisher* and *Hubbell*; it sought the files being withheld, which was the case here. Therefore, the decryption and production of the contents of the drive were testimonial. In regard to the second point, the court needed to examine whether the testimony was a foregone conclusion. However, the court reasoned that the government only showed that the storage space could contain the sought-after files and refused to accept the argument that just because the devices were encrypted meant Doe was attempting to hide something.

In the court's analysis, they stated that this case would be far closer to the *Hubbell* end than the *Fisher* end. In *Hubbell*, the government had not shown any prior knowledge as to the whereabouts of the files it sought. On the other hand, the government knew exactly what documents it sought in *Fisher* and knew that they were already in the possession of the attorney and had been prepared by the accountant. Although prior case law does not require the government to know the exact contents of what it is seeking, it does maintain the subpoena be executed with reasonable particularity. Both *Fisher* and *Hubbell* require that the government demonstrates that the files exist at the very least. In sum, Doe's Fifth Amendment rights were infringed when he refused to decrypt and produce the contents because the act would be testimonial and the government could not show the "foregone conclusion" doctrine applied.

Lastly, the court examined the immunity that was given to Doe by the government. Despite properly invoking the Fifth Amendment, the court concluded that Doe was not given the proper immunity under the Fifth Amendment and 18 U.S.C. §6002. The government claimed that it would not use Doe's act of production against him in future prosecution and that it would only use the contents of the unencrypted drives in any prosecution. The act-of-production immunity given to Doe was not the type of immunity mandated by 18 U.S.C. §6002, nor was it synonymous with derivative-use immunity. The act-of-production immunity was not sufficient to compel Doe to testify. Citing former precedent, the court stated that derivative-use immunity establishes "the critical threshold to overcome an individual's invocation of the Fifth Amendment privilege against self-incrimination. No more protection is necessary; no less protection is sufficient."[28]

However, as stated, the government never gave derivative-use immunity. This does not allow the government to obtain immunity only for the act of production and then subsequently introduce the contents of the production. It is irrelevant whether the contents are characterized as testimonial; introducing the contents would allow the use of evidence derived from the original testimonial statement. Requiring Doe to produce the contents of the drive would require immunity co-extensive with the Fifth Amendment and §6002. An act-of-production immunity would not suffice to protect Doe. Accordingly, because the immunity offered did not correspond with the Fifth Amendment, he could not be compelled to decrypt the drives. Doe had properly invoked his Fifth Amendment right and the District Court erred in finding Doe in contempt.

This case established *Hubbell* and *Fisher* as starting points and two ends of a spectrum for Fifth Amendment and cloud computing jurisprudence. When applied to litigation and situations involving the compelled discovery of potentially self-incriminating electronic communications or other stored electronic data, *Hubbell* demonstrates a case in which the government was not able to show that they had prior knowledge of the contents of the physical documents. *Fisher* was the opposite in that they already were aware of the documents and who had possession of them. Because Doe was being compelled to produce a combination, the court spent ample time in its analysis in discussing an individual being forced to use the contents of his own mind. This was described as touchstone as to whether an act is testimonial, and the court discussed the dichotomy between this concept versus compelling a physical act. The court ultimately held that his knowledge of the location of the files, his possession of the files, and his capability to decrypt the files would amount to more than just a physical act. In examining the facts of *Boucher*, the Government was able to satisfy the reasonable particularity requirement, unlike the present case. Although the circumstances were factually similar, the court reached opposite results.

The cases demonstrate how fact-sensitive each inquiry is for the court in Fifth Amendment jurisprudence. While it is generally agreed that divulging a password constitutes a testimonial act, for example, courts such as the one in *Boucher* that compelled Boucher to produce previously encrypted files have shown that there is no general bright-line rule for something such as password-protected files. Protecting a defendant's right against self-incrimination should be of the upmost importance for courts and as a result has produced ample litigation with respect to cloud computing. This balancing act will only become increasingly taxing on courts unless definitions and standards are clarified and courts become more consistent in their approaches to Fifth Amendment jurisprudence.

Notes

1. U.S. Const. amend V.
2. Vivek Mohan and John Villasenor, "Decrypting the Fifth Amendment: The Limits of Self-Incrimination in the Digital Era," *University of Pennsylvania Journal of Constitutional Law Heightened Scrutiny* 15 (2012): 11–28, 1.
3. *U.S. v. Doe*, 465 U.S. 605, 608 (1984).
4. Mohan and Villasenor, 4.
5. In addressing the workpapers, the Court stated, "whether the Fifth Amendment would shield the taxpayer from producing his own tax records in his possession is a question not involved here; for the papers demanded here are not his 'private papers'."
6. *Doe*, 465 U.S. at 610.
7. Mohan and Villasenor, 13.
8. *Ibid.*
9. *Doe v. United States*, 487 U.S. 201, 209 (1988).
10. *Id.* at 209.
11. *Id.* at 210.
12. *Id.* at 215.
13. *United States v. Hubbell*, 530 U.S. 27, 31 (2000).
14. Several documents were exempt based on respondent invoking attorney work-product privilege.
15. *Hubbell.* at 32.
16. *Id.* at 42.
17. *Id.* at 40.
18. *Id.* at 41.
19. *Id.* at 42.
20. *Id.* at 42–43.
21. Erica Fruiterman, "Upgrading the Fifth Amendment: New Standards for Protecting Encryption Passwords." *Temple Law Review* 85, no.3 (Spring 2013): 16.
22. *In re Boucher*, 2009 WL 424718, 1 (D. Vt. 2009).
23. *Id.* at 3.
24. Mohan and Villasenor, p. 5.
25. *In re Grand Jury Subpoena Duces Tecum*, March 25, 2011, 670 F.3d 1335, 1340 (11th Circ. 2011).
26. *Id.* at 1345.
27. In such instances, the individual is not called upon to make use of the contents of his or her mind. An example of this is compelling the key to the lock of a strongbox containing documents, an example also used in *Hubbell*.
28. "Id. at 1351."

ABOUT THE CONTRIBUTORS

Matthew P. Breuer, JD

Matthew P. Breuer is an associate at Cendrowski Corporate Advisors in Bloomfield Hills, Michigan. He provides consulting and advisory services to clients in the legal, private equity banking, corporate, and nonprofit industries.

Prior to joining the firm, he served as a clerk to the Honorable Judge Lisa Gorcyca. He is a member of the Michigan State Bar Association and Oakland County Bar Association. He received his undergraduate degree from Michigan State University and his law degree from Wayne State University Law School in Detroit, Michigan. He currently serves on the Executive Counsel of the Young Lawyers Section of the State Bar of Michigan, and is a member of the American Bar Association Business Law Section.

He has authored articles appearing in *Smart Business Chicago*, *The Value Examiner*, and other publications. In addition, he was a contributor to *The Handbook of Fraud Deterrence* and *Private Equity: History, Governance, and Operations*, both published by John Wiley and Sons.

Deirdre Fox

Deirdre A. Fox is counsel at Scharf Banks Marmor LLC in Chicago. She concentrates her practice in commercial disputes, intellectual property and restrictive covenants, and product liability. She lectures on developing social media and data privacy issues. A former partner of Kirkland & Ellis, Ms. Fox is a graduate of Northwestern University, the School of the Art Institute, and University of Chicago Law School.

Virginia Kim

Virginia Kim is an Associate at Scharf Banks Marmor LLC. She concentrates her practice in employment litigation and counseling, class action, pharmaceutical defense, toxic tort, product liability, franchise and trademark enforcement, and commercial disputes. She earned her AB (History, Philosophy, and Social Studies of Science and Medicine) and JD degrees from the University of Chicago.

Sarah Marmor

Sarah R. Marmor is a founding partner of Scharf Banks Marmor LLC in Chicago. She concentrates her practice in employment law, commercial disputes, and product liability litigation. She has developed a particular interest in social media law, and has lectured throughout the United States on this developing subject. A former partner of Kirkland & Ellis and Jenner & Block, Ms. Marmor is a graduate of Princeton University and Northwestern University School of Law.

Christopher Thieda

Christopher Thieda is a business technology analyst specializing in evaluating and improving technology environments and processes. He has spent his career working in the information security industry and has experience relating to data protection, assurance, and compliance. He has a particular interest in emerging technologies and privacy issues.

He has a bachelor of science degree in finance from the Eli Broad College of Business at Michigan State University, where he participated in the Broad College Student Senate and was a member of the College Capital Committee.

ABOUT THE AUTHORS

James P. Martin, CMA, CIA, CFE
Managing Director, Cendrowski Corporate Advisors, LLC, Chicago, IL, and Bloomfield Hills, MI

James P. Martin is frequently involved with litigation support matters involving fraud examinations, divorce, and professional malpractice. He additionally specializes in providing comprehensive risk assessments, focusing on the evaluation of operating effectiveness of business processes and the internal control structure and the development of recommendations for improvement. In many cases, these services were provided to companies where basic internal control lapses had led to financial reporting and operational issues. He has performed forensic examinations of numerous business arrangements to determine the accuracy of recorded transactions and presentations, including the healthcare, durable equipment, real estate, and construction industries.

He holds a BBA in accounting and an MS in accounting information systems from Eastern Michigan University. He has served on the faculty of Davenport University, Walsh College, and the University of Detroit–Mercy, where he instructed courses in fraud examination, managerial accounting, internal auditing, and information technology. He is the head coach of the Michigan State University ACHA hockey team, and is the treasurer of the American Collegiate Hockey Association. He has authored numerous articles in various professional journals, and is a co-author of *The Handbook of Fraud Deterrence* and *Private Equity: History Governance and Operations*, and a contributor to *Computer Fraud Casebook, the Bytes that Byte*, all published by John Wiley & Sons.

Harry Cendrowski, CPA/ABV, CGMA, CFF, CFE, CVA, CFD, MAFF
President, Cendrowski Corporate Advisors, LLC, Chicago, IL, and Bloomfield Hills, MI

Harry Cendrowski is a founding member and managing director of Cendrowski Corporate Advisors (CCA). He is also a founding member of Cendrowski Selecky PC and The Prosperitas Group. Over his 30-year career, he has worked hand-in-hand with public and private businesses, private equity and venture capital funds, attorneys, and nonprofit organizations to address their needs. He has helped businesses mitigate risks, streamline their operations, and deter fraud. In the legal community, his experience has allowed him to serve as an expert witness in numerous economic damages analyses, contract disputes, lost profit analyses, business valuations, and partnership disputes.

He sits on boards of numerous nonprofit and charitable organizations. A passionate advocate for assisting families and children in need, he is currently on the advisory board of the Schiller DuCanto & Fleck Family Law Center at DePaul College of Law and an active trustee for La Rabida Children's Hospital. He is also a supporter of higher-level education and served as the chairman of the Madonna University Foundation, vice chairman of the Madonna University Board of Trustees, and chairman of their Finance Committee and Investment Committees. He received a "Committed" award from the Association of Fundraising Professionals for his dedication to the educational community. He is a co-author of *The Handbook of Fraud Deterrence, Private Equity: History Governance and Operations*, and *Enterprise Risk Management and COSO: A Guide for Directors, Executives, and Practitioners*, and a contributor to *Computer Fraud Casebook, the Bytes that Byte*, all published by John Wiley & Sons.

ABOUT THE COMPANION WEB SITE

The companion web site (www.wiley.com/go/cloudcomputing) offers links to laws, regulations, and case documents cited in this case.

The companion site also includes a link to an up-to-date LinkedIn discussion group addressing current events on the topic.

Technical Considerations

- Developments in digital forensic tools related to cloud applications
- Development of accepted procedures to perform extraction of cloud data
- New cloud solutions and storage locations
- Discovery standards
- New legal cases setting precedent or affecting the discovery process
- Updates on pending cases covered in the book

Regulations

- New regulations and laws that change the standards for discovery of cloud data
- Proposed legislation updating the Stored Communications Act

The password to enter the site is: martin123.

INDEX